Your Negro Tour Guide

Truths in Black and White

Kathy Y. Wilson

emmis
books

1700 Madison Road Cincinnati, Ohio 45206

Your Negro Tour Guide
Copyright Kathy Y. Wilson 2004

Published by Emmis Books
1700 Madison Road
Cincinnati, OH 45206

ISBN 157860-143-6

Library of Congress number TK

Cover photo: Chris Lowry
Cover design: Stephen Sullivan
Interior design: Dana Boll

"I have no greater joy than to hear that my children are walking in the truth."
--III JOHN 1:4 NIV

(PRINTED ON A REFRIGERATOR MAGNET GIVEN
TO ME BY MY MOTHER.)

Dedication

For my mother and my
father for teaching me to sing
a Blues called Truth;
for Kennedy Anne Wilson,
I'll see you when I get
there.

And for lirpA.

You incite me to chorus.

Acknowledgments

Since this is my first book, I'ma shout it out like I just won a *Soul Train* award.

In lifelong succession four women kicked my ass with the truth.

First, my mom, Gladine Rosetta Hill (disrespect to all the men she gave up her name for) was the first person who told me I could write. You kept me warm and warned. By your example I learned to love Jesus, Angela Davis, my family and myself.

Mamma is a verb.

Next, Cathleen Arnold more than 20 years ago read my poem, "And Christ Climbed Down," at Greenhills High School.

Instead of laughing in my face she called me a writer.

I thank her every time I see her.

I thank her again now.

Then thundered Tammy Ramsdell at the long-ago *Hamilton Journal-News*.

She gave me a chance and no choice.

Tammy first put me in the columnist column.

I am indebted to her. Wherever she is.

Finally, Bev Lenicky's empathetic probing is largely responsible for my sanity and my ability to know when it's being threatened. Bev, we did some difficult work together. Thank you for teaching me that to be told, truth does not need us. It is mutually exclusive of all else.

Now the rest.

Weezy told me to get offa my ass and live and to seek God in everything.

I take her One-A-Day(TM) everyday. We do what sisters do.

Shelle, never let me go. We are discriminating.

For a white woman, Holly Wilson, you're the blackest man I know.

And I mean that as a compliment.

Al and Sidney Jones are my surrogates, and they kept me together when no one else could. You give love a good name. Alfie, Darrell and Michael, I should've dated one of you and married the other two but it's better that you're my brothers.

To the Wentzels, of the Louisville Wentzels, you gave me refuge back in the day when my poems sucked and my clichés were cloning. Time is on our side.

Nicole Greene had my back way back when I didn't know what I was doing.

We down but we ain't out, Vincenza, so welcome to the Welcome Table, where all are welcome.

"Stay with me and I will bless you."

Hamilton and Cincinnati have my DNA smeared all over them. I appreciate everyone who ever speculated, congratulated, sneered and prayed. To the artistic collectives of 144,000 and Liberated Souls — *muchas gracias* for letting me house sit.

Reparations, mates.

Dani McClain: Call it a haiku/Even though Kofi says no/You make perfect sense.

I grew up and became a badass at *Cincinnati CityBeat*.

Those were the times that tried white men's souls. Hang in, gang, and get in the fuckin' game!

John "Paychex" Fox, my *CityBeat* publisher, whipping boy and friend, gets a big up for giving me free reign to roam the country in 850 words or less. John, you're a kind and generous man, and I'm a better woman because of our affiliation.

Gregory Flannery, I'm not mad; only now well informed.

I owe Sara Sarasohn, my producer and friend at National Public Radio's "All Things Considered," for pursuing me once she heard "a new thing" in my voice. Sara, you chase me when you shouldn't. Thanks for teaching me to believe in my words and for concisely directing me to speak them well.

Your patience and vision are frightening.

Me want more.

DKO, whatever happened to Deacon? Thanks for letting me listen to black music one day a week.

Richard Hunt risked some shit to put this down. Where would I be without your faith, money, vision, connections and determination? Not here. Let's go forward.

My editor Jack Heffron is as far from my experience as I am from his. But we made love and birthed a book.

Dana, Katie and Howard at Emmis Books are strange and brilliant bibliophiles and I'm glad we're teammates. You made it real.

Sean Hughes...patient, diligent Sean Hughes, the ugly lesbian father...you made the work easier. I woulda been a typin' ass without you.

Kitty Morgan, let's fuck 'em up!

Thanks, Lena, for losing me at Coney Island when I was 5 or 6. It was my first taste of self-reliance. Denise Martin, God loves even me.

I owe every staff member during my tenure in the Literature Department at the Main Public Library of Hamilton County. You freaks grew me up and schooled me.

It turned out to be my college education.

Darlene D'Agostino I will tirelessly acknowledge you for burping "Your Negro Tour Guide" from my belly. You saw it for what it was and you made me see it, too.

Zora Neale Hurston and James Baldwin book end my soul.

Rita Dove signed my journal and her genius across my poetics.

While writing for my life I shoplifted bravery from Ursula Rucker, Saul Williams, Carl Hancock Rux, Paul Laurence Dunbar, Donnell Alexander, Victor D. LaValle, Sarah Jones, Junot Diaz, Hilton Als, Nikki Giovanni, John Edgar Wideman and Toni Morrison. Because of them I know there are no new roads, only new paths.

I call my core Randy, Kenny, Devin, Kelly, Kyler and Ken Wilson, Jr.

Can y'all believe this shit?

Look at what you made me do.

I don't know how you all put up with my strange, uppity Blues woman ways. I'd adore you even if you didn't.

We'll ask the ages.

(Mary, don't you weep.
Tell Edward not to moan.)

"I'm not taking anybody's word for my experience.
For that, you'll have to take my word.
They've been describing me for too long.
Now I'm describing them."

--JAMES BALDWIN, *BLUES FOR MISTER CHARLIE*

Table of Contents

II. What Fresh Hell Is This? Cincinnati, Its Dickless Mayor, His Riot & Going Back to "Dead Nigga Blvd."

III. A Funky Potpourri: Goin' Up Yonder, Dreams and "Kunta's Compensation"

Introduction

I've been the only one for most of my life.

The only girl/woman, the only black, the only black girl/woman, the only woman without a college degree, the only, the only, the only....

It's a relic, this only-ness intersecting gender, race and class.

No complaints or carping.

Only observing.

I've fashioned razor-sharp defense mechanisms from seemingly always standing out like, well, me at a Klan rally.

I found an odd neighborhood. I'm comfortably anxious.

That is, while majority culture makes sport of observing and appropriating from The Other I've made sport of—and, most importantly, a living from—observing and then reporting the truth of *them*.

Life as a black American is mostly like 12 months of Black History Month with its pockets turned inside out—all white all the time. So, to buffer and buoy I create language, a lexicon I wield to whittle through and then reclaim tired stereotypes which I ultimately refashion to more appropriately fit my time and place.

I rip off the thieves.

I fear the co-opt.

I cringe at the thought of parts of myself being parceled out to further another's agenda. Gays and lesbians try the hardest and are the worst at it. Broke-down and voiceless Negroes stepped up a time or two but I've swatted them away like sweat bees.

It's whites who are the most subversive, the slyest at the co-opt.

In the winter of 1994 I began a five-year stint at *The Hamilton-Journal News*, the daily newspaper for Butler County — a sprawling, partially rural/partially overdeveloped county 25 miles north of Cincinnati, Ohio. Butler County — farms ringing strip malls nudging developments and apartment complexes — suffers the obligatory identity crisis like similar burgs run by politicians pressured to develop land mass for money which ends up smashing the classes farther apart.

The *J-N* is also the newspaper of Hamilton, the hometown I left once my folks split up when I was 7 years old.

Separation is my life's recurring theme. A three-time college dropout who majored in English — not journalism — I applied to the *J-N* on a fluke and a prayer at the insistence of my then-stepfather, the paper's staff graphic artist and illustrator.

Hamilton is geographically sectioned off into brownie-like chunks of race and economics; of poor blacks and whites, middle-class whites and then stinkin'-ass rich whites.

A river ruins through it.

The Great Miami River separates the city into unequal halves and have-nots. Separation's what I grew up on so it was hard shaking the 22-year-old classist monkey of my girlhood when I returned the conquering (s)hero reporter.

Ashley Young, an ambitious married black mother with an icy wit, had just departed the *J-N* for a corporate writing gig with more money and stature but less stress. We'd missed one another by a matter of weeks.

However, Linda Wright, a passive/aggressive single black mother who appeared defeated by life and was viewed by many of our colleagues as dead journalistic weight, was still toiling at the paper when I got there.

Linda championed me in a sideways glance.

The culture of American newsrooms breeds anxiety and mistrust among the minorities those newsrooms half-heartedly pursue yet are disproportionately dependent upon for reporting stories on culture, gender and race.

It's survival of the brownest.

My arrival for Linda meant she was no longer the sole Negro at the cocktail party.

I threatened her paradigm, whatever it was.

Another of The Other.

J-N editors and managers immediately began figuring where Linda and I were going to land once they fed us through the Salad Shooter of beats and reporters. She floundered, authoring overwrought, magazine-length articles that busted deadlines like flood waters over saturated sandbags.

I floundered, authoring overly writerly, hymn-like articles requiring sandblasting and buffing like mud-encrusted gems.

Our editors eventually tired of the tedium of constantly working with Linda, of working around Linda and of working her over. Watching City Desk Editor Ron Fonger daily massage Linda's ego for the sake of birthing a 10-inch story on a boring county comissioners' meeting was like watching a postmodern Sisyphus push his (lethargic black female) boulder up the mountainside only for Linda to roll back over his ass by day's end.

She was fired.

I was The Lone Other.

Tammy Ramsdell, the newly christened managing editor who'd fired Linda, methodically and maniacally restructured the newsroom, redesigned news sections, hired and fired editors and reporters and terrorized the city that'd been sleeping soundly.

Not long after Linda's firing, Tammy abruptly fired me — a little-known fact — for "not working out."

I'd not even hurdled my probationary period; I didn't even have an insurance card yet.

Before I could pack my desk I published a feature story about the two long-time black barbershops in town. I documented the gossipy nature of black men and the faux-Africanness of barbershop storytelling. I wrote of the disparate class status of both shops, cobbling together along the way a loose historical structure of the Second Ward, Hamilton's main black neighborhood.

That story blessed and cursed me with a reprieve.

In it Tammy read my potential.

She peeped a gold mine of future tours through the colored section.

I was her one-stop shop for stories emanating from the blackest places — black churches and the black-run Booker T. Washington Community Center. She also depended on me to report (black-associated) social woes like AIDS, crack and black-on-black homicide.

Tammy gave me free reign to infiltrate.

Obviously, she expected something in return; freedom ain't free.

"Perspective," she called it.

Vantage point, I call it.

So, infiltrate it was.

I nearly choked to death on the adrenaline of my own reconnaissance missions.

I felt like the target in a game of dodge ball where everybody had a red rubber playground ball cocked to pummel me. I became a gas station coffee-drinking speed freak; after I guzzled the 48-oz plastic tumbler of coffee laden with sugar and milk, I moved onto Mt. Dew and Pepsi.

Green and brown fuel.

By the end of every day my eyes ached, my jaw was clenched tight and I recoiled, laying in wait to bite someone's head off.

My dukes were always up.

Since nearly every black Hamiltonian knows someone in my large extended family of halves, steps and bloods, I traded on my family name for tips, secrets and entree. I was invited into meetings, households and circles heretofore roped off from previous *J-N* reporters who were either too lazy, too frightened or too white.

And The Pull loomed in my rearview mirror.

The Pull is what happens to minorities elected as spokesmodels for our respective races.

In this case there are two models of the minority spokesmodel — professional and racial.

Who we are while we're at work and who we are when we're not.

I guarantee it ain't the same person.

My editor hired me to represent the paper in the neighborhood and the neighborhood raised me to represent them at the paper.

The Pull is racial guilt vs. impressing the bosses; it's everyone assuming you speak for them when you barely speak for yourself.

At the behest of The Pull and to appear "neutral" and "fair" we act standoffish within the racial ranks. Truth is, as we descend deeper into our chosen professions, we're consumed with guilt over the tricks we employ — insincerity and cultural theft — to gather the information we're paid to report back to the front.

The Pull immediately hit me upside the head in Hamilton.

Thankfully, I just as quickly identified and railed against it.

I somehow convinced black folks throughout Hamilton I wasn't a spy, an Auntie Tom or race traitor.

And despite being asked—and declining—in the aftermath of the O. J. Simpson verdict to "introduce" white reporters to potential black sources at the two barbershops I'd written about, I showed my white bosses I'd no intention of being their spy, their Negress Provocateur.

While all this was going down, I slowly morphed my appearance to fit my growing hostility and professional burn out.

I came to the *J-N* with a closely shorn and meticulously manicured smoothed-down Caesar haircut. I wore oval-shaped, horn-rimmed glasses and elegantly preppy clothes and shoes.

By my third year I'd lost count and track of the beats I'd bounced between. As punishment for a reporting mishap I was busted down to the purgatory of permanent weekend reporter. I covered manmade and natural disasters, grisly teenage murders, strawberry festivals, an annual authentic German Oktoberfest and every piddling neighborhood street festival Butler Countians could dream up.

People were either so happy to get in the paper that they fawned all over me (and I guiltily shat out a forgettable non-story), or they were so discombobulated by the sight of my black face they'd turn tail (and I angrily shat out a forgettable non-story).

Once I realized I'd been dropped off by my editors at the intersection of Fuck You Ave. and You're On Your Own Blvd., I let my hair speak.

I grew a gnarly, voluminous Afro that spiraled into kinky, gray-tipped black stalks jutting catawampous from my head.

My 'fro had a mind of its blown.

In summer I wore shorts, gyms shoes and baseball caps, and in cool months I wore khakis, jeans, turtlenecks and boots.

I felt fenced in so my appearance became a fence; it kept the right people out.

Then, dreadlocks happened.

After pulling, separating and twisting my hair—sometimes obsessively for hours at a time—I'd fucked around and cultivated 'locks that grazed my shoulders. My burned brussel sprouts fucked everybody up. Sources pretended not to notice, yet answered questions to my hair.

Potential sources blanched. My colleagues either shucked and jived me with fumbled Soul shakes, ignored me further or pelted me with stupid-ass ethnic hair questions.

("Do you wash it?" "Does that hurt?" Or, my favorite Top 10 Stupid Whitey Trick, "Can I touch it?")

I'd developed the patented Angry Black Bitch Combo Pack Response to the last question, which was always accompanied by a raised white hand hovering above, then lighting against, my crown of spun black cotton.

With agility and quickness I'd automatically dip to one side and slide slightly back on one foot, as if dodging invisible karate kicks to my dome.

In the first of countless Quaker Instant Language mixes, I came up with what I assume is an original phrase.

First, I'd dip, then: "I am *not* your Negro petting zoo," I'd sniff.

A young white *J-N* staff photographer from Kentucky schooled me one day in the newsroom.

In one blink-of-an-eye, uninvited motion he fucked it up for white people everywhere.

I'd been through the emotional ringer already at the *J-N*.

I'd stood nose-to-nose with Tammy, dodging the sucker punches of her emotional takeover of me as she secretly tried to make me her protégeé. I nearly lost my mind during a marathon mind fuck with one of the city desk editors.

So by the time my 'locks locked up everybody's common sense, I was weary but not yet cynical.

The photographer and I were standing in front of my WWII-issue orange metal desk.

I'd long since been assigned to squat at the front of the newsroom. I'm to this day convinced the seating assignment was meant to both fool visitors into thinking I was the receptionist and to show off to all others my boss's prize lawn jockey.

Either way I was the spook who sat by the door.

The photographer was an arrogant asshole whose youth—this was his first post-collegiate gig—exacerbated his annoying self-love.

Mostly I humored his ignorance.

By faking interest in his cultural drive-bys (the way he'd ask blacks "black questions" instead of making black friends) I duped him into thinking: a) he was cool, b) I gave a fuck and c) he was cooler than he thought.

They're all lies. He wasn't cool, I did give a fuck (I was cruising a little cultural drive-by of my own) and he wasn't as cool as he thought.

I averted my gaze from blacks and started really checking out white people. I mean, I took notes.

Apropos of nothing, the photographer ran his spindly fingers through my 'locks, dropped his hand and wiped it against his Gap Outlet jeans.

All in full sight; all without invitation or warning.

Fade to black.

After I regained my eyesight, I lost my memory.

I still cannot remember if I cursed him out, laughed it off, ignored it altogether or glared at him. I like to think I hit 'em with my ol' trusty "I'm not your Negro petting zoo" but somehow I think I lost control and flew into a niggerbitchfit. If I'd killed him I'd have claimed insanity.

That's how internally enraged I'd become over the subtle vulgarities of white male entitlement.

And it goes a lil' somethin' like dis: *Who the fuck asked you? Oh. Now you're disgusted? Then backdafuckup!*

I didn't quit until a full two years later but I was already gone.

My spirit had left not just the building, but the county.

I'd written a widely read, despised and syndicated (and award-winning) column at the *J-N,* so I thought I was done with that shit. My photo ran with it, and I'd received death threats, mean mugs in line at McDonald's, back slaps and horn blows. I was ready to be incogNegro by the time I left the paper in the winter of 1999.

Then, *Cincinnati CityBeat* founder, co-publisher and editor John Fox made good on a long-running promise. He hired me full-time after five years of paying me as a featured contributor to his fledgling alternative newsweekly, duties that overlapped and augmented my *J-N* gig.

John also did something that irrevocably changed both our lives. He redesigned the front of *CityBeat* to make room for my new column. He helped me from my noose.

"It can be anything you want," John said. I yanked my column-writing skills—ideas, truth and stankin' sentences—off the charger.

I wrote a few evergreen pieces to see if my eye and ear were any good now in Cincinnati where I'd lived but grown a benign relationship with after five years of spending 12 hours a day in Hamilton.

At the *J-N* I only read Cincinnati's two dailies to see how badly I'd been burned on my own beats.

Otherwise, in Cincinnati I wasn't a player, I didn't know who were the players and they didn't know my ass, either.

I was so B-list I didn't even register on the radar.

That worked deliciously to my benefit.

Cincinnati's self-appointed high-post Negroes don't know it's better to be anonymously autonomous, a nobody without allegiances, debts or a Tailhook of asses to kick and kiss.

That was me.

This is me.

"Anything?" I asked, testing John's definition of the word.

I waited to hear "...*except*...."

"Anything," he said.

"Can I curse?"

I've not asked John's permission since.

"Your Negro Tour Guide" debuted in *CityBeat* in July 2000 with the overstated headline: "In the Beginning."

A week before its premiere the column lacked a running header, a strong identifier.

Darlene D'Agostino, was *CityBeat*'s aggressive/progressive young reporter fresh from college and a year of travelling the world. Darlene is a Phish fan and follower, a nouveau hippie unafraid of differences.

She's prone to frequently saying "Heeeeey maaaan" but she's fluent in world and current affairs and she fights to write better.

She'd started listening to hip hop and borrowed De la Soul, Common and A Tribe Called Quest CD's from me.

Every time she returned a disc she lobbed questions at me.

"What does it mean when they...,why do they always wear..., what does...mean?"

I'd softened.

My dukes were down at my sides.

I answered her questions colorfully and with great humor and detailed examples.

Until one day.

CityBeat is a small shop.

Your bedroom's bigger than our former newsroom.

Some bug had flown up my ass the day Darlene came in giddy and loaded with hip hop questions.

"Like, why are they always calling out names and neighborhoods?" was, I think, the question that broke the black woman's back.

"Damn, Darlene! It's called a shout out, you know? Reppin' homeboys and 'hoods."

I felt like an out-dated idiot, spewing slang circa *Krush Groove*.

I was angrier with myself.

"Don't come in here no more askin' me no dumb-ass black questions," I bellowed before a room bustling with interns, copy editors and writers.

I made quote signs with my fingers when I said the word "black."

I tried to sound well-meaning. Like I wasn't pissed off.

"Darlene, get a black friend."

Beat.

"I'm *not* your Negro tour guide."

The room erupted with chortles and snorts.

"That's it! That's the name of your column!" Darlene said. "That's it, man. Man, I'm tellin' you! That's it!"

I took the idea to John, re-enacting the episode that birthed it.

He was reticent, deflecting my enthusiasm for this brilliant name—No! Concept!—at every turn.

"What are you going to do, explain it every week? What if people haven't read it since the beginning and they don't know about the title? It'd be pretty tedious to have to re-explain that week in and week out," John said.

"It's a tour!" I said, excited and not backing down.

"Every week I'm pulling up and either you're taking the Tour or you're not," I said. "Either they're gettin' on with me and I'm pulling out or they're not.

"If they're not, fuck 'em!"

*"If white people are pleased, we are glad ... If colored people are pleased we are glad. If they are not, their displeasure doesn't matter either."**

I've written of riots, white and black lies, black hair, white appropriation, Negresses and police misconduct.

I called our mayor "dickless," outed myself as a lazy diabetic and a lesbian.

But I knew I was a bad-ass when, after chastising an errant black councilwoman in print, she flew into a public rage and threatened to unleash a legion of her black firefighter friends against me in retaliation.

Whew!

And that was only the first 18 months of "Your Negro Tour Guide."

Herein lies the truth.

During three years I've gotten better at telling it—mine and ours.

I've garnered national attention and a few awards for it; however, I never thought I'd be all the way here from all the way over there.

From all the way from Hamilton, Ohio.

Here we go.

Be mindful of the implications of language as you traipse through this mind field of rants, accusations, letters, commentaries and nightmares.

Please recall the labor pains that ached all these words to life.

Be especially cognizant of the scenario three years ago starring Darlene D'Agostino and I.

Mind the implications.

And remember.

I'm nobody's spokeswoman—not all women, all blacks or all lesbians.

Remember.

I speak for myself.

I'm *not* your Negro tour guide.

Aug. 15, 19 and 20, 2003.
Cincinnati, Ohio

* Langston Hughes originally either wrote or said these words. They were reprinted in the *Village Voice*. (issue of Jan. 8–14, 2003)

Blacker Than Thou

Rants, Riffs and "The Scarlet 'L'"

Blacks Like Us

Doug, my white coworker, wanted to hear some driving-while-black horror stories.

Negroes call 'em lynching stories.

"I know you, of all people, have some," he said. "You've got to."

Of course I do.

I don't know a black person regardless of age, gender or income who can't, on demand, recall at least one.

But I blew off the question then and there, knowing, though, that it'd acid reflux its way into another conversation.

Just because the pitfalls of blackness are collectible mammies to The Other don't make them fun for me/us. Toni Morrison talks of eschewing from her mind the peculiarity of the white gaze on black literature.

I'd amend that to include trashing the strangefruit feeling I get when white folks wanna hear about how fucked up it is to be me.

Doug regurgitated the question while we were out drinking at a bar where the eclectic jukebox (Billie Holiday, Johnny Cash, Punk, Reggae) that doesn't attract a similarly diverse clientele.

There's always a crush of same-looking people, those intentionally nerdy white people trying to look poor but who aren't.

This night wasn't different.

I was the only black person and, to make matters more culturally tricky, I'd just come from the symphony with another white co-worker at my side.

I must have smelled funky considering the stares.

So, yeah, I had a full (nappy) head of steam by the time I got to the bar.

I was culturally overloaded, imploding at the thought of pending race-laced bullshit.

Doug was poised with anticipation, waiting for me to turn my stories into easily digestible slapstick shtick.

Shit.

What a gimmick.

I'm black and I drive in America.

I have horror stories.

But I stalled.

Stalling, see, is power.

Make 'em wait then don't deliver.

His question set me thinking about the traps of being deemed a spokeswoman for the race; of how people in my own sphere, my own family, are tired and hostile because they fell for the okey-doke of speaking for us *all* and therefore lost their own voice and their own way.

In times like these I feel like a Mini Me is inside somersaulting, pushing against my innards, Stretch Armstronging me into a perpetually new me saying: "Girl, don't buy it. Make *them* do some work."

"What's the big deal?" was the recurring question of my interior monologue.

Astounded disbelief that racial profiling exists distracts whenever it pops onto the national radar—from Rodney King's ass whippin' heard the world over to deadly encounters played out here in Cincinnati to my very own.

Trust.

It does.

Cities from left to right coasts wouldn't be constantly settling racial profiling lawsuits if it's not real.

Fuck the findings of some study.

It is true and frightening that some cops target/profile/detain/question/arrest blacks disproportionately to white drivers; that they get us on a humble, because of equipment failure or expired tags so they'll hopefully find drugs, weapons or that we're wanted on warrants.

It's also true and telling that my black friends don't venture into some white neighborhoods after nightfall because they'll be hassled by (usually) white cops.

And we don't mark our boundaries based on speculation.

We base boundaries on experience.

Our conversations about neighborhoods to avoid, alternate routes and where the boys are would be hilarious if they weren't fact-finding sessions.

It appears paranoid.

It feels shameful.

Only when I'm at my bad-ass best (when the trifecta of my license, registration and insurance are all up to snuff) do I drive wherever I wanna.

See, the illest part of racism is that it fleeces Negroes like me of our be all we can be-ness that our parents spent years slathering on.

I'm confident a middle-class white driver doesn't think about where she'll drive for fear of being pulled over by a black cop who'll ask her in a sniff, "What are you doing in this neighborhood?"

Which I was asked by a white cop late one night as I got into my yellow 1974 VW Super Beetle on the side street of a toney, old-money white neighborhood. The car was parked legally and I wasn't committing a crime en route to my car.

I was nonetheless detained and released after a barrage of haranguing questions.

I had too much identification and that was suspicious.

Trying to convince non-believers that racial profiling exists is a distraction from the perilous micro management of postmodern Negro life with all its entitlement and opportunity.

Let's talk about walking while black.

Like the day in the summer of 1999 I almost came to blows with the white man who, in an instance of urban synchronicity, stepped on the same section of sidewalk with me.

By the way he positioned his body, he expected me to step off the sidewalk to let him pass. By my old-school upbringing, I expected him to let this lady pass.

"Stupid! Nigger! Bitch!" he hurled as if spitting.

Just then I had a flash of the filmstrip of my mother refusing, to her grandfather's dismay, to step off 1940s Alabama sidewalks for white passersby.

He'd reduced me to three please check here boxes small enough to fit inside his world.

Then there's shopping while black.

I've been eyeballed, followed, and questioned while browsing large department stores and boutiques so many times I go out of my way to appear *not* to be stealing.

Let's break it down to blood stains and molecules.

Let's rap about breathing while black (environmental racism), living while black (sickle cell anemia, diabetes, AIDS, hypertension), and, hell...*existing* while black.

Taken together, it can feel like a bear sitting on a black woman's chest, conspiring itself into hostility and depression.

Remember, this is America.

Do not be fooled by the attack of the Killer Black Middle Class.

Life's not the same for us all.

It's been curious, at best, since we booked passage, landed and realized that if we separate into classes we could outmaneuver one another and find favor with the officer/overseer.

I know. I know. There goes that slavery thing again.

When we gonna get off that?

Me? Never.

It all boomerangs back to ownership, to being stripped of culture while being clothed in blackness as a substandard commodity. It makes for colored schizophrenia, for healthy distrust when a white someone wants to be entertained by the horror of our daily drive-bys on normality.

This city and this country did this to me and others like me.

We're standing on the verge of gettin' it on, waiting for the high sign.

So, yeah, I've got one too many driving-while-black horror stories of epic proportion.

And you should hear me tell 'em.

They're hilarious.

But ain't shit funny.

Of Hair Weaves, Short Sets and White Flight

❖❖❖❖❖

I'm one of those schizo Negroes.

I loathe and love this time of year each year.

Likewise, I loathe and love black folks this time of year each year.

And it's for the same reasons: Every year, the last weekend in July brings out the best and worst in us. It always reminds me why I love my black self and black people.

It also reminds me why my black people sometimes make me recoil, horrified at the parade of spiraling, store-bought hair, flashy, rim-fitted rides, outlandish outfits and the outbreak of violence in pockets of bored hangers-on.

The last weekend in July makes me laugh at who I'm not, who I'm from and every gradation of what I could be if I weren't someone else.

The weekend illustrates our potential to make and generate income, to be creative, to be soulful and Soul-filled. To just be black—that is, to just be ourselves.

Why?

It's the weekend of the JazzFest.

And the Ujima street festival—the source of so much people watching—rides along.

For those of us who graze and don't go to the festival, Ujima is African for: Whitey get outta downtown before sundown or else you might get caught in the crosswalk with a gaggle of lavishly dressed black folks! You might get lost and have to ask a faux African vendor for directions!

Talk about culture clash.

This is the one time here where the lines of race and class are so clearly drawn that once the sun sets on Friday, downtown is in full black-out.

It's lights out.

It's whites out.

Why is that? Are we that frightening? I mean, it's not like we're not downtown every other day of the week.

Black women either don tame hair and wear sensible Proctor &

Gamble casual career separates or they're loud, young, stroller-pushing banshees running for the bus. And black men are either staidly corporate or border on thug life—pants saggin', gold teeth shining and cornrows pulled tight.

But come the last weekend in July, black folks break out the fake, sky-scraping, shellacked hair; the airbrushed nails; the almost-but-not-quite silk short sets; mirror-heeled shoes; booty-flossin' shorts; and booming systems.

And that's just the men.

All of this must explain why some downtown businesses close early, why some restaurants complain about a lack of customers or why there's nary a white face to be seen.

Or maybe it's easier to shut down than to try to be accommodating.

Perhaps it's easier to just be closed than to try grappling with black stereotypes in the flesh, like the one that says we don't tip well, if at all.

Why not just stay open—seeing green and not black—and risk the experience?

We're like Jehovah's Witnesses.

Nobody's home when we come calling.

Who knew a little music festival masked so much animosity and misunderstanding?

We all did.

Think back on this weekend.

Has it ever passed without incident during the last decade?

At the very least it's rife (and synonymous) with urban legend come to rest at postmodern lynching stories.

If you're black, someone you know either received shoddy restaurant service or got price-gouged at a hotel.

If you're white, you've probably seen the news reports of bottlenecked traffic, pockets of violence and general mayhem that, if attached to any one of the city's popular white festivals, would not be cloaked in racial doom.

So where are we?

Money-makin' music festival aside, we do not get along.

The divisions are chalk-outlined by race-based fears. Whites get ghost during the downtown festival and it's proof that many whites don't wanna stick around long enough to see if they *can* get along with us.

If Negroes dipped every time we were racially outnumbered—and packed up our wares as we left—there'd be a collective whites-only, neck-snapping double take heard 'round the world.

Any event so exclusively and inherently black is bound to bring out the best and worst in all of us.

And that's cool.

We can't all be me.

It's just this: The worst among us — black or white — impede the best from shaking the stereotypes and from movin' on up like the Jeffersons.

Meanwhile, the city waits for weekends like this one to come and go.

When it's over, that sound you hear is a collective sigh of relief.

And come Monday morning, street sweepers clean up our mess and white people reclaim their whiteful positions.

Last one out, turn off the lights.

Blacks Like Y'all

White people take everything.
You call it corn; we call it appropriation.
Let's start with the hair.
Rewind the tape.
Bo Derek did not invent nor did she enhance the beauty of cornrows and braids.
In fact, her silky white hair throughout *10* looked like it was loosening at its roots.
But that just may be the badblackcattiness in me.
Attend a hip-hop or jazz concert anywhere and most of the audience comprises majority people.
Black folks are notorious for taking our culture for granted.
Some of us prefer spending Benjamins on nails, hair, rims, Timberlands, gold fronts, time shares, cheap Caribbean vacations, crack, still over-priced happy hour drinks or platinum rather than to buy back a few hours with ourselves at a jazz show.
Then we complain about the lack of black events.
It's not that they're scant.
We're just broke, having spent all our ends on what we're wearing and driving.
Some of us hold narrow definitions of culture.
The symphony?
The opera?
They're "white."
They hold little appeal.
Meanwhile, boat rides and dances sponsored by mediocre black radio stations literally and figuratively sell out.
We're wack and our priorities are out of whack.
While we over-think ticket prices to events that rest somewhere off our cultural radar, white folks pack clubs and concert halls absorbing our culture. They emerge with superficial, drive-by knowledge of us.

33

To the uninitiated, it appears whites know more of us than we know of ourselves.

But it's usually just a drive-by.

It gets deeper still.

First, white America has very little original culture of its own, so it steals.

Again, appropriation.

Second, blacks are sometimes embarrassed and frightened by what we really embody.

Like the blues.

And I don't mean no Eric Clapton.

I mean the blues.

Like many of his generation with similar education, Darren, a white friend in his 30s, has an encyclopedic knowledge of black culture.

He co-owns with his brother a successful independent record store.

During a local blues festival, the two brothers stocked a stand with CD's hand-picked from their record store and sold them at the festival.

The festival annually boasts a mixed line-up of national and local acts.

It attracts a predominantly white audience.

The scant black patrons come to hear gospel acts.

White festival patrons worship the Holy Trinity of the White Man's Blues: Clapton and Jimmy and Stevie Ray Vaughn.

A white man, dressed, says Darren's brother, in his best Stevie Ray get-up, sidles up to the bins of CD's.

He flips through.

"John Lee Hooker's got a lot of albums for somebody I ain't never heard of," says the faux Stevie Ray.

Now that's a cultural drive-by if ever I've heard one.

But still, that's not my point.

For an upwardly mobile black family living in the hinterlands of white suburbia with two kids and two SUVs, the blues is scary.

It requires too much work; there's too much remembering.

So add the lack of cultural originality to self-hatred, and you get a gaping hole.

And here come whites to fill the hole with a cartoon—a caricature, really—of who and what they think we are.

Blacks chuck into this hole a little caricature of our own—and of ourselves. It's our own apathy, a rat-in-a-wheel quest for material wealth and the constant comparisons to elusive and silly white standards.

I don't advocate racial separatism.

I'm not saying we shouldn't mix.

Some of my best friends are white.

What I am saying is that before we complain about this being a white world or that the white man's got his foot planted on our collective neck, we need to get off our asses and back that thang up.

Support black culture in its disparate forms.

Plays don't all have biblical underpinnings set to a gospel soundtrack screamed by a morbidly obese, B-list has-been black sitcom actress from the 1970s.

Neither should we assume that support from non-blacks—that is, well-meaning whites—will keep our arts and us alive and vital.

And white folks, before you grow your version of dreadlocks, pull your pants down past your ass and then mean-mug a sista for staring or pump your fists at a hip-hop show, please stop.

Stop and think about how many black folks you actually know.

What's your interaction with blacks outside the office based on?

What's your motivation?

Are blacks welcome at your dinner table, in your son's or daughter's bed?

Are we allowed in your grandchildren's bloodline?

Think about how much black literature is on your bookshelf.

How much black history do you know?

How do you spend Martin Luther King's birthday?

Do you appropriate because you're bored, because it's funny, because it's hip or because you don't know any better?

Or are you really down?

If so, I wanna be like you. White and a'ight.

If not, you give me the blues.

The Beauty Politic

Q: What did the black woman with the raggedy fingernails and the suspect weave say to the Korean beauty supply shopkeeper?

A: Gimme the airbrush background *and* the glitter tips this time, Ms. Kim. And throw in a bag of hair.

It wasn't supposed to be.

But you get the picture?

Beauty is different for everyone.

However, isn't it disconcerting that black women purchase European versions of beauty (and exaggerated black ones) from a plethora of Asian nail, hair weave and beauty supply stores located in and around black neighborhoods?

Used to be they only dotted poor black neighborhoods. Back then, it was easy to take because class kept it neat and ordered. Not poor? Then don't look at it.

Now they're everywhere —from the newfangled strip mall in similarly newfangled neighborhoods infiltrated by New Negroes, to the downright ghetto-ass bodega on the corner that also sells sugary drinks and bags of barbecue chips.

It is hilarious and surreal to see Asian shopkeepers adrift yet fixed in black culture and neighborhoods.

It's mainly so because rarely do these business owners live where they make their money. Moreover, it's rarer still that black patrons like the Asian shopkeepers or, at the least, even understand their culture.

The only exchange is the money for the product.

Blacks in fact resent The Other.

Truthfully, many blacks border bigotry when it comes to our foreign-born hair and nail suppliers.

In the words of Prince, "What's this strange relationship that we hold on to?"

It's so commonplace, barely anyone bats a false eyelash.

In the distance between where I live and where I work, there are several of these joints. When I walk past, sistas splay open their fingers like the wings of a wounded bird on hot pavement. They fondle their gold hoops, twirl their store-bought hair and eyeball Ms. Kim, making sure she's hookin' those nails up.

It's so '80s.

Don't misunderstand. I'm all about a black woman gettin' bitched out. We're naturally beautiful, but the right paint in the right place never hurt, either.

But what's perplexed me for years is how black women have become nearly orgiastic in our quest for beauty.

We stalk a European definition of beauty laden with the gimmicks of self-hatred. We're paranoid and anxious we'll never get it precisely right so we settle for aberrations and low-rent imitations. So busy on the prowl for more of the latest beauty tools, we deny our children our full attention.

Beauty is important. Any woman with any self-esteem wants to look good. It makes us feel good. The problem rears its weaved head when we want to look good according to someone else's definition and at the cost of our comfort levels.

How stupid is it to have 2-inch nails when you're a word processor or you can't change your baby's diaper without some apparatus?

Just how ridiculous is it to have weaves and falls sewn and glued into your head when the addition of someone else's hair requires an extra 45 minutes of grooming in the morning?

Some of us are walking around like victims of postmodern hairagami.

Funnier still, the Asian shopkeepers don't "do" the hair they sell and it weights down the lop-sided relationship with the black beauty queens.

I'm not saying all black women have to look like me: *Essence*.

It'd be cool for about a week, and then I'd get sick of seeing myself—all those Stepford Kathys with their short, nappy/curly natural Afros or peach-fuzzed and nearly bald heads and neatly trimmed Lee Action Length nails.

Even I am not beyond the reach of the world's additives for the sake of feigned vanity. I recently had my barely there hair dyed reddish-brown.

I feel sassy now. Stronger, really.

It troubles passers-by unaccustomed to seeing—those accustomed to *seeing through*—who dares to shave her head and who strengthens herself by what she loses and not by what she keeps.

Likewise, when I cut all my hair off 11 years ago, I knew I was in for it.

That's because the length of a woman's hair in "the black community" (dis)orders some secret, unspoken social (dis)order.

The longer the sista's hair, real or rented, the higher her standing, the more valid and enticing her feminine sexuality.

So I rank low. But I do not mind because I've figured it out.

Beauty is a burden.

The store-bought kind is, anyway.

Still, we must admit that there's some degree of self-hatred at the core of this ritual of the low-rent makeover. It's nothing new, though.

Ever since Madame C.J. Walker stacked millions off potions, lotions, hair grease and hot combs, black women have been dyin,' fryin' and layin' our tresses to the side. And I speak as a former Oprah Winfrey hair double.

What exactly does all this have to do with Asian hair and nail joints in black neighborhoods?

It's time we looked in our own mirrors instead of everyone else's.

And we'll see ourselves first as everyone else subsequently should: *au natural*.

The Clean-Up Woman

❖❖❖❖❖❖

There's an all-white boys' club in Hamilton.

My hometown is 25 miles north of Cincinnati and on the way to the college town of Oxford, home to Miami University. It is a burg sequestered from the rest by its longtime refusal to be connected to or by an expressway.

Finally today there is the Mike A. Fox Highway, named for the native son who held forth against small-town resistance and got the stretch of road built.

A former representative in the Ohio House, Fox was rewarded with a post as a county commissioner. And he returned from the state capital feigning humility and salivating over the chance to annoy his formerly long-distance foes.

But Hamilton's flirtation with modern times hasn't kept it from its backward self.

The city subsists on the basis of its unspoken fraternity.

White frat brothers—bankers and millionaire landowners don't have an official meeting place, no Honeycomb Hideout, no secret handshake.

There are fewer of them than everyone else. Like its sister cities everywhere else in America, Hamilton is owned and operated by a powerful minority born of the majority.

Black folks in Hamilton have lived under this pall—with a few lackluster exceptions—of majority government and the subsequent skewed media representation since Hamilton's settler days. Racially, socially and economically delineated by the river running through it, Hamilton is also divided on far subtler levels.

Again, unspoken.

Growing up there, I always knew something wasn't quite right, that as blacks we had a "place."

"They" were over there and "we" were someplace else, usually in the Second Ward, an area literally at the bottom of the city.

My family moved out while I was still in elementary school, but as an adult I went back to work there as a reporter for *The Journal-News,* the medium-sized daily serving Butler County. Working there proved all my childhood inklings about race, gender and economic politics done up the Hamilton way.

The city has machinations all its own, and they'd been played out by the daily paper.

Back in the day—including my mid-'60s childhood—the only time you'd see a black person on the front page was in profile holding a placard with a police serial number on it.

Either that or on the obituary page.

Dead and otherwise disappeared were the sum total of our worth.

And the *Journal* played it up.

When I got to the paper, a black female reporter had just left to work at Miami University. That left me and another black woman, who was soon fired for a hodgepodge of reasons that amounted to the new managing editor's house cleaning.

And that left me as the Spook Who Sat by the Door, literally.

Seating me by the newsroom's main entrance felt like a publicity stunt that lasted five years. *See? We got one!*

The title of this book was my code name while I worked in Hamilton: Your Negro Tour Guide, or *Their* Negro Tour Guide.

I was a conductor.

Sometimes by choice, sometimes subconsciously and other times out of anger and frustration, I led the ignorant, misguided, misogynistic and myopic alike through a landscape of hot-potato issues ignored and overlooked.

Because of what my managing editor called my "perspective" (read that as "black opinion" or, worst still, "race spokeswoman") I landed a weekly column.

Meantime, I was batted from beat to beat.

There was the purgatory of the police beat, the "you take her" general assignment beat and the "let's see what happens with this" education beat.

My favorites were the urban affairs and minority affairs beats.

These are where brown reporters end up because we are experts on urban issues and also naturally interested in them since we're preoccupied with our minority upbringings in the ghetto.

I hadn't had any professional newspaper training before *The Journal.*

I was baptized wearing ankle weights.

My tenure was gimmick-laden and I bought into most of it by taking on spokeswoman status and resenting the role whenever others looked at me as such.

I ended up nearly insane, weighted from saddling the responsibility of enlightening the city's backward-thinking citizenry on my back while I played games with and out-maneuvered my crazed city desk editor.

He is a white man from Hamilton who almost permanently scrambled my marbles by undermining my self confidence and destroying my professional character to the managing editor.

In the wake of the O.J. Simpson verdict, he directed me to facilitate "introductions" between white reporters and blacks. The white reporters had been dispatched to get reaction from patrons of one of the black barbershops and apparantly they hadn't been taught in journalism school how to talk to black people.

They needed me.

I declined.

No white reporters were asked to make similar intros when I went to Ku Klux Klan rallies, to meet armed militia members or to trailer parks to interview white families about neighborhood murders.

Life's dicey for a black woman at that paper.

I was intrigued recemtly when Edwina Blackwell Clark, the 38-year-old black woman was named as editor and publisher of *The Journal*.

Only three years older than me, Clark had been in the game a lot longer, having spent 14 years at *The Dayton Daily News* as well as a stint at *The Cincinnati Post*. She's a native of Springfield, a city I know nothing about but I'll wager is nothing like Hamilton.

Whatever her intentions, plans, outlook or agenda, I wished Clark fearlessness, rest and sturdy mental health.

I hope she kicks butt — whatever that means for her.

Mostly, I hope she goes in and cleans house.

Since several of us from my beleaguered era jumped ship, from what I can tell of the paper that house on Journal Square is filthy.

Its managers are void of ideas; editorial morale is in a morass of apathy.

Someone needs to prop open the doors with wind machines and throw the switches.

I hope Clark's briefcase can accommodate a bucket, a mop and a broom.

Maybe even a compass.

Hamilton — and *The Journal-News* — could use another guide.

Black Is/Black Ain't

"You better think
Think about what you're trying to do to me
Yeah, think
Let your mind go, let yourself be free."

-- ARETHA FRANKLIN

It is long past midnight.

I have insomnia, so my television babysits me. There's an endless trail of commercials—black folks eating hamburgers, driving cars, buying insurance, frolicking on beaches, guzzling Coca-Cola.

At first I think I'm dreaming, that I've died and gone to the colored section of *Jet/Ebony/Essence/Black Enterprise* hell.

It must be a dream.

Too many Negroes.

Then that familiar dread.

It's Black History Month—the 28 days of the year when Negroes are lulled into thinking that majority culture gives a hoot about our culture because we "get" middle-of-the-night TV specials, culture-specific displays in book and record stores and the obligatory news features.

Black History Month might be the biggest farce since reparations and the most disingenuous try at reparations since the lie of 40 acres and a mule.

Remember America?

We're the country that dragged its feet with Liberia and, before that, turned its back on Rwanda when the Hutus were cutting a heinous swath of genocide through the Tutsis.

Neither country is a nuclear or military threat.

There's no oil, gold or other natural resource worth exporting, so we left our United Nations troops there, unarmed and idle, while black folks murdered tens of thousands of other black folks.

This is the culture to which we're beholden to respect our culture, heritage and legacy.

I know the argument in favor of Black History Month.

Namely, that black history is scarcely integrated in curriculum; therefore, Black History Month is 28 shots to the dome, a whippin' put on students who may not get black history anywhere else or any other time.

It's cultural catch-up.

But if you're black, you should be living black history.

If you're white, get off the black history I.V. Make a black friend; get to know a colored co-worker.

Other races? Join the reindeer games and good luck.

I may be appeasing myself when I say that when Carter G. Woodson invented Black History Week we needed it then more than we do now.

History is like a bookstore.

It should be inclusive.

What's with the colored sectioning of culture?

Like the bookstore that relegates black studies and literature to that far-away corner of the store, so have we similarly ghettoized Black History Month.

Black History Month makes me feel that integration has failed or, at least, is limping.

And us?

Black folks need to stop waiting for a week, a month, a Black History Month moment.

We are a minority.

The root of that word is "minor."

And we help perpetuate our own marginalized status.

Chances are, our children in public schools won't be taught the literary contributions of Zora Neale Hurston, James Baldwin, Jamaica Kincaid, Octavia Butler, Charles Johnson, Paul Laurence Dunbar, Ishmael Reed, John Edgar Wideman, Sapphire, Gwendolyn Brooks, Gayl Jones, Toi Derricotte and many others sidestepped in favor of the Black History Month All-Stars.

More than likely they'll be force-fed Alice Walker, Maya Angelou, Langston Hughes and, if they're lucky, Ralph Ellison, Richard Wright and Toni Morrison.

They're the safe Negroes, the ones allowed throughout the house.

And shame on any Negro who, like pulling up to a spit-shielded buffet, fills up on blackness during Black History Month.

Black History Month ain't gonna make you correct or invigorate you enough to sustain you for the other 11 months you're asleep.

Neither is it substantial enough to fully embrace all of who we are.
And white folks, you're not off the hook.
Our history is yours and vice versa.
Now let's make history together-

Prison for Bad Pigs
(A blues in the key of Jill Scott)
❖❖❖❖❖❖

"The price of hating other human beings is loving oneself less."

-- ELDRIDGE CLEAVER

I should've expected it would be a bust.

My oldest brother wasn't even there.

Randy is the Original Negro Tour Guide.

He's been stomping down the blues for more than 40 years.

He brought me out.

He gave me permission to tell the truth about black folks.

The poster child for the Angry Black Man, Randy's anger is smoothing over.

He's either tired, jaded or both.

I should have turned and left when I didn't see him on Fountain Square—gathering place for the Ku Klux, Klan and ice skaters in winter and rallies and protests in summer.

Not even the New Black Panther Party's lame ring around the rally lured Randy out of retirement from anger management therapy.

That the event was so scantily clad in attendees that my brother's absence was noticeable tells on the turnout. There were the usual suspects: a few fringe Negroes, several more curious black onlookers, Asian sightseers, the brown-bagged white lunch crowd and a few old-school black activists on the busman's holiday.

These days they sidestep involvement, preferring the sideline view of what's not getting done in the name of revolution.

Me, myself personally?

I could care less about the New Black Panther Party. I rank them with the Rev. Al Sharpton and Minister Louis Farrakhan in the trifecta of (un) necessary evils derailing and distracting New Black America.

Once I'd remembered about the rally, I went to Fountain Square out of black guilt, a self-diagnosed condition far more critical than its cousin, Jewish guilt.

45

I got off the bus, heard the shouting from Sixth Street and saw some black folks heading toward and leaving the square.

I wanted to be pleasantly surprised.

Same shit, different day, parts I, II and III.

In the end, it was like patronizing a black business for the sake of race. The price? All the merchandise is tagged with non-existent customer service, surliness and substandard product.

But you go, anyway. Some tired tune about recycling black dollars rings in your head like that ugly-ass song you can't shake.

Same thing happened during the rally.

It was like an open casting call for a Wayans brothers production spoofing the glory days of black activism, rage and revolution now diluted a muddy green with the blackening of corporate America.

The underlying message was weak the few times it was discernable.

Something about bad pigs or crooked pigs, black unity and black love, a tumble of disjointed statistics about the disproportionate amount of imprisoned black men.

A black protest rally isn't a black protest rally without the tangy zest of song and dance.

There was a politically correct exhibition by a multi-racial drill squad of young girls. They gave us some half-hearted, rhyming, quasi-Jesse Jackson rhetoric about unity, freedom, justice and being "somebody."

The stage was flanked by a few crudely written signs, also difficult to figure.

"Prison for bad pigs" was the most prominent.

It especially resonated because as soon as one of the speakers said he'd attended the "Jewniversity of Cincinnati" then, voila! We got ourselves a failure to communicate and a soundbyte for the evening news.

"Jewniversity" does whom what good?

Cultural criticism is one thing.

Dropping idiot bombs to infuriate people into a froth is another.

The New Black Panther's intent fell short if it was supposed to light fires under the 10 or 20 people who actually listened.

See, mobilization requires a platform, and it isn't just a thing you stand on.

Secondly, to articulate that platform you must be, well, articulate.

If you cannot speak clearly about the machinations of police brutality without reading a poorly constructed speech, then sit down or step aside.

Finally, lobbing racial stereotypes like water balloons is lazy and irresponsible.

Anyway, what makes the New Black Panther Party think anyone will "win" the race race when they're in the relay?

They become who they claim to detest most: bigoted hate police.

And to that, I flip the script.

I say for every "Prison for bad pigs" sentiment there is "Bad pigs for niggers."

It's equally myopic and inflammatory.

So what if the factions who have similar contempt for the other—white racists (cause) and black race baiters (effect)--what if they teamed up in an *Amazing Race*?

Who'd end up as *Survivor*?

That's some reality TV worth watching.

On second thought, already caught the reruns.

It's the 40 Cs!

"Dude looks like a lady."

-- AEROSMITH

There oughta be a name for people like me.

You know, people straddling perception and reality because of interpretation.

This is about hair, breasts and identity.

Let me tell you what it's like walking around as a black woman with barely there hair and 40 Cs. I mostly keep my hair buzzed short not out of any confusion over identity, self-hatred or penis envy, but because I'm lazy and it's cool looking.

And I'm cute this way.

Yeah, I've got a pretty, round, brown face and dark eyes. Lest you think this is a singles ad, let me move on.

I had hair—lots of it, in fact. But it's overrated and sometimes a security blanket. I never felt freer than when I first cut my hair off in, I think, 1989. Even when I had hair, I never could relate to those commercials with flaxen-haired white girls throwing their manes around.

My point is, people get so twisted over female presentation and what exactly *is* feminine that my bald head is cause for pause.

People actually stop.

Their physicality changes.

Some stare and, when I attempt eye contact, look away.

Then there's the case of the two white guys—one we'll call Ice Cream Man, the other we'll call Redneck Man.

I'm addicted to those butter cookies at Graeter's, a local ice cream shop pedaling hand-dipped homemade ice cream. One day I was waiting in line with a 50ish, silver-haired matron at the Graeter's in Hyde Park, a toney, posh neighborhood where white people either jog or drive luxury SUVs everywhere.

The clerk—Ice Cream Man--was on the telephone while servicing patrons at the counter.

The lady perused the cases. Hyde Park Man, phone tucked between his ear and shoulder, glanced up at me. "What can I get ya, sir?" he said.

I'm accustomed to but not immune to this kind of hurried assumption.

"Just these," I said, handing over the bag of cookies for purchase.

"Oh...uh...uh...oh, I mean, ma'am. I'm sorry, ma'am." He fell all over himself.

What's best in instances like these is one quick apology.

Either that, or we should all just act like it never happened, like a booger hanging from a friend's nose, an impolite public fart or the open zipper.

The lady next to me was outraged.

"I cannot *believe* that!" she snorted, her voice hushed like we were at the opera.

"There's no way you could be mistaken for a man. You have such a pretty round face. Those cookies should be free."

I giggled.

I love well-meaning whites.

"Forget the round face," I said, "What about the 40 Cs? How could you *not* see these?"

Unimpressed, she kept her focus on the pastry selection.

Weeks later I was walking into Joseph-Beth, an independent bookstore in a shopping center in Norwood, a working-class white neighborhood bordering Hyde Park.

It was mid-afternoon, so hot I felt delirious.

I thought a skate through the bookstore would inspire me to write.

Plus, I was killing time before returning to the barbershop.

Al, my barber, has an uncanny ability to estimate haircuts to the minute so there's rarely a backlog of uncut heads clogging the waiting area.

You come back, it's your turn.

I couldn't wait to get into the bookstore.

Like an outtake from *Deliverance* appeared a shirtless, raggedy white man driving a raggedy white van.

Yes, it was Redneck Man.

As I walked through the parking lot, we made eye contact.

He slowed down. I slowed down.

Aaaw, I thought. *Bring it on.*

Just as I set foot on the sidewalk to the bookstore, he yelled from his window.

"Take your boy-lookin' ass on somewhere!"

His timing was perfect. He'd waited 'til I'd reached a clearing so everyone within earshot could see the bald black bitch he'd caught in his sights.

I felt like I used to in the fourth grade when Robert, son of a Klansman, put pictures of black folks hanging from trees on my desk, trapping me and then smothering me.

I felt ambushed.

I was angry and confused.

How could he just yell out what he thought of me when I'd squelched my classification of him?

I wanted my say.

I turned and walked up the embankment, waiting for him to enter traffic and drive past on the main thoroughfare. Maybe he'd get caught at the light and I could have a word with him.

I remembered a long-ago image of my mother—tall, black and proud with fists fitted on her waist like an Angela Davis action figure. Throughout my childhood, she was always somewhere setting someone straight. While it was thrilling to watch, it almost always left her drained.

And I caught myself about to disrespect the urban nobility of my mother's sass.

I was 'bout to be a straight nigga.

Then Redneck Man turned the other way. Lucky for both of us.

Laughing at the absurdity of Redneck Man's shout out to my presumed identity, I walked into the bookstore and cooled off. I couldn't shake it so easily, though. I seriously reconsidered cutting my hair again.

Then I stopped myself when I realized I almost let some fool have power over me.

I am a black woman whose bald head makes me invisible to some, boyish to others and beautiful to me.

It makes me unfettered and unadorned.

Mostly it makes me free.

And without it my name is all woman.

Harlem on My Mind

❖❖❖❖❖❖

"It's a gift to feel this good."

The New Black Aesthetic has arrived.

Our grandparents, Zora Neale Hurston and James Baldwin, bequeathed it.

They got it from and gave it to folks like Romare Bearden, Gordon Parks, Josephine Baker, Miles Davis, Paul Robeson, Ossie Davis and Ruby Dee, Sidney Poitier, Duke Ellington, Nina Simone, Donny Hathaway and Jelly Roll Morton.

I discern the spirit of the NBA these days in MeShell NdegeOcello, India.Arie, Savion Glover, Common, Mos Def, Bahamadia, Jill Scott, Erykah Badu, Saul Williams, Carl Hancock Rux and in all their imitators and haters.

I live the NBA vicariously through Cincinnati black nerds like artists Joe Bailey, Ken Leslie, hip hop trio IsWhat?!, and Jazz trumpeter Mike Wade.

Soundscapists The Five Deez DJ the soundtrack.

Shelle Clark, Dani McClain, Bobbie Corbean, and Bug Williams are all muses who have NBA DNA.

Their names mean nothing to you, but they're equalizers when bad news threatens to prevail.

Their lives manifest truth and they don't subscribe to gimmicks. ·

No more okey-doke. Status quo is a guaranteed whuppin'.

They ain't takin' or talkin' shit no more.

No crybabies or victim language allowed.

Dues are due the first of every month.

Late fees come as lies.

The NBA is head bangers.

They carry change.

They strange.

The Cincinnati members of the Hurston and Baldwin branches of the tree have a clubhouse, a space to validate.

Ever been to Harlem? Me neither.

But Harlem has as its twin East Walnut Hills, my mixed-race, mixed-income neighborhood situated in central Cincinnati. And like 125th Street in Harlem, New York, East Walnut Hills is getting a storefront-by-storefront facelift along its main corridor.

Simone's, a restaurant-cum-art gallery and performance space, is the anchor that started it all. Once nearly hidden from sight by its locale on the inside of a rear-facing, nearly empty plaza that time forgot, Simone's is now the anchor of a swank new development with high-end rentals towering above it and specialty shops at each elbow.

So we sojourn to truth at Simone's.

We go there to strategize, confer and confirm.

I laugh a lot while I'm there. I love everything about my blackness every time.

The southern fried tilapia sandwich isn't the only draw.

Atif Kemaz is Simone's brain trust, court jester, publicist, sometime cook, waiter and bus boy.

Owning and operating Simone's is the "oh yeah!" to his tangential conversation peace.

This is a lifestyle review.

Atif is as close to James Baldwin as I'll ever get.

He's black, gay and non-traditionally outrageous. His urban sophistication stifles his flamboyance just right, right before it starts to grate.

He's unapologetic about his mission.

Get with Atif or get out of his way.

Back in the day, I didn't understand adulthood. Simultaneously, I play-acted at being myself. What was happening? What was to become?

During this time I ran into Atif at the Loft Society—Bug Williams' spooky electric acid test tube spot with all them jazz hoes in its creamy center.

We sit Indian-style on his floors and swig jazz.

Atif was hawking homemade jewelry and greeting cards in the kitchen next to a skyline of pots of greens, pans of meat and pedestals of homemade cakes.

In life's ebb and flow I'd see him, then I wouldn't see him.

When I did, he'd be just back from Israel, Amsterdam, Egypt.

Meeting Atif reminded me I could do as I pleased.

He gave me permission to be free.

One day in the late '90s, I was hoofing it to my hooptie with fresh laundry from the Family Affair Laundromat.

I was cold crushin' a blue raspberry Slushee when I saw Atif coming out of Salaam East, a little almost-but-not-quite bistro next door to the hair salon that's next door to the laundromat.

Salaam East? Atif invited me into his unfolding dream/nightmare with its dark walls, mud cloths and postmodern Black Arts Movement canvasses by Jean-Michel Basquiat's babies. Later he told me melodramatic tales of inspections, licenses, cash flow, no cash flow and on and on.

Back then, it was open but only privately for book club meetings and Loft Society gigs.

Then came an e-mail inviting me to an international Sunday brunch at what's now Simone's.

I always suggest Simone's.

The food is the ambiance.

Sunday's the best day to sightsee the colored section.

Old black church ladies eat sautéed sweet potatoes; white couples share desserts and map out the day. Rastafarians bring their children to the vegetarian menu.

But this NBA thing ain't rocket science, especially not here and now. It's easy to be a Negro making moves in Cincinnati because there are so few of us using our powers for good, so few who don't fall for the hype of small-town talk-radio notoriety.

In this thicket, NBA members find one another.

For the sake of diversity, non-traditional New Black Aesthetic Negroes must remain in Cincinnati. When we leave, the pendulum of power tilts to the other side.

And we must stay knowing we'll be excluded from conversations about the flight of the city's creative class.

NBA members are used to being see-through. Still, we see through you.

I'm often asked when will I leave town. Surely, they ask, New York, Los Angeles or Chicago beckon a Tour Guide.

I used to ask it of others in the NBA.

Why would I leave? Doesn't mean I won't—just means I'm in no hurry to dip out. I'm ambitious but I believe in playing my position.

The NBA and I have work to do here, mainly to accurately document our times.

We take responsibility.

We disassociate.

Do not confuse us with those champagne sippin' moneymakers like media mogul Ross Love or athlete Ken Griffey Jr.

We are not Stepford Negroes. We step off.

This is our stop.

Here's where we get off: We take chances, we ain't scurred, we travel abroad and we return broad, we make legacies while others merely plan.

We rock worlds, and tectonic plates are shifting beneath us, readjusting the Earth's foundation to fit our needs.

Paths mark themselves for us. Tomorrow knows us by name.

And Simone's is where we rest our heads and replenish for the rest of the trek.

Our souls *have* grown deep like the rivers.

But we swim.

Demystifing Davis

Angela Yvonne Davis is a militant bobble head.

An easily recognizable pop culture icon.

When I was a little girl Angela Davis was first just an Afro, like Don "Love! Peace! And Soul!" Cornelius.

Like the Chi-Lites.

Like my mother.

Then Angela reminded me of danger.

From *Jet* headlines and the way street soldiers invoked her name like a verb, I cobbled together that the early 1970s was no place for a black woman like Angela Davis.

She was a professor at the University of California, Los Angeles, and an outspoken member of the Communist Party. She was fired, ran from the feds on dodgey charges, got thrown in prison, served a 16-month sentence and was finally acquitted.

Her clinched fist raised in defiance above the red sunrise of her 'fro is the visual refrain to "I Have a Dream."

It burns and resonates.

She's now a tenured professor of history at the University of California, Santa Cruz, despite then-Gov. Ronald Reagan's vow she'd never again teach in California's college system.

From 1970, when Davis was on the FBI's 10 Most Wanted List, to her 1972 trial my mother looked a lot like Davis. When I was between 5 and 7 years old, my mother found part of herself, especially her post-divorce self, in Davis' aesthetic and inher defiance.

She mimicked Davis from the circumference of her Afro to the ring of her bellbottoms

If Davis had dispatched a lieutenant to battle sexism and racism, she would've hired my mother. I secretly called Mom a "store counter soldier" for her militancy during The Battle of Being Overlooked at the counters in our small town stores.

Like Davis, my mother is statuesque. Their influence on me intersects somewhere at the corner of mother and heroine.

One summer I made my way to an African merchant downtown during Ujima, an annual street festival. I'd heard he had Angela Davis T-shirts. I snagged a brown one. It's a full frame of Davis' face. I wear it when it matches my feelings. It's only a T-shirt but I take it seriously.

When Davis addressed a near-capacity crowd at the University of Cincinnati, I was finally under the sound of her real-life voice.

"Standing here at this podium at UC and in Cincinnati, I can't help but feel that, in some sense, I'm standing at the center of the world," she said. "There are some [aspects] connecting Cincinnati with Palestine and Kabul."

She addressed us where we are, twice invoking the name of Timothy Thomas, the 19-year-old unarmed black man shot April 7, 2001, by Cincinnati Police Officer Stephen Roach.

The shooting invoked looting, fires and showdowns with the cops.

We were catapulted to international news blotters as yet another powderkegged American city seething with racism.

An economic boycott is underway and some entertainers and artists have by-passed us, choosing not to cross over. Many more have come, anyway.

"I have never crossed a picket line or violated a boycott," she said, "so I did come after I was assured this is being done in the spirit of building restoration to . . . end police misconduct and economic apartheid in this city."

Applause ripped through the auditorium.

I've always liked the way Davis' mind moves around at will.

She deconstructs complicated ideas. She unravels and restitches thoughts into wholly digestible blocks.

She demystifies academia.

Maybe what always made her dangerous is her insistence upon inclusion.

"Knowledge is produced at many sites," she said. "It's not only produced at colleges and universities. One of the most important sites is at radical activism—activism against racism, against gender bias, against homophobia and activism against war on terrorism."

She tethered male dominance to racism.

"We continue to be told this is the end of racism, and that we no longer need affirmative action. Much of the racism explicit in the law has been eliminated, but does that mean racism has ended? Racism doesn't only express itself in the law. There are *structural* forms of racism."

Davis then took off on prison reform/abolition, women's health, white male privilege and voters' apathy surrounding George W. Bush's presidency. Davis said there are "historical links" begging us to make the right moves.

"Where are we at the beginning of the 21st century? Are we more able to act upon those links and connections or are we less able?

"The forces of oppression count on the parochial and provincial nature of our character. Let me be more specific. The Bush Administration relies on a certain kind of common sense that assumes we'll act upon a simplistic thought process as in a division of the world into legions that do good and those that do evil.

"Bush claims so many of our problems will be solved by revisiting marriage as an institution of male dominance as a panacea for welfare mothers.

"His presidency is about regression. So how do we exist in a post-Sept.11th society? I'm reluctant to use that term, 'America,' because there are so many nations in America. How is it we got bamboozled by the notion of a multi-cultural America?"

Navigating the loitering mostly black and white attendees afterward, Davis questionslingered unanswered.

She'd made me feel mighty and small, empowered and beleaguered. Heroine worship does not pacify reality.

Guess Who's Coming to Dinner?

❖❖❖❖❖❖

A white man purchased me.

The slave metaphor is tired, but it's true.

I thought I was doing a good thing by offering myself 'at auction' to benefit a reading program of the Unity House World Peace Center.

Dianna Brewer, Unity House Jillito-of-all-trades, asked some months ago. To add leg irons to injury, she'd planned the event at that bastion of white, gay male divadom — The Dock, or 'The Dick' as the gay club is known around these parts.

"You know the irony is not lost on me that I am being sold in front of a bunch of white men at a white, gay male club?" I told Brewer.

I waffled, laughed, hemmed, stammered.

Finally, I said yes. I wanted to use my powers for good.

Dread and fatigue conspired against me and, on the night of the auction, I fell ill. My dead-end obsessing over not being able to justify traipsing the catwalk in front of a bunch of money-clutching white men got to me.

Even in my absence I was still bought. By a white man.

From what I hear around town, he's cool enough — politically active, with all the 'correct' boxes checked on his membership forms. I'll be the guest of honor at a small dinner party in his home.

I'm expecting it to actually be an honor.

During our two or three phone conversations, he's sounded reasonable and open-minded. He reads my column, laughing and taking offense in all the right places.

This writing marks Gay Pride in Cincinnati, a time when mainly white gay men and lesbians line parade routes and party in a street-festival atmosphere as a show of, well, gay pride. When I say such events are mainly white, the included majority mistakenly takes offense, and no one bothers to consider that the absent minority bears as much, if not more, accountability for their exclusion as the people reveling in their privilege.

When segments of our city are broken down in specialty groups — gay,

Latin, Catholic, black, poor, etc.—it's obvious how separated we are once we try to reconvene around issues of humanity.

Witness the boycott group Black United Front's (BUF) near repulsion at welcoming Stonewall, a mainly gay human rights group, into its fold. Likewise, check Stonewall's own foot-dragging when the BUF came to Stonewall and solicited help with non-gay and non-lesbian issues.

We're splintered.

There has been, however, fragile progress in mending our relationships.

Negroes in the fight for racial equity crave the privilege and organizing tactics white gays and lesbians utilize, while white gays and lesbians covet the scratch-off instant angst and attention Negroes garner when we gather to sing our tales of woe.

See, people more readily believe and are attentive to racism. Overt racism lost its en vogue status somewhere in the mid-1980s.

Conversely, many more people can be homophobic and it's somehow acceptable.

And the struggle for "cause" attention between gays and blacks is the ultimate *Survivor* played to the soundtrack called "Your Blues Ain't Like Mine."

It's like comparing the atrocities of the Holocaust to those of slavery.

When I walk into this dinner party, I will not behave like commodity, like property. '

Course not.

I will give the host his money's worth. I will be the me of these columns—appropriately impolite. Honest. Real.

Maybe more of us from different camps should have dinner at one another's homes. Maybe we could all stand to buy and sell one another for a night.

It's not like we'll have to live together.

And it's not like we've never bought and sold ourselves before.

Only this time, no ownership.

Only fellowship.

Leviticus: Faggot (No. 65)

❖❖❖❖❖❖

"Hey faggot, better run, run, run 'cause Daddy's home
Daddy's sweet little boy just a little too sweet and every night the man showed
the faggot what a real man should be."

-- "LEVITICUS: FAGGOT," MESHELL NDEGEOCELLO

The soon-to-be murder suspects in the dark blue Cadillac couldn't leave gay enough alone.

Discontent to let the year dissolve without resolving their homophobia, they eked out the city's 65th homicide for 2002 with a few hours to spare.

Gregory Beauchamp, 21, stood on the corner of Vine and West Liberty streets on New Year's Eve with at least three friends, the caller told me. The dark Cadillac pulled to the light.

Beauchamp and his group stood there, perhaps reveling and maybe a little tipsy already. Maybe they flamed like flamboyant gay men do: Arms flailing, hips thrust forward, heads cocked back—gay, proud, outrageous and excited about the night ahead.

Two in the group were transvestites—"he-shes," the caller said—and they were on their way to the Venus Club, to bring in the New Year. They were noticeable; gay men who interpret themselves this way are conspicuous.

But on a corner in a neighborhood where black men sport the "uniform"—jeans two sizes too big sagging nearly to their knees, hoodies, Timbos and bubble coats making them identical and profileable—a gay man hanging with two transvestites sticks out like me at a Klan rally.

And the butch black male ego recoils at, then reviles against and finally eradicates, such outlandish behavior because gay men are antithetical to his outlandish butch posturing. There's no room in the 'hood for faggots.

But ask the faggots under assault, and they'll tell you many of the homies vomiting gay-bashing hate speech at them are the same ones—Tupac-bumpin', Courvoisier-sippin' brothas—now populating a subculture of B-Boys trolling gay clubs for head. But that doesn't make them faggots.

They receive. That makes them men.

While under the cover of darkness and with some anonymity they enjoy the game of sexual subjugation, these "men" despise what, in broad daylight, they might become. Then a cycle of violent self-loathing ensues that absolutely must be transferred onto the lowest on the food chain — the faggot.

For a black man dwelling in the ghetto of his myopic mind, a faggot is the worst possible thing he can become. Faggot is the worst word he could ever call his enemy.

To banish a faggot with words and bullets is the ultimate form of rebellion against the powers that have conspired against him. It says this: If I'm nothing according to them, the faggot is even less according to me.

Back to life and death. The four or five young black men in the dark Cadillac yelled epithets at the group on the corner.

Surely Beauchamp, an affable and openly gay man to his friends, was accustomed to verbal assaults.

The caller said the car circled the block, returning with still more passengers. More vitriol is vomited from the car.

Then came the only thing left to do for a 'hood rat who's trying to impress his colleagues and secure his membership in this distorted brotherhood: Beauchamp was shot once in the chest. He died on that corner.

A burned-out metal skeleton matching the dark Cadillac was found later on New Year's Day, and the alleged perpetrators have scattered like roaches.

They should be proud, though. They had a hand in ensuring our city would top its previous murder record.

They added Beauchamp to the age bracket (18- to 30-year-olds) most affected by the murder rate. Plus they increased to 56 the number of men murdered in 2002.

And they killed a faggot.

But there's no statistic for black-on-black hate.

What's Matter with Self?

White T-shirted niggas look like pigeons. They flock and clock on corners and in doorways pushin' death onto white and black likewise niggas. Then these peddlers swagger past one another, Biggie-sized uniforms won/one with the win of sin. They all look alike/like we do to whites.

They look away from palms pressing cash only long enough to check the score.

White T-shirted niggas are so bad, so stealth and so cold-blooded they serve in God's broad daylight. What for?

For death, for cash, for rims, for babies, for they mammas, for life. Maybe because it's all they know. But they know better—they just can't do better.

They've got corner offices cornered. Their balls are briefcases; beneath is where they stash stashes. They're always bringing work home. Cell phones chirp orders: Buy! Buy! Buy!

They're up in arms like heroin. It's scary when they drop guns in garbage cans, scared to carry the weight whenever cops chase quotas.

I'm unarmed. Got no statistics and no police reports. No official government statements, poll results or disingenuous political concerns. I don't even have interviews.

I just see white T-shirts. So many white T-shirts, it's like clotheslines stretching above ghetto sidewalks.

Like you, I'm afraid to approach and talk to any of the brothas within the swarms of posturing and jostling crack and cocaine dealers. Besides, they ain't feelin' me.

I might as well be five-o. Anyway, I got my job and they've got theirs. We're both seers. I see cause and effect; they see supply and the man. Still this feels like betrayal. Until now they've counted on us to always consider them invisible.

I hate to disappoint. Something says: Speak.

The threat of racial excommunication—of wearing The Scarlet Sell-Out—will be worth it in the end, because maybe someone will do something. Meanwhile, I'll write more sentences than they'll serve, and up above my head *"I'm a P.I.M.P."* repeats, depletes, defeats.

It's beats, rhymes and life. And I can spot 'em a black away.

I know them by their white T-shirts—those awnings hewn from Hanes declaring them to be merchants selling crack and powder cocaine. I know them to be black, mostly boys and men.

Sprinkled among them are young black girls donned with the androgyny of white T-shirts, jeans and boots. Trying to fit in, the girls nudge at the periphery of street-level drug trade, swapping their bodies for slang and rocks. Either that or they're customers working sex for leftover crumbs and dust.

They exhale blowjobs. They inhale suicide.

White T-shirts got little use for a real woman. They reek. They weak.

I know 'em, but I don't want to get to know them. Our long-distance relationship is better. It's more comfortable to check each other across the pain of half-closed car windows.

If we talk, we'll have to break it down about disappointment and stereotypes, about joblessness, illiteracy, AIDS and homophobia. Our exchange will be all about absentee mothers and fathers and broke-down grandmothers, child support payments, subsidized housing, Kobe Bryant, bitches, hoes and being locked up. We'll have to go there.

Really I am already there, and every direction I turn there's nothing but white T-shirts. Thirteen- and 14-year-old black boys tagging behind twentysomething black men, and they're all wearing these shirts, sometimes in layers of three at once.

I recognize them, yet they're anonymous. Maybe it's genius. Maybe the more alike they look, the harder it is for cops and robbers and victims to call them by name.

They are proud. Maybe it's professionalism. Maybe the whiter the shirt, the purer it is to smoke and snort and cook to get all coked up.

There's an infestation of dealers and addicts. Vermin. Pure roach.

All around I see them clamoring. If I know what they're doing, why don't the cops?

Why isn't the racist anti-loitering ordinance effective? Why are its targets left congregating? What good's an unenforced statute?

At what point are we terrorized to submission. Why does the monotony of a white T-shirt make the rest of us appear abnormal?

I'd ask 'em, but I feel more comfortable just keeping my eye on them.

Thank God they're wearing white T-shirts. It makes them easier to see.

That Negro Problem

When I was a young girl, I'd burst home, breathless tales of school-mates swinging between my pigtails. "Mom, Jeffrey, this white boy at school ..." or "Karen, this one white girl ..."

I didn't make similar distinctions for black classmates. The behavior of white kids seemed different, and I had to say so.

My mother, born and raised in segregated Appalachian West Virginia, where she refused to step off sidewalks for passing whites and read from hand-me-down texts discarded from the white high school, stopped me cold at the outset of each racial description.

Exasperated by her insistence that I start the stories over, this time without the "white," I eventually stopped. Not because it was right or correct, but because it pleased my mother.

I was profiling. Even then.

See, my white classmates behaved in ways my black classmates just didn't. Cultural? Social? Stereotypical?

I don't know. But race-specific behavior exists.

There are things whites do (coatless in winter, convertible tops down when it's sunny but cold, close talking, beer festivals as excuses to get drunk) that black folks shun. Likewise, Negroes have ways whites appropriate (sagging pants, Rap, barbecue and, well, anything else cool you can imagine) but don't dare permanently adopt.

Deeper, though, are crimes we commit.

Yes, there are "black" and "white" crimes, but mainstream media don't report this aspect because it's intangible. Negroes don't publicly cop to the relief we feel when school shooters, rapists, baby-killing mothers and serial murderers are white. Conversely, Negroes barely bat a resolved eye when gang bangers, home invaders, drive-by shooters and baby-mamma beaters are black.

Such black crimes lean to the lean. That is, we commit reactionary and passionate crimes and it's nearly, if not absolutely, a stereotype to say so. With exception, criminals of color tend to be blue-collar, low-rent offenders, whereas whites commit time-consuming crimes studied by Federal Bureau of Investigation profilers.

Negroes have been accustomed to discomfort since the Middle Passage. We violate in response to violation.

On the other hand, whites commit crimes in direct correlation to the disruption of their comfort—from Wall Street and S&L scandals to shaking and drowning needy babies. To paraphrase James Baldwin, whites have less tolerance for discomfort and therefore mean to correct it immediately and at anyone's expense.

But a *black* Muslim *sniper* in Washington, D.C.? Ain't enough bean pies in the world gonna spring this brotha.

C'mon, admit it. You were surprised. Even the cops first looked elsewhere and investigated Latino leads. *¿Que?*

I, too, was in that number of the Negro non-believer. I assumed the sniper to be a white, paramilitary Ruby Ridge-dwelling separatist or a fanatic Bin Laden lieutenant waging second-tier terrorism.

Why? Because, like a bag of Skittles, the victims ran the rainbow.

When the news came, I pursed my lips and raised an eyebrow. I sang a song of "hmmmmmm."

You know the drill: Maryland officials arrested 42-year-old Muslim convert John Allen Muhammad and John Lee Malvo, his 17-year-old brainwashed stepson, in connection with 10 D.C.-area killings and possibly a liquor store killing in Montgomery, Ala.

Now comes word the pair are suspects in the February 2003 fatal shooting of a Tacoma, Wash., woman whose aunt once worked as a bookkeeper in Muhammad's car repair business. They're also liked for a May shooting at a Tacoma synagogue.

But since the first shot rang out, investigators went looking for hate in all the wrong places. Led by the shell-shocked Montgomery County Chief Charles Moose, investigators had composites of white vans.

They told Latinos not to fear deportation if they'd come forward with information. And the media speculated, insinuating the sniper, when nabbed, would have an alphabet-soup name and sport a turban. Meanwhile, Muhammad and Malvo—M&M to you—were camped out in Muhammad's blue 1990 Chevrolet Caprice maybe sharing a KFC two-piece meal with an extra biscuit.

Muhammad was pulled over a day after and 50 miles from one of the shootings but was released after he came back "clean." And this isn't the first time America's hunted the wrong man. Remember when cops looked for a brown man as Ghost Dog Timothy McVeigh drove away from the Alfred P. Murrah Federal Building?

Back to the middle. Where is the notion born and how is it belched up that Negroes are incapable of high-caliber, calculated evil and heinous crimes against humanity? We, too, suffer mental illness, hatred and fanaticism frothed up to the level of sociopath. Excluding ourselves says we don't live in the world or we're somehow exempt.

People, black and white, still are saying they don't think cops got the right people. Unless another gunman suns himself in the light of a confession, it's true.

Now say it loud: We black and ain't proud.

Movin' On Up

❖❖❖❖❖❖

Oh, those party conversations.

It was said wistfully, in passing.

Still it carried heft. *Whooomp!* Like a steaming sack of hot do-do it splattered down.

The affluent black woman at the holiday gathering confirmed the quiet fears and anxieties of upwardly mobile, scorched-earth Negroes everywhere. She hoped her pre-adolescent son, though surrounded by white children, wouldn't grow up to marry a white girl.

And this from a mom living so far east that Negroes probably carry passes to drive around in their own neighborhoods.

Negroes living in suburbs to the far north and east are hilarious. And they don't realize it.

They move as far away from us as their myths, aspirations, fears, money and sweat equity will take them. They show their children otherness and recoil when the offspring covet that otherness.

Then they wake one day and realize that a) their (white) neighbors resent the assimilation, b) their (blackwannabewhite) children are rapidly aping their assimilation, c) they've created a paradise lived from the underside of a glass ceiling or d) their sons appear destined to give 'em the sweetest taboo—marrying a white girl.

Gasp! Clutch the pearls.

But don't stay in a state of permanent Mayberry. What can you expect when you've socialized your children to be as far away from themselves as possible? When white is the paradigm, it will be the reality.

Let's get one thing clear: I don't advocate separatism.

I'm not a honkey-hatin' Black Nationalist. I don't subscribe to the notion that to be black—I mean reeeaaallly black—a Negro must be down by street decree. You know, an urban dweller raising nappy-headed children who stayed put in the ghetto to prove a point.

Nor am I a playa'-hatin' sista begrudging any black person their share of what and how they consider the American Dream. Dream on.

I am a Myth Buster. I'm taking out the gimmicks in my range. I'm here to remind that *The Jeffersons* was a sitcom created by a white man starring black characters so bitter, bigoted, hostile and self-loathing we *had* to laugh.

Maybe it reminded us of ourselves. Wasn't it secretly delicious the way George could snort "honkey" and call the Willises "zebras?" Perhaps we dreamed of being simultaneously rich and hateful.

Why, it was white flight in reverse. We could move on up and hate *them* instead of them hating *us*.

All I'm saying is, when you move on up, don't be surprised when your self-inflicted alienation comes back to bite you in your newly acquired Burberry.

But black sprawl is more serious than Negroes moving away, acquiring and then questioning. It creates and manifests unnatural competition between us in a society that delights in its people killing themselves softly so they can own what they can't afford.

Unless Negroes are independently wealthy or entrepreneurs who don't have to make hellish commutes to the city to make more money, black sprawl might actually contribute to the fraying of the New Monied Black Family (NMBF). And though NMBFs tend to remain intact, they're not healthy units. We don't discuss them the way we denigrate single-parent black homes.

Why? Simple.

The more we make the more we (think we) need, and the more we (think we) need means the more we must work and the more we must work means the more time we spend away from the home we're killing ourselves to pay for but it's a home we're never in except maybe on the weekends and then we're so exhausted we don't want to be bothered with the family we *say* we're providing a better life.

And it don't stop. If the mounting stress grows disproportionately to the rest of their lives, I'll bet one SUV, one private school education and one nanny that these Negroes are pulled taut to the point of implosion.

I bet they're self-medicating to numb it down. They're overwhelmed and perhaps questioning their identity while all the time measuring themselves against a standard they neither created nor even fully comprehend.

But it's OK. It's OK to show our children we did better than our parents and that they can do better than theirs.

How much should that lesson cost? What's the price tag on identity, and will a second mortgage cover it?

The point is we don't have to go so far to find ourselves or to prove points. When we do, we end up threatened, classist, hostile and alienated. Separate and still unequal. Just like *The Jeffersons*.

Head Job

I use humor. I use it to diffuse the stereotype of the angry black bitch and to stunt my hate-filled, presumptuous and bigoted growth. I guffaw to keep from screaming.

Seth wanted to rub my head. He should've asked first. The answer still would've been a *hell* no. But I deserve the option.

I was in Boston with more than 1,000 other journalists for the Nieman Conference on Narrative Journalism. Intentions to learn strained beneath the groan of being with award-winning and internationally acclaimed talent.

There were so many Pulitzer Prize-winning writers that, if we'd been bombed, the resulting brain drain on America would've caused a collective black out.

Friday night Jason, Linda, Seth, Maureen and I convened at the hotel's over-priced spinning rooftop restaurant. Jason and I entered the ring of the oft-sidestepped topic of police misconduct. I ran it down like a commercial for a crooked law firm: Caton, Jorg, Roach, Twitty, Thomas, Owensby and Streicher.

Seth and Maureen got the *Reader's Digest* Award Tour of Cincinnati. Jason defended the cops. I didn't.

The only black person, I reminded Jason I'd done the Police Tango. I'd danced the Profile, the Detention, the Follow-the-Nigger and, my favorite, the Interrogation—a dance Negroes do when we're stopped for being in the wrong neighborhood.

The checks came and Linda retired, while Jason, Seth, Maureen and I reconvened to a lounge. Seth looked to be either a Seattle-born Indie musician, a med student or a New York barfly—but he's a magazine editor. He's tall enough to skulk.

The four of us talked about our writing processes and their downfalls. After enough, we said our goodnights and split.

After a detour, Jason and I made our way to the elevator. Seth, Maureen and four or five other whites—all men—were already crowded in.

I stood next to Seth. Before I knew what was happening, I saw, in my peripheral, his long arm and the left hand of his pair of Edward Scissorhands rising over my head. His spindly hand, palm down, rubbed my newly shorn head.

I recoiled. "What are you *doing*? I have *no* desire to rub *your* head," I said.

"You don't need to rub my head," he said, smiling and satisfied. "I just wanted to see how it felt."

The other white men seemed to hold their breaths, hoping they wouldn't witness a fight.

"You messed up my hair," I said, exiting.

The laughter at my back was nervous and tight. "Thank God" hung in an invisible thought balloon above their heads. That protective humor spared us. But wasn't funny.

In Jason's room, I vomited the scene in a run-on rant. Seth's reducing me, in the rub of my bald head, to a subliminalgooddarkiemammy stunk not only of low-level racism—it was a flash of white male privilege in an instant gratification egg roll. During our conversations, I'd not given him any indication his invasiveness was welcome or appropriate.

And this wasn't the first time I'd been caged in the Negro Petting Zoo. During my tenure as the only black at the *Hamilton Journal-News*, a young male photographer blanched after he touched my hair. He didn't have an invitation, either.

I was cultivating dreadlocks when, during small talk at my desk, he reached out and felt my hair. He quickly pulled his hand back, wiping it slyly yet repulsively against his Gap jeans.

I can't remember how I handled that one. Probably asked, in some faux Chris Rock squeal, "Why was white folks always tryin' to touch black folks' hair?"

Exasperated, I told Jason I was sick of making white men feel comfortable in response to my own discomfort.

"If I'd been, say, bell hooks I bet Seth wouldn't have pulled that," I said. "Does he know who I am? I'm a 37-year-old professional woman!"

As all innocent whites must who associate with known disgracers of their race, Jason took it.

I'm not a fur coat, a puppy or the manifestation of the exotic black woman. I'm beautiful, yes, but my boundaries are clear.

Saturday I spied Seth across the room. I played my position. God waited until Sunday morning. (Isn't that just like Him?)

On a double take, I recognized Gerald Boyd, the black former managing editor of *The New York Times*. We both got on the elevator.

"Ohmigawd, you're from *The New York Times*? Gerald Boyd?"

He laughed. In a few minutes, he would tell us about building two major projects, "How Race Is Lived in America" and "Portraits of Grief."

Seth and I coincidentally converged on the same sad pastry table outside the ballroom. We exchanged polite greetings and small talk.

I looked over and saw Boyd again. Nearing the ballroom's door, I pointed out Boyd to Seth.

"I just came down in the elevator with him," I said.

"Did you touch him?" asked Seth.

"No," I said, "that would've been inappropriate." My voice was loud, agitated. "And I didn't rub his head, *either*."

Sitting in the row nearest the door, Maureen was in full laugh at my comments by the time I'd stepped inside.

"I knew that was you," she said.

Exactly. It's me.

So don't think because you're whiter, taller, more privileged and presumptuous or just a stupid man that you can ever get away with doing a job on my head.

Volunteer Slavery

"You know, there's nothing worse than being wrong around white folks."

-- JILL NELSON, 'VOLUNTEER SLAVERY'

I still wince. Yanked off car crashes, fires and dog attacks, I was anxious to prove my worth not as a writer but as a reporter.

The exact date now fails me, but back in 1993 or 1994 I was thrust into my first major story as a daily general assignment reporter at the *Hamilton Journal-News.* I'd been given the task of following the demise of the Community Action Agency. Shoddy leadership, mishandling of state monies and a discordant board added up to boisterous, sometimes violent meetings and the threat of people without basic social services.

I was a nervous wreck throughout, but I compensated my anxiety with energy and hard work. I wanted to please my bosses and prove they'd made the right decision by hiring a good writer who was an inexperienced reporter.

I was present when it came time for the board to finally vote to accept or decline the state's offer to temporarily dissolve and rebuild. I filed what I thought I understood.

It was all wrong, up to and including the headline that read something like, "Board votes to end CAA." I royally and with vigor screwed up that story.

After all three editors ripped me a new one, I spent the entire day tracking down and apologizing to each board member. The next day we ran a correction/apology the same length as and in the same spot as the original erroneous story.

And I stayed off the radar, keeping my head down and doing grunt stories nobody would notice until I again felt confident and redeemed.

The embarrassment was intense because the *Journal-News* is my hometown paper. Besides facing peers and sources, I had to face all those well-wishing black church ladies who reminisced over my pigtails and dimples.

It was my first hard-knock journalistic lesson. In such cases — I was then one of two black reporters and ultimately the only black reporter — there's the rush to frame the tangle in racial polemics.

What will white people think? What *will* they *think*?

It's a gimmick.

There's something misleading, however, about the nobility and inclusiveness of journalism. Journalism is like police work; it's ignoble and rife with blame. Newsrooms are like neighborhoods; they're classist and sorely lack diversity.

Class, blame, ignobility and diversity? Smells like *Times* Spirit.

I want to sit down in a bookstore with 27-year-old Jayson Blair, the defrocked *New York Times* reporter accused of leaving a "long trail of deception" from October 2002 to April 2003 fraught with "widespread fabrication and plagiarism," according to *The Times* itself.

I'd talk to him about being depressed (he clearly is), playing the race card in the newsroom (he and his editors did), shabby newsroom management (he excelled, then suffered because of it) and lying in the name of a "good" story.

Blair and his editors should know that nobody bought their disingenuous push for "diversity" because swaddled in that rank egg roll was their brand of the old-boy network. Just because they made room for a colored boy makes it no less a network that closes rank around access and privilege.

Blair was mismanaged and pushed along because he cozied up to top editors. And it got them all in hot water.

Blair should take solace, seek cover and heed this advice. First, don't make future mistakes but expect to and, when you do, take full responsibility. Editors' stars rise vicariously through their writers, so when a writer crashes in flames a substandard editor will piss the fire out but won't blanket the writer in guidance.

When a black writer screws up, we do — right or wrong — carry the weight of Ida B. Wells and the rest of the race on our narrow shoulders. This, too, is a gimmick. When our white counterparts make missteps, there's no public discourse over the character of all white people because one of them did something stupid.

Finally, I found comfort in the pages of *Volunteer Slavery*, Jill Nelson's manifesto documenting her rocky tenure at *The Washington Post* and published around the time of my fiasco.

"Not that there's anything inherently horrible about making a mistake, but when you're a Negro in America it's usually not just you who's making the mistake, it's y'all, the race, black folks in toto," she writes. "One individual's fuck-up becomes yet another piece of evidence that affirmative action equals incompetence, that people of African descent somehow just don't fit in, that America cannot rely on spooks to do the right thing, no matter what Ossie Davis and Spike Lee say."

Jayson, bro', you messed up. You lied. And now that's on you and no other Negro I know.

But I feel your pain and alienation. Because I know what volunteer slavery feels like.

Instant Vintage

I live in column time.

My clocks tic snatches of conversations and tocks moments when humanity notices itself. Suddenly war, AIDS, famine and empires make sense.

This is dedicated to all those times when nobody sees it but you.

"There's something in the way of things," says Amiri Baraka.

The morning of my 38th birthday, I woke still drunk from hours before. Birthdays ego-trip us into believing perfection is a birthright and a day without revelry is a failure.

Intoxicated, I stepped into my day. Vinnie lawn jockeyed on the stoop, and I stooped to conquer our past hostilities. We joked with the mailman.

"Don't bring me no bad news," I said.

I ripped a bill to shreds and moved my lips as I read a card from my beloved mother. God cooperated and pulled back the curtain on His son/ sun.

Black men sagged on corners. They didn't avert their eyes when I looked to size them up. Some smiled. Some watched until they lost sight of me, and we weren't at odds.

Vine Street was mellow like late summer and cats counted their loot, leaning to the side to shield us from the sight of someone else's money.

I ambled into Tucker's. The boxer at the counter stole my nut. "It's her birthday," he said to the room. He never said how he knew.

David DJ'd a mix tape from the mid-1980s, and I ordered to the blue-eyed popcorn Soul of Tom Tom Club's "Genius of Love." (*Whatcha gonna do when you get outta jail? I'm gonna have some fun.*) None of it mattered once Lee brought the steak, eggs, grits, toast and lemonade.

I matched music trivia with Rick while The Cure's "Close to You" played me back to the University of Colorado circa 1985. David sent me off with carrot cake.

At Findlay Market people recognized me from my "Hot Seat" schtick. I felt black by popular demand when the short white lady told me she rarely agreed with me but liked the way I express myself. How nice for her.

At my car a derelict and dirty black woman with a beard asked for seven or eight dollars. I derided her for passing on to me the inflation of homelessness, crack addiction and mental illness. Remember when a buck panhandled your guilt? I gave her $1 and told her to be careful.

I sailed home to sort clothes. The laundry swishing, I camped out next door at Simone's. Atif and I solved the world's problems slouched in the employee booth. I begged for a kite from AmeriStop and, while I folded pajamas, received a fistful of kites wrapped in the plastic sleeves of my girlhood. We kidnapped the African man doing his laundry and flew kites in the parking lot.

Back home, my cell phone chirped and it was my brother, Kenny, recuperating from a bicycle accident. He said he's fine but sounded tired, small and scared. He wished my birthday happy. My brain percolated toward night.

April, Nicole, Nikki and Courtney showed up, delivering a church-basement-grandmamma-good 7-Up pound cake commissioned from my aunt Janice. The quartet of black women who live at *106 & Park* in a *Real World* reality coerced me into Thai food.

I broke camp for The Greenwich and the Ra Session, where Eric Steins split my wig with vowel movements borrowed from Gil-Scott and Baraka. Then i.e. croaked the "Happy Birthday Song" and Dani from Camp Dennyson battled flaming B-52 shots that made her dance down demons and that blazed down my throat and settled sunrises behind my breasts.

Nas made us look on the way to Lava, where sweaty white men thanked me fallettinmebemicelfagin and the DJ eulogized Nina Simone in a sorcerer's remix of "See-Line Woman."

A filmstrip of Napoleon woke me Sunday and I told him so in an electronic Valentine. "You don't even have to call back," I said.

Welcome to the colored section. Tears well up my throat. All the commitment, promise, shame, power and beauty of being 38 floods my dining room like shafts of black sunshine and I cry over spilled ilk of this dichotomy—abundant blessings and anorexic praise.

Everything is OK, and strangely that's not OK. And it goes on like this.

'Dead & White'

"I gave my promise to the world/ and the world followed me here."

-- "TESTIMONIAL," RITA DOVE

This is the antidote to war.

Burgeoning into poetic brilliance, Rita Dove thought all writers were "dead and white."

The revelation elicited polite titters.

"I loved to write, but I thought of it as play," the Miami University alumna (class of 1973) said in a crowded Hall Auditorium. "And it *is* play. Serious play."

Dove fell pen over poem in love with writing when, at the outset of a back-in-her-day creative writing class, she realized she could "take a class in the thing I love to do."

She cares for words, carries a torch for them. She toils so words might praise her name. She is an elegant thesaurus who nails down glabrous moments.

It's why poets live among us. They straighten abstractions and make obviousness abstract. They remind us life without poetry overwhelms.

Life swallows us whole without the lasso of the deft/Def poet. Successful revision, not name-brand recognition, is Dove's hallmark of success. She told us priorities are obvious once you find what you love. Her priorities are ordered.

This was some Big Name Lecture masquerading as a love song. Imagine Jessye Norman singing "Amazing Grace."

'Twas Dove who taught my intellect to rear, and Dove my fears relieved. When I first read about Thomas & Beulah, I anticipated a whuppin.' She won the 1987 Pulitzer Prize for poetry for the book-length cycle that eye-spied her grandparents—just 14 years after graduating from Miami.

Dove vividly remembered when she first tripped the white fantastic. New to MU from Akron in 1969, she wandered, wondering "where are they?" about her fellow incogNegroes. Despite some memorable racial insensitivities, undergrad went OK.

"All the black students, we knew each other," Dove said. Her tone assuaged and dispelled. "We knew each other well. We got together and taught one another to dance."

She took a master's of fine art from the University of Iowa. In 1993 she began a two-year stint as Poet Laureate. She's been a Fulbright Scholar. Her husband is German and resembles a holdout from *This Is Spinal Tap*. There's a daughter mastering art history. Years ago their house burned to the ground, but some librarians taught them to identify charred manuscripts, which survived as "charcoal blocks."

Dove and her husband study and practice ballroom dancing. The poem "Brown" was born after a travelling saleswoman tried to convince Dove to buy a ballroom gown.

"Any color looks good on you," the woman chirped.

Dove, 52, prefers her brown skin. It rules polite spaces.

She is sleeker and more air conditioned than the dated black-and-white book cover photographs brimming with an unruly Afro that lost a fight with a hot comb.

Her scientist father taught Dove and her brother that learning never ceases and just getting by was intolerable. "Flash Cards" tells it:

What you don't understand, master, my father said.

And the faster I answered, the faster they came.

I had to guess.

"10," I kept saying.

I'm only 10.

"These are poems that trace the education of an artist who didn't know she was going to be an artist," she said.

But for a writer the nougat is hearing of another writer's process. It's conspiratorial validation.

"I write poems in fragments, letting them dangle for a while," she said. "Poems also have a way of completing themselves when they're good and ready."

Hers are dense. They're directly antithetical to the flim flam of the brushfire of poetry slams, which she credits so long as they foist "something good."

Dove's poems ignore the laziness of obvious rhythm and burdensome metaphors. She calls this delving "deeper than logic," as she told a student questioning the tricky imagery of one of her poems.

The former cellist forges poems in the guise of classical scores expansive as Greek mythology. They demand work. It's only reciprocity. Dove worked them.

We rewarded her with a standing ovation. I milked watered-down prominence and got ushered to 20 seconds of uninterrupted audience in the lobby.

On a page in my favorite journal where, during note taking, I'd already twice scrawled her name, she wrote "Rita Dove." Who's dead and white?

James & Annie (and Me)

❖❖❖❖❖❖

I left during intermission.

I got half a play buzzing through my brain.

Growing up I couldn't understand why my mother, born in 1934, never got excited about TV movies and documentaries that retread racial paths she'd literally walked along.

I was all over anything on PBS or network television about America's screwed up race relations. I remember *Roots* quieting my whole neighborhood and generation.

We were spellbound by how real slavery looked.

It wasn't a myth, a lie or a history book footnote. We'd come from somewhere.

Likewise with PBS's *Eyes on the Prize* and *Slaves in America*. They titillated my starving intellect and filled in the crevices left by my stingy public school history lessons.

I still love watching black people testify about where we came from and what we made along the way. And the art, families, literature, travels, laws and love are always a salve to racism.

The most divisive and the trickiest parts of racism are the lies it tells.

Racism makes its sufferers defensive. It makes its victims believe they're insane because, surely, this clerk isn't following me through this store and I know this realtor isn't showing me only homes in black, high-crime ghettos.

Racism makes its underclasses crave invisibility and, once that's achieved, forces those underclasses to act out so they can again be visible if only for the purposes of the statistic.

Negative attention's better than none.

In 1979, I was in the first class bussed to a predominantly white Greenhills High School and I lived through the blunt trauma of *"Guess Who's Coming to Study Hall?"*

At Heritage Hill Elementary School in Springdale, I was daily terrorized by Robert, the black-haired white boy across the aisle who quietly showed me some strange fruit—grainy photographs of black people limply hanging from trees. He and his dad were going to do the same to me, he whispered.

For weeks I thought this was my lot, that this must be what the fourth grade is supposed to feel like. I finally told the teacher and emancipated myself. Robert still lurked, but I wore down his resolve by tricking him into thinking I wasn't afraid of him.

Travelling through sequestered parts of the Midwest, I've been told the public bathroom wasn't available for me or that I'd better get my nigger ass away from wherever I happened to be. Working at *The Journal-News* in my Hamilton, Ohio, hometown, I got death threats so often I thought "nigger" was my name.

I'd long given up persuading my mother into seeing those televised re-tellings of her past starring other people.

Not out of frustration.

Out of respect.

"I don't need to relive that," she said. "I lived through watching my grandfather step off sidewalks for white people, coming to back doors and reading from second-hand textbooks passed down from the white high school."

She sucked air through her teeth instead of cursing. "That was painful *then*."

And now I get it.

Last week I went to see *James & Annie* by Warren Leight, also known as a producer and sometimes writer of *Law & Order*.

Or I *tried* to see it.

There were some funny lines, some good sentences. I was relieved to laugh, and I laughed too loud. I do that when I'm nervous.

I was nervous because I knew the road was soon to bend into coal-black misery for James, the naïve, gung-ho and blindly patriotic black World War II veteran chasing an honorable discharge. In a fit of end-of-war passion he'd fallen for Annie, an equally naïve white woman chasing her own set of freedoms.

And this is where the dramatization of history turns back on itself and lands at reality.

For blacks, the enactment of America's racist past (and present) doesn't end when the final curtain falls or with after-show drinks to wax poetic about the play or this and that.

I'm silenced and haunted by the nuanced realities of post-war life for black war vets—white soldiers crossing the street to keep from saluting black brass who ascended the ranks in empty appeasement of Eleanor Roosevelt and whose lives were forgettable when they weren't cooking and cleaning for the white armed forces.

James got caught up because he bought into the American Dream, and he choked to death on its nightmare.

There are times when I'm steeled against sorrows without happy endings, victimization without redemption and realities with no escape hatches.

But not during this play.

James & Annie did what good art's supposed to.

I was uncomfortable.

I didn't get answers. And I was reminded.

But it was just one of those days when, like my mother, I couldn't look right into the face of it.

So since I couldn't switch the channel, I left.

But I'll go back and see the other half.

I don't run from the sight of strange fruit.

Just ask Robert.

Call Me Chad

I knew I was a nerd when, way back when, my brothers ridiculed the way I talked.

Just like fellow black nerds, I got clowned for "talking white."

In case you've taken a lifetime cultural commercial break, talking white means using good diction and enunciation capped by a European vocabulary.

No Ebonics or lazy slang.

Good *English*.

In my case, I'd said somebody at school got "socked" in the mouth instead of "hit" or "punched." And Randy and Kenny hit me with a one-two punch of "White girl! White girl!"

That had to be 30 years ago, and in the name of black nerdiness I've been taking left turns ever since. I've consciously decided not to join, belong, fall in line or be beholden.

Anyone who's arrived at herself knows it's hard to be who she is.

Being a female black nerd is especially foreboding, because there's an extra box of invisibility: female.

Like all movements and subcultures, women are subjugated and relegated to support positions.

You should be here, the invisible rules state.

Black men forget that because they've been dismissed by the world it's not OK to externalize their rage by further dismissing women once they get home.

Cultures are inclusive.

I've found some solace in my black nerdiness because, unlike mainstream popular culture, black nerdiness doesn't require status quo approval and there's no secret handshake.

Class distinctions are non-existent and there's nothing to aspire.

We are merely *in*spired.

There's no dress code, no checklist to say you're in. It's the Me Phi Me.

I can rock Kathy any way I wanna, and it'll always be correct because the ink's perpetually drying on the blueprint of my me-ness

But don't get that me-ness wrong.

Black female nerdiness has its desert island loneliness.

I try to wear sneakers everywhere, my glasses are an accessory, I've never owned a car manufactured the same year I bought it and Bobby Brady and Michael Evans are my fashion idols.

And when I was teaching myself to skateboard and leaving DNA on the street, my girlfriends were laid up on their parents' phones listening to and telling lies throbbing with prepubescent sex.

The day 25 years ago I got my first pair of glasses—tortoise-shelled Ralph Lauren ovals—was more momentous than when I passed my driver's test. I have more books and records than clothes, shoes and everything else combined.

I'd rather be fighting with a good sentence on a Friday night than chasing an olive at the bottom of a glass in some bar or club.

Besides my mother, all my heroes are artists.

Though I distrust all politicians, I vote so my grandfather won't yell at me when I get to heaven. I believe in God, but I question all religions.

Other than the Brownies, I've joined only one club in my life—the Ohio Newspaper Woman's Association—and that was so I could enter a journalism competition.

Even then my editor had to strong-arm me into it.

I read over-priced European music magazines and I've been thinking of starting a 'zine about...what else? Me!

I can count on one hand the furniture in my apartment that was purchased brand new. The rest was found curbside or negotiated for at thrift stores and yard sales. I learned more from reading and talking to people than I did during the sum total of the three times I tried and failed college.

Anywhere I am is where I'm supposed to be.

It was only two years ago after my first trip abroad that I realized I'm a citizen of the world.

I thought this was all there was.

I picked prominent local blacks to illustrate a feature story on black nerds because they transcend the emerging trendiness and instead embody the spirit of black nerds through the ages.

While interviewing each of them, I learned things about them I didn't otherwise know and saw myself through a lens darkly. They're fearless, entrepreneurial, questioning and ultimately ostracized and misunderstood because of it all.

Yet they thrive.

Maybe not how you'd define thrive. But they're free becauuse they self preserve. And they don't apologize or barter in order to fit in anywhere.

Further, with all the brouhaha over the (white) creative class and its I'm-too-sexy-for-this-city mass exodus, the black nerds have been overlooked.

We've stayed. Nobody's bothered to ask us why or how, especially unnerving considering the city's embarassing track record with Negroes.

And we stay because we know that, without us here, a black hole would suck down progressive politics, art, music, protests and socioeconomic change. We build communities and do so without the benefit or glare of media attention or self-congratulatory limelight.

We comprise The Other.

We're the ones who show up looking out of place but who nonetheless will always belong.

I've been nicknamed Chad by intimates who can't quite finger my tomboyish, white frat boy daily uniform of T-shirts, cut-offs, old-school sneakers and baseball caps.

Call me what you wanna.

I'm going with Kathy.

The Scarlet 'L'

Black talk radio in America is the new black church.
And I don't attend regularly.
Dwight Patton, splintering ad hoc/half-activist member of Black United Front (BUF), a grassroots activist group, spitted and sputtered his venomous way through outing me on the radio on *1480 Talk with Courtis Fuller*.

Fuller, a former TV news anchor and mayoral candidate, hosts the daily show on WCIN, the nation's longest-running black radio station and one of two black talk stations in Cincinnati.

I was shocked but not surprised. Though winded from the punch in the gut, I was prepared.

Don't he know I've been blind-sided all my life? Been in sorrow's kitchen and licked out all the pots. Sticks and stones, brother, sticks and stones. I know I am, but what are you?

Patton can't hurt me. And to make absolutely certain, I stole his thunder. I snatched back my freedom. I came before him. I got mine and rolled off.

My sexuality has long been among a grocery list of judgment-heavy words like speculation, discussion, debate, horror, fear, damnation and prayer. Perhaps yours as much as mine.

As such there are people who even think my sexuality invalidates my intellect; that it backspaces me to the child's table. Some people say I don't speak for Negroes or anyone else.

Why, they're absolutely right. I didn't sign up to be spokeswoman for anyone but myself. Nothing about me gets co-opted. Still, it's fodder.

"Eck! She's a dyke," they whisper. "Nobody's listening to her."

Most of these homophobic naysayers connecting the incorrect dots are Negroes. Many in that number are Christians. They've forgotten that we collectively and individually have so much work to do that fretting over who's in my bed is not only counterproductive but silly and dangerous. It shows a real lack of focus.

I do, however, understand such obsessive/compulsive behavior.

They're looking, turning over rocks hoping to find something. There's nothing in my closet but ugly clothes and too many pairs of black shoes. So I don't owe y'all anything.

I owe my family—especially my two young nephews and a sister 13 years younger—the benefit of certain truths. That is, when they look at me I want them to see me finally standing comfortably in my skin.

Two parents who labored in the church raised me in a nearly devout Christian home. They've made mistakes and woke the next day to try again. Save a prayer 'til the morning after. I know I live outside the full grace of God in more ways than one.

So drop those stones, 'cause your house is transparent, too—I see you. But I digress.

"I wanna ast you a question and you don't have to answer it. You can tell me it's none of my business," Patton said, sounding like a manic street preacher. "You don't have to answer."

Patton blathered something about the BUF and Stonewall, the largely gay and lesbian human rights group. My first red flag went up.

There are Negroes in the BUF who want no affiliation with the gays and lesbians in Stonewall. They think if homosexuals are in "the fight" they'll soak up some of that precious struggle spotlight from "black causes."

Black civil rights leaders in the 1950s and 1960s stiff-armed James Baldwin back in the day. Forget that Baldwin was a pied piper for racial and social equality whose pen wielded significant influence. He was an ugly black faggot.

"I wanna know—you can tell me it's none of my business—with Stonewall, and it don't have nothing to do with the look," Patton said, getting excited.

Hmmmm. "The look." A second red flag.

"But are you a le-le-le-lesbianbisexual?"

I leaned into the microphone. My throat was relaxed, my voice clear. "Yes, I am," I said, while he tripped around, still muttering.

He muttered some more: "You don't have to answer."

"Yes, I am," I said again.

He kept talking.

"The question has been asked and answered," I said. "We're talking today about terrorism, Lt. Col. Ron Twitty and the international ballet. What's the correlation between those three things and my sexuality?"

Then a tennis match ensued between Patton and Fuller. Fuller won, shutting Patton down and maintaining control of his show. Patton hung up in a huff.

I'm not gloating. Sarcasm is my defense mechanism. It's kept me from catching a case.

I respect and protect a person's right to express an opinion. But this was an ambush.

I am the O.G. Punxsutawney Phil, poking my nappy head from my hole only so far and exposing only so much. I'm normal that way.

But whom I love doesn't make me any less loyal as a friend, doting as an aunt, honest as an artist or devoted as a daughter and sister. Whom I love makes me a lover. Whom I love makes me fallible as a Christian.

Don't go yelling "Bingo!" so quickly. You still know only as much as I've let on. How you process the information is up to you.

I'm moving on. Except to say this.

Your plan worked, Mr. Patton, though I still wouldn't know you if you sat down beside me on the No. 69. Yep, it worked. I'm free.

But the scarlet "L" stands for "Loser."

Now look who's been outed.

Talking Black to the Screen: Black Folks at the Movies

❖❖❖❖❖❖

Announcer: Last weekend, Kathy Y. Wilson went to see the movie, *13 Ghosts*.

She didn't like the movie very much and she knows just how everybody else in the theater felt about it, too.

Y'all shut up, hear?

When I heard the black woman in the back of the theater say this to her two black male companions before the start of *13 Ghosts* I was again hanging with another crew of NWB—Negroes Who Blather.

Negroes Who Blather aren't new; they're just another kind of Rap group.

Depending on your vantage point, Negroes Who Blather either add value to the price of your movie ticket or they're singlehandedly responsible for another cultural phenomenon—The Mean Muggers; the people who turn a stern face to the talkers in hopes of killing them softly with silent daggers.

If you've ever been to see a certain genre of movie—you know, any drug-related/hip-hop laden/monster/*The Matrix*/Kung Fu/*I Know What You Did Last Summer*/*New Jack City*/gangsta/you better have my money/*Boyz 'N the 'Hood*/baby mamma drama flick—then you've heard the NWB.

Movies are meant to be escapism.

But to black folks movies are like buffets. We visually pick and choose what we want and anything we don't like we verbally throw it back. Anything we dig, we applaud, laugh and holler at.

Call it verbal seconds.

Flicks are to the murderously mundane black existence what the Underground Railroad was to slavery—a way *out*.

And with the advent of discount multiplexes, the 'hood rats who count themselves founding NWB members have still more, cheaper chances to get their chatter on.

They come on busses. They come in hoopties. They come in droves.

Forget those industrial, gimmicky trailers with the faux-techno music and the "No talking, please," instructions.

Talking black to the screen is as *de riguer* for the movie-going NWB as procuring a babysitter is for the YUPPIE.

When I saw *13 Ghosts*, a movie dripping with blood and special effects about a group of unsuspecting, postmodern ghostbusters in the guise of a family who inherits a haunted glass house from an evil, not-quite-dead uncle, the NWB chimed in at all the right—and wrong—times.

Don't go in the basement! That's where all the trouble is, y'all.

Girl! Turn around!

Man...oh naw!

They killed the punchlines and laughed at the wrong times, like when characters were crushed, slashed and dismembered.

See, that's what the NWB do.

They cackle. They talk back. They talk black.

It's a form of rebellion.

Yeah, rebellion when black folks normally silenced in the outside world by crack addiction, misdirected corporate aspirations and a general feeling of self-hatred and disenfranchisement talk black to the screen.

OK, OK, it may not be all that serious.

Wait a second, yes it is.

Peep this: A darkened movie theater is a place where black folks simulataneously rise up and recline.

Somewhere in all this cultural genuflecting we are the best and worse of ourselves.

We talk back 'cause we can.

'Cause we're black.

'Cause we got soul and we're super bad.

Shutchomouf.

Bush's Lott: State of the (Racist) Union

Announcer: In case they're burning the midnight oil at the White House tonight in preparation for tomorrow's speech, we've asked some of the people who've written commentaries for this program over the last year for their suggestions for the State of the Union Address.

Racial issues have come up frequently for President Bush and the Republican Party in the last couple of months.

There was, of course, Sen. Trent Lott's praise of Strom Thurmond's segregationist presidential campaign.

But, also, the Bush Administration's legal brief on affirmative action and the President's renomination of Judge Charles Pickering, which is opposed by the NAACP.

Commentator Kathy Y. Wilson isn't sure what President Bush might say on the topic of race in tomorrow's State of the Union speech.

And not knowing is what concerns her.

My Dear President Bush:

This isn't calculus.

But you've been calculating.

And boy, oh boy, have you got some 'splainin' to do.

What better time than your State of the Union Address? We'll all be there and we'd like new answers to old questions. Like, what's your stance on Sen. Trent Lott?

Where do you *stand*?

Your silence is deafening surrounding Lott's "Song of the South" for America's segregated past.

There's no doubting where Lott stands on the color line.

Frankly, he said it.

But you, Mr. President, you've dodged bullets, you've been slippery, hands-off and even passive.

You've let GOP underlings dog Lott off his high post.

Yet, during the 2000 election you grubbed for southern votes by declining a stance against state capitols flying Confederate flags. Tie these together and we're beginning to wonder about you, sir.

I imagine your speech writers and advisers scrambled after Thurmond's birthday party and they came up with, well...nothing.

And the GOP, the new white nationalism, has reared its rednecked head.

And mum's been your word.

Therein lies your problem.

You gotta talk.

We're left wondering whether this New Century Republican Party really loves its Negroes. Or, are they just lawn jockeys?

Not to worry. Mr. President, I've got ideas.

Here's how you can let America know: A) where you come down on Lott's lot and B) that you're serious about not slapping blackface all over the Republican Party.

First, endorse affirmative action.

Merely shuffling Negroes to greater visibilty within your administration, that's fine. But they're already there, so that's not really outing yourself as anything other than what you are. Your vocal support of affirmative action spells decisiveness and progressiveness.

But I know you won't do it.

Or, try telling America you'll propose a bill to begin a commission to study the feasibility of slavery reparations. It won't make you a coddler. However, it would show your seriousness in addressing and eradicating the time-honored racism that got Lott in trouble in the first place.

But I know you won't do that, either.

Here's what you can do.

Apologize.

Not *for* Lott. Rather, apologize for your guilt by association, for not stepping up quickly and for leaving us to this guessing game.

In case you didn't know it, apologies go a long way with Negroes.

Simply assure us that Lott's America is not your America, and that Lott's GOP isn't your GOP.

Because we already know neither one belongs to us.

Sincerely,
Kathy Y. Wilson

What Fresh Hell Is This?

Cincinnati, Its Dickless Mayor, His Riot & Going Back to "Dead Nigga Blvd."

Cincinnati UpSouth

Cincinnati is the southern-most northern city.

Yet, in our uppity northern ways, we make fun of all things southern.

But they've made visible strides since sprayin' niggers with hoses was a sport.

And just how far have *we* come?

Our attitudes about class, race and gender are as southern as a plantation.

It's a tired but true metaphor.

This city is, as my friend April, says Cincinnati UpSouth.

Federal numbers bear the truth of who we've become.

But our actions tell on us, too.

According to 2000 U.S. Census figures, Cincinnati is the sixth most segregated city in America, up from No. 18 a decade ago. Census takers use complicated equations—segregation and dissimilarity indexes—to figure that we really can't stand one another.

Despite a population of 331,000 that's 53 percent white and 43 percent black and in spite of the fact that two high-ranking city officials—vice mayor and city manager—are black women, No. 6 means we're not mingling. `

We don't co-exist. With few exceptions, we don't live together.

At work we maintain water cooler friendships with people of different races, if we work together at all. And at the first sign of trouble—cross or menorah on Fountain Square?—we show our true colors.

After reading such a depressing/oppressive government statistic, it'd be easy to point a crooked finger at banks for redlining certain neighborhoods based on race and class.

I wanted to rail against City Council for always setting a sad example of leadership and unity and for marching us *straight* to the crapper.

And I wanted to tell the cops to stop terrorizing everyone and then maybe, just maybe, whites would stay put and Negroes wouldn't be so angry, so riotous ... so *black* .

But our segregation is bite-sized. It's how we treat one another when the chips are all the way down.

When I say "we," I mean us—black folks.

My own people.

Blacks are equally guilty on the road to perdition. Somehow we don't think so.

It's part socialization as perpetual victim and part chronic fatigue syndrome from centuries of servitude that make us this way.

Together it's a heady cocktail.

One hit, and we become what we've loathed and seen at work, play and in the neighborhoods and families we've integrated—technicolor bigots.

Suddenly we're bigots of the loud-mouthed variety. We make generalizations based on revisionist history to further our own agendas and to reclaim the sick-hot spotlight of "they done done me wrong."

Case in point: The "rally" on Fountain Square by the Black Fist, an ad hoc group of protesters and hangers-on who demonstrated against the placement of a menorah. This year it was a menorah and not a cross in the ongoing holiday festivities I like to call "Who's on First, and Is It a Religious Symbol?"

That we annually consider the Ku Klux Klan's cross on the Square says as much about the lethargy and passivity of City Council as it does about our collective threshold for pain and bigotry.

Speaking of pain and bigotry, members of the Black Fist held signs demeaning Jews, and there were other signs that were just plain senseless. "KKK babies born with monkey tail and breast fed by black moms and dogs," read one. Wha?

"Jews killed Jesus, had black slaves, stole our black identities!!!" read one carried by Amanda Mayes, co-chair of Coalition for a Just Cincinnati.

Blacks think we can't be bigots. We're getting away with semantics. We're confusing bigotry with racism, hatred of a different hue based on the rich greens of economics.

We can be bigots, and we are bigots with vigor more than we'll admit.

Black folks perpetrating hatred and oppression is nearly laughable, especially against Jews. And if protesters had a beef with one Jew or two, why curse them all?

What if whites carried signs on Fountain Square that said, "Niggers sell drugs, rape our women and overcrowd our prisons?" There wouldn't be enough mic time at City Hall.

Blacks manipulate biblical history to curse Jews, forgetting more recent history such as the Civil Rights Movement when Jews marched with us, fed us and bled and died with us. Further, cursing an oppressed colleague—Jew, Native American, Asian and Latino—gives grist to the larger hate mill.

And *that* is the point and the proof of segregation.

Those craving a racially divisive status quo rejoice at your ignorance and your tactics. The point is segregation isn't relegated to whites getting away from blacks or vice versa. Segregation is a tentacle of racism and its bastard brother, bigotry. We've all been reached.

At its base, segregation is akin to terrorism. Though quiet, it still effects us. Though not exploding, burning or murderous, it remains on our lips, in our hearts and guiding our subconscious.

Who needs the Klan or Bull Connor when we've got one another?

Just remember that two wrongs don't make a white.

What's in a Name?

◆◇◆◇◆◇

Pooh hadn't been expecting us so early.

But there we were—three hot, hungry, tired and sun-baked black women and a 1-month-old infant—collapsed in a rear booth at the Queensgate Frisch's.

Queensgate.

Its name suggests royalty and exclusivity.

Queensgate reps another time and place for Cincinnati when rails replaced SUV's as major forms of transport, shipyards were turn-of-the-century parking garages and the West End brimmed with immigrants who hustled like their modern-day counterparts peddle phone cards, 40 ounces and fake hair.

Queensgate today is mainly the gateway to the urban Appalachia of Price Hill, which is jammed with poor whites and Mexican day laborers; it's home to office supply stores, a gas station, warehouses, fast food joints and printing plants.

We'd just come from perusing the 12th Annual Black Family Reunion at Sawyer Point, a manicured park spanning the banks of the Ohio River. Discouraged by the snaking food lines and sudden influx of the ultimate 80,000 total attendees, we dipped out early to find a place we could sit and get our grub on.

So here came Pooh to take our orders.

Barely occupied when we came in, the restaurant, too, filled up.

"They said it was gonna pick up, but not 'til after 6 o'clock," Pooh said, already dirty and exasperated only five minutes into her shift. "Yeah. They got the Reds and Bengals playin', Kidsfest and the BlackFest all downtown."

Wha'? We raised our eyebrows.

BlackFest? Hmmm.

Being black in Cincinnati means never having to say "I know you."

Know what I mean?

No?

Black Cincinnatians are slightly paranoid about our identities because we're identified by the events that cater to us, how we respond to police treatment and, finally by where we reside. And regardless of zip code identity—our blackness—forces us to overcompensate.

In doing so we're constantly wondering if we're being disrespected.

The *least* this white girl could do is get right the name of one of our festivals.

I bet either of us could tic off one of her festivals.

It's silly but this is how we get down.

We waited for Pooh to get herself together.

We pretended we didn't hear her so badly mispronounce the Black Family Reunion that she boiled it down to a name closer to a dashiki and Afro pick party.

BlackFest.

It was just lazy.

It was just diresspectful.

It was just *wrong.*

It was like being called "Jackie" repeatedly when I know I'd enunciated K-a-t-h-y.

But you know how that goes—whenever someone says something so wrong, chances are they'll repeat it.

With certainty.

So we made small talk.

Something like, "Yeah, there's a lot going on today."

And sure enough, Pooh ran down the list of events, again landing lastly on BlackFest.

Speaking for everyone, as I usually do, I said, "When you say BlackFest, do you mean the Black Family Reunion? It's *Black Family Reunion.*"

My friends chimed in. "It's the Black Family Reunion. Where'd you get BlackFest from?" It wasn't an attack, just a correction.

Pooh threw up one chubby white hand, ordering pad in the other. "Thatswhatthey toldmeintheback.

"Thatswhattheytoldmeintheback.

"Thatswhatthey toldmeitheback."

She ran her words together like she was declaring her innocence.

It was no big deal, really.

Just telling.

Here we'd just come from the city's most celebrated and well-attended black-specific event, second only in instant name recognition to the JazzFest, and Pooh just messed over the name.

I think it was culture shock for all of us.

Unlike the stadium festival, which encourages and focuses on excess and breeds division (see "Of Hair Weaves, Short Sets and White Flight," Section I), the Black Family Reunion promotes unity, prosperity and strength through family and community ties.

Also unlike the stadium festival, the Black Family Reunion extends beyond corporate, social and class borders, reaching for inclusion.

White families strolled side-by-side with black families, and white businesses tended booths between African vendors and those selling fish and chicken wings.

Cool.

Back at Frisch's, my friends and I poked fun at Pooh's nervousness at having slurred the name of such an important event into a glib bastardization of what she (or somebody "in the back") perhaps thought it should have been called:

BlackFest.

We waited until Pooh left and amongst ourselves made falsely angry demands to "speak to the manager" for being seated in the back near the bathrooms. Laughing, we "refused" to pay for our meals because we were hyped up after having just come from BlackFest.

We jokingly assumed every aspect of Pooh's service was somehow a sepia-toned slight.

See, that's what black folks do.

When white folks demean, ignore or smear what's important to us, we drain our pooling anger by laughing at them and at ourselves as they see us. Blacks to whites. Ha, ha, ha.

The only thing in this scenario more surreal than leaving all that black beauty and unity to light upon a Naugahyde booth at Frisch's was watching Pooh change her demeanor and language as she dealt with white patrons in her section.

When she waited on us, she lazily and intrusively leaned her body on the table, spoke in some slurred, quasi-slang and was way too casual.

I watched her take orders from the table of middle-aged white customers in the booth behind us and, except for the dirty rumpled uniform, she was like a page from the corporate training video.

Where I stay at they call that switching.

I know what you're thinking.

Who cares about how some white girl in Queensgate takes an order? Get over it.

The point isn't how Pooh took our orders.

It's about how Pooh talked "black" to us but was culturally clueless.

When she switched she reduced us to disrespected caricatures.

But maybe I should cut Pooh some slack.

After all, she wasn't expecting us.

Death Becomes Us

✧✧✧✧✧✧

"Anything to help a kid along, he went the extra mile."
— FELLOW BLACK OFFICER OUTSIDE POLICE OFFICER KEVIN CRAYON'S SEPT. 6 VISITATION

The above quote is damage control if ever I've heard it. Sincere and ironic, no doubt, but damage control nonetheless.

In fact, nearly every word publicly uttered and written since 12-year-old Courtney Mathis dragged Officer Kevin Crayon to his death and was shot to death by Crayon has been little more than a sick sundae of damage control topped by flakes of news bytes.

There have been countless press conferences held by all sides concerned, including one by Crayon's family during which his sister gave a poignant and moving portrayal of Crayon as a father, brother, husband and son.

I felt bamboozled. Then again, I guess I shouldn't have expected the sister mourning the death of her brother's highly publicized death to own up to the fact that Crayon acted rashly and prematurely.

Had one of my brothers been in a similar situation, I now feel comfortable and confident in saying I'd first have to own up to the mistakes that took him away from us before I could publicly honor the man. C'mon, people! It's called accountability.

I'm not trivializing Crayon's life or his personal legacy, but the officer acted so irresponsibly that it's truly heartbreaking and even baffling.

Add to that the speculation as to what would have happened had Crayon not tried to reach inside the maroon Ford Taurus to thwart Mathis from illegally driving out of the parking lot of that United Dairy Farmers, and what do you get? Mass confusion, cynicism and gaping holes where two black men—one an established family man, the other a young life with infinite potential—used to stand.

Should Crayon, who ordered Mathis several times to stop, have reached inside the car? Absolutely not. If a 12-year-old kid is driving around, he's undoubtedly high strung and will react likewise.

This isn't the movies, and judging by Crayon's picture, he wasn't Clint

Eastwood, so he should have left the heroics for Hollywood. From what I've heard, police aren't trained to jump in through the windows of moving cars. That's left to their discretion, but Cincinnati cops seem to like to do that. Why?

Should Crayon, who was dragged by Mathis more than 800 feet, have pulled his service revolver and shot the kid in the chest?

Again, no. In hindsight, however, who's to know what Crayon—who no doubt saw his life, his family and his career scraping by in the pavement beneath his body—was thinking in those last moments? Perhaps he thought he'd shoot out a tire. What he ended up doing was shooting out a future. Two, actually.

But neither mourning family needs to hold another press conference. No, we don't need anymore follow-ups, no "year after" pieces. Let these families rest in peace.

What we do need are detailed explanations from the Cincinnati Police Division explaining how it trains its cops. Further, the division needs to let us know if the collective mental and emotional temperature of its force is taken after such a debacle.

Are cops told to calm down after an incident like this or are they, like Mathis, jumpy and paranoid?

And why, for God's sake, have the streets of this city been turned into the Wild West? There are too many cops grabbing their weapons. It's almost as though they're told at the police academy to shoot first, hold a press conference later.

Wait a second. OK, I'm back. I had to peel the target off my back.

Right now I fear for my two young nephews. God forbid should they ever stray from their parents' Christian love and guidance and do something as stupid and reckless as Mathis. If they did, would a cop also panic and take them out?

Would we be holding a press conference outside my brother's home to explain, puffy-eyed and broken-hearted, what "good boys" they were? I certainly hope not.

What this all comes down to is that young lives aren't expendable and, once again, black folks are afraid to say when one of us has messed up. Meanwhile, white folks are just glad it wasn't a white cop pulling the trigger. Who needs that?

If Crayon, who was a father, had been thinking clearly, he'd have treated Mathis just as he'd have wanted another cop to treat his own children. And everyone still would be alive.

Note to Readers

MICHAEL CARPENTER, AN UNARMED BLACK DRIVER, WAS STOPPED MARCH 19, 1999, BY CINCINNATI POLICE FOR DRIVING A CAR DISPLAYNG AN EXPIRED VEHICLE REGISTRATION STICKER.

DURING THE STOP CARPENTER REFUSED TO EXIT THE CAR AT THE COPS' REQUEST.

CARPENTER DRAGGED THE OFFICER WHEN A COP REACHED INSIDE THE CAR (TO GRAB THE KEYS, TO SAVE THE DAY/NIGHT?).

MEANWHILE, ANOTHER COP POSITIONED BEHIND THE CAR FIRED ON THE CAR THROUGH THE REAR WINDSHIELD, STRIKING AND KILLING CARPENTER.

THOUGH A FULL ONE YEAR AND EIGHT MONTHS BEFORE ROGER OWENSBY, ANOTHER BLACK MAN, DIED IN POLICE CUSTODY, CARPENTER'S DEATH ELICITED A COLLECTIVE "DAMN!" AMONG CINCINNATI'S BLACK CITIZENRY.

BY THE TIME OWENSBY DIED OF MECHANICAL ASPHYXIA ON NOVEMBER 7, 2000, DURING A VIOLENT TAKEDOWN IN A GAS STATION PARKING LOT BY POLICE, BLACK FOLKS WERE YELLING: "WHAT THE FUCK?"

"BURN THIS SHIT DOWN!" CAME THE WAR CRY FROM THE STREETS THE NIGHT OF APRIL 7, 2001, WHEN OFFICER STEPHEN ROACH CHASED, SHOT AND KILLED TIMOTHY THOMAS IN A DARK ALCOVE IN OVER-THE-RHINE.

CARPENTER, OWENSBY AND THOMAS WEREN'T THE FIRST BLACK MEN KILLED BY CINCINNATI COPS.

BUT THE RAPID AND VIOLENT SUCCESSION SHOVED MANY BLACK FOLKS BEYOND THE BRINK OF RATIONALE.

AND MANY WHITES RETREATED.

AND WE ARE STILL REELING.

I HAVE GROUPED TOGETHER IN BUNCHES THE COLUMNS ON THE KILLINGS OF OWENSBY AND THOMAS, THE ENSUING RIOTS, BOYCOTT AND RACIAL POLARIZATION IN THE POST-THOMAS ERA. THERE IS ALSO A GROUPING DISSECTING THE INEFFECTIVE LEADERSHIP OF CINCINNATI MAYOR CHARLIE LUKEN.

CONSIDER YOURSELVES WARNED.

Try & Try (Him) Again

❖❖❖❖❖❖

Cops talk too much.

Like gossipy hens across the backyard clothesline, they squawk about what went down with this perp and what was done to that one.

I'm betting that, right about now, Robert Jorg wishes he'd kept his trap shut about what kind of hold he used on Roger Owensby Jr. that fitful evening.

Owensby died of mechanical asphyxia during a takedown by Jorg, then a Cincinnati officer, and officers Patrick Caton and David Hunter Jr. in a gas station parking lot.

Jorg was closest to Owensby. Directly on top of him.

When Officer Victor Spellen showed up moments after the arrest, Jorg replayed the tight restraint he used on Owensby. During Jorg's trial last October for assault and involuntary manslaughter, however, Spellen testified that Jorg used a loose 'head wrap' restraint on Owensby.

Spellen later flipped, telling internal investigators he'd lied to protect Jorg, his training officer.

If you're keeping score, Spellen is black, Jorg is white and Owensby was black, as are the two jurors who held out for a guilty verdict on involuntary manslaughter.

More on that in a minute.

What goes through a cop's head during a pursuit and takedown?

What are cops thinking when they decide use of physical force is appropriate?

And who knows what goes through a cop's head when he decides, in the heat of the moment and tanked up on adrenaline, to tell another cop the truth?

Does the cop assume his fellow officer won't later cross that thin blue line and come clean with crime-scene details? Or does he look into the face of the man he helped train and assume the conversation will remain between them and follow them to their graves or, scarier still, to other police forces?

By now you've figured out that, although the time is long gone (as are

Jorg and Stephen Roach, the former Cincinnati cop who killed Timothy Thomas), we're still stuck in the quicksand-like aftermath of their actions.

We might well be for years to come.

That's because the written and unwritten rules governing American police (mis)conduct might as well be transcribed in Chinese for as much as they deploy justice in real time.

There exists a cult of personality among cops—black, white or other.

Take police loyalty, which transcends race, as in the case of Jorg and Spellen.

Spellen thought he was doing a good thing when he lied for Jorg.

Forget a dead man.

Forget justice.

Forget telling the truth and letting the process come down on one side or the other.

Spellen thought he'd help it along by corkscrewing the truth.

What are the implications when a black man lies to save the skin of a white cop implicated in the death of a black man in a city ignorant to its own racial strife?

More profound, what are the implications when two black jurors hold out for Jorg's conviction only to be steamrolled over by the 10 white jurors who just want the whole thing over with?

I'll tell you. The implications in the former are that black life is indeed expendable when blacks cannot and will not stand up to defend it and instead fall for the okey-doke of uniform, blind loyalty.

No wonder we drop like flies.

In the latter, the implication is, 'Why bother?' It's why black folks mistrust direct inclusion in the doo-doo process of justice. We often end up in it face down and ass out.

Last month Jorg filed a $30 million federal lawsuit, claiming prosecutors hung him out to dry as a 'scapegoat' in Owensby's death. Jorg says city and county officials blamed him as a means to 'appease' Negroes (my descriptor, not his).

If that's so, I say we file a lawsuit against the judges and jurors who let Jorg and Roach off the hook. That was textbook appeasement we're still paying for in mistrust, hostility, boycotts and empty prayer fests.

Those suits wouldn't have any teeth, of course, and they'd get us nowhere.

Retrying Jorg, however, would turn this train around and show the citizenry that Cincinnati is serious about its brand of better-late-than-hardly ever justice.

The U.S. Department of Justice could file federal civil rights charges against Jorg.

Now that Spellen has recanted, Hamilton County Prosecutor Mike Allen could retry Jorg on involuntary manslaughter charges.

And why not?

Spellen's truth-telling is like saying he not only found the murder weapon but he knew where it was all along.

As for Spellen, he's exempt from perjury prosecution because he signed a police document granting him immunity when he finally spoke truth to police investigators.

As for Jorg, he's an artful dodger.

He skated off the city force and avoided lingering investigative questions. He's now sunning himself in downtown Pierce Township as a newbie on their force, welcomed by former Cincinnati Assistant Chief and current Township Chief James Smith.

As for Owensby, he's dead.

Members, Don't Git Weary

❖❖❖❖❖❖

'Members, don't git weary/ Keep your lamps trimmed and burning/
We're going down to the river Jordan when our work is done.'

—MAX ROACH

When 29-year-old Roger Owensby Jr. died Nov. 7, 2000, his mother, Brenda, knew her oldest son was dead.

She knew before she got to University of Cincinnati Hospital and saw for herself his battered and bloated body in the morgue.

Someone called that evening asking if Brenda and her husband, Roger Sr., had seen their son.

Little Bit, the caller called him.

Roger Jr. got the nickname because he was a tiny baby.

He had just been home a few hours earlier laughing and joking as usual.

He was supposed to return. Roger and his father were going to work on Little Bit's car. Father-and-son stuff.

Roger was at the neighborhood Sunoco, the caller said. But there was trouble up there.

When the Owensbys got to the hospital, they waited 90 minutes before anyone spoke with them. They were told to 'see the social worker,' a signpost of imminent grief.

Once they saw Roger, they weren't allowed to touch him.

Roger was evidence.

Officers Robert Jorg, Patrick Caton and David Hunter Jr. responded to a drug bust next door to the Sunoco. An officer spotted Roger, thinking he was a man who previously eluded police.

Jorg, standing spread-legged in a riot stance, blocked the Sunoco entrance. When Roger approached to exit, Jorg frisked him long and vigorously.

Other cops approached.

Roger dipped like a scared rabbit.

Outside, the cops took him down.

'Is he fucked up?' one unidentified cop asked.

By then, according to later police testimony, Roger had been wrestled down by five cops, handcuffed, Maced, hit in the back by Caton and hit again by Caton while still handcuffed in the back of a cruiser.

Jorg walked past a cruiser's camera.

His sleeve was smeared with blood. He ripped it from the shirt and flung it into the trunk of his cruiser.

In the morgue, Roger's stomach was fully distended. His body, face and neck were criss-crossed with bruises and abrasions. Blood flowed from the back of his head onto a hospital pillow. The official cause of death was mechanical asphyxiation.

Then his eyes

April Martin, the *CityBeat* intern and fledgling filmmaker, called the Owensbys for interviews to use in her documentary, *The Color of Justice*.

It's a history of the legacy of riots in Cincinnati centering on Officer Stephen Roach's April 7, 2001, fatal shooting of Timothy Thomas, the ensuing demolition of Over-the-Rhine and the little boycott that could.

It's also about how police police us and politicians politic us.

The Owensbys have everything and nothing to do with April 7, 2001.

"If you want to know the end look at the beginning," goes the African proverb.

Interviewing the Owensbys wasn't my gig.

April asked me to ask the questions so she could run the camera.

I didn't take notes.

This is painted from memory.

But one detail hovers: *Then his eyes*.

"Roger looked more like his father, but he had my eyes," Brenda says.

We sit around a modern dining room table in the Owensbys' middle-class, split-level home. Myesha, Little Bit's 11-year-old daughter, sits beside her grandfather.

As Brenda undresses the details of her son's corpse, Myesha bows her head and weeps.

"His eyes were always happy and what struck me was the fear in his eyes," Brenda says. "They were wide open and so full of fear."

I ask her to take us through those details as a means of separating Roger Owensby, Jr. from the monotony of dead black men in Cincinnati.

Roger Sr. reminisces over how his son was really his buddy and about how, as a 22-year veteran of the U.S. Army, he'd taken his family across the globe.

His son was a citizen of the world unafraid of different cultures.

As mourning black parents grief-stricken over the death of their boy at the hands of cops, the Owensbys are a cliché.

It takes one to describe them: They're a study in contrasts.

Brenda and Roger have known one another since 1969. They married a decade later.

Where Brenda is gentle, soft-spoken, positive and leans on her faith in God, Roger is brash, outspoken and angered to the point of brittleness by the truth of their predicament.

Brenda's eyes are bright; Roger's are dark. She folds her fair-skinned hands gently or gesticulates for effect when she talks about Little Bit. Roger drops his head and wrings his dark hands; he bites back tears, his jaw tightening at the mention of his son's name.

Yet he laughs, easily and mightily.

Even as he harangues cops, city officials and prosecutors for answers — a report, a word, anything — Roger Sr. says he's learned from his son's death.

He cherishes his family.

He's laughing more.

He honors his son's memory and legacy by pursuing justice.

It drives him to distraction and obsession.

He gets tired.

He's biting his tongue more these days and waiting for answers, though he feels justice has already evaded his family.

Roger Owensby Jr.'s parents are to be marveled.

If they don't get justice, maybe they can get a piece of peace.

They deserve rest most of all.

Dead Man Walking

❖❖❖❖❖❖

"You're blind, baby/ Blind to the facts of who you are."

—FLAVA FLAV

There's an explanation for why former Cincinnati Police Officer Robert Jorg hasn't been retried and indicted in the death of Roger Owensby Jr.: Fear is a loathsome thing.

What leaves truth seekers hanging like strange fruit is that the evidence against Jorg isn't *mounting* so much as it is *piling up*.

That is, it's always been there. Now it's repetitious.

I've seen two tapes—the surveillance video from inside the Sunoco where Jorg first encountered Owensby and another from a police cruiser picking up the confusion of Owensby's takedown.

From this abridged *Behind the Hits* video collection, Jorg looks like a rogue cowboy cop standing in a doorway, then shaking down Owensby and landing and coming to rest on Owensby's back with his knee. In the second tape, Jorg walks past the cruiser camera, Owensby's blood and DNA smeared down the length of his sleeve.

Mechanical asphyxia was deemed the official cause of Owensby's death when Jorg and fellow cop Patrick Caton were tried for and acquitted of assault.

And while the ruling is specific, it's awfully general.

Then nothing happened.

Except that Ownesby's parents went a little stiffer with grief and some of us went a little more apathetic with disbelief.

Even when Jorg's police trainee, Officer Victor Spellen, swapped his original testimony for the truth that Jorg had indeed used a tighter, more brutal restraint on Owensby, the evidence remained insufficient to Hamilton County Prosecutor Mike Allen and juries alike.

Fear's got Cincinnati by its citywide balls. But for how much longer?

Dr. Cyril Wecht, a forensic pathologist and coroner from Allegheny County, Pa., isn't double-dipped in our politics, fear, racism and classism. He released a report, commissioned by the city's Office of Municipal

Investigations, deciphering the specifics of Owensby's death.

Reports are fine.

Yet they frustrate folks like Owensby's family and the rest of us sick to death of the cult of personality of Cincinnati cops.

We know and see the truth, and we've been patient. So what? Another report?

Will it galvanize prosecutors into action and stop surrounding jurisdictions from hiring Cincinnati's tainted cop castaways. Will it gag Jorg's mouthy and insensitive attorney?

Nope.

But Wecht's report seems different in its sameness because it names names and points fingers: " . . . the cause of death of Roger Owensby Jr. was mechanical asphyxia due to compression of his chest by Police Officer Robert Blaine Jorg, who was kneeling on his back," Wecht reports.

This is from an independent medical examiner credited with unearthing truths in a gaggle of famous deaths, including a couple of Kennedys and Elvis Presley. This should be the final report we'll ever need in the death of Owensby.

This is the final word. There's no doubt about who killed Roger Owensby Jr.

Allen said he wouldn't retry Jorg's case.

What's so wrong with justice, and why is Cincinnati immune to it?

What's so frightening about admitting a cop did horribly wrong and then convicting that cop based on his actions, especially when the evidence bears out the obvious?

William Gustavson, Jorg's attorney, embodies what's rotten/rotting with this entire incident. He blames, as he has all along, the victim.

"The entire concept that Roger Owensby Jr. died on the pavement, during the arrest, is absolutely incredible," Gustavson told a local newspaper. "At least six persons saw (Owensby) walk to the car after he was up off the pavement, and numerous people saw him in at least three different positions while in the back of the car. The last time I checked, dead men don't walk, and dead men don't move around in the back of a car."

Exactly.

If they did, then Jorg wouldn't be chest deep in trouble.

I wouldn't keep writing about his head fakes around justice

And Roger Owensby Jr. and his family could rest in peace.

AS YOU READ THE FOLLOWING SELECTIONS FROM "LET MY PEOPLE KNOW" THROUGH "IF YOU BOOK US, WE'LL COME . . . NOT" COVERING THE APRIL 7, 2001, POLICE SHOOTING OF TIMOTHY THOMAS, THE ENSUING ECONOMIC BOYCOTT OF CINCINNATI AND MY OPINION OF THE MAYOR, YOU'LL NOTICE THE RECURRANCE OF CERTAIN NAMES.

THIS IS A CAST WORTHY OF A CHITLIN' CIRCUIT MUSICAL, *SAY, MAMMA, DON'T LET 'EM SHOOT ME!*

YOU'LL NEED TO KEEP TRACK. THEY ARE:

MAYOR CHARLIE LUKEN AS HIMSELF, THE HOSTILE AND OVERWHELMED WHITE FRAT BOY WHO INSTITUTED TWO CITYWIDE CURFEWS DURING RIOTS. THE FIRST APPLIED ONLY TO POOR BLACK NEIGHBORHOODS. DURING IT, WHITES, IN A "WHO ME?" MOVE, TOOK TO THEIR STREETS LIKE MARDI GRAS.

THE SECOND IS MORE EFFECTIVE.

POLICE CHIEF THOMAS STREICHER PLAYS IT HARD, CLOSING RANKS ALONG THE THIN BLUE LINE OF THE CULT OF PERSONALITY OF POLICEMEN AND WOMEN. HE DOESN'T FLINCH OR OFFER REASON WHEN, AFTER THOMAS IS SHOT AND KILLED, POLICE OFFICERS WORK IN ONE OF TWO MODES—EXCESSIVE FORCE OR NO CONTACT AT ALL.

OFFICER STEPHEN ROACH, WHO SHOT THOMAS, WAS EXONERATED AND LEFT THE FORCE TO POLICE IN A NEIGHBORING VILLAGE. IT'S SAID HE ONCE PULLED OVER ANGELA LEISURE, THOMAS' MOTHER, IN A ROUTINE TRAFFIC STOP IN HIS NEW JURISDICTION.

AFTER RUNNING HER PLATES HE NEVER EXITED HIS CRUISER.

LEISURE PLAYS THE LONG-SUFFERING, GRIEVING BLACK
MOTHER BLAMED AND REVILED FOR THE FACT THAT
THOMAS HAD MULTIPLE MISDEMEANOR TRAFFIC-RELATED
WARRANTS. SHE'S ALSO BLAMED BECAUSE THOMAS
RAN FROM ROACH, SEALING, MANY BELIEVED, HIS OWN
COFFIN.

LEISURE SAVES HERSELF FROM THE CLICHE OF THE
WAILING "MY BABY NEVER HURT NOBODY" BLACK MAMMA
BY CALLING FOR CALM DURING THE ROUGHEST PARTS OF
OUR PERFECT RACIAL STORMS.

THE ECONOMIC BOYCOTT WEIGHS IN AS ITSELF: DIVISIVE,
RACIALLY CHARGED AND UNENDING. ITS CO-STARS
INCLUDE THE REV. DAMON LYNCH III AS THE REV. JESUS
CHRIST SUPERSTAR AND NATHANIEL LIVINGSTON JR. AS
A RABBLE-ROUSING BOYCOTT ORGANIZER OSTRACIZED
FROM EVERY GROUP BUT HIS OWN. TOGETHER,
THEY'RE THORNS.

THOUGH INITIALLY ORGANIZED AND INSTITUTED BY
BLACKS THE BOYCOTT WAS NEVER ABOUT RACE.

BUT THE QUESTION: "HOW DO YOU FEEL ABOUT THE
BOYCOTT?" BECAME THE LITHMUS TEST FOR RACE AND
CLASS LOYALTY.

WHEN ASKED OF A BLACK PERSON—EVEN BY ANOTHER
BLACK—THE UNDERLYING QUESTION WAS REALLY:
"ARE YOU A GOOD NIGGER OR ARE YOU ON THE SIDE OF
THOSE TROUBLE-MAKING NIGGERS?"

YOU ARE NOW UP-TO-DATE.

GOOD LUCK.

Let My People Know

❖❖❖❖❖❖

To: Cincinnati City Manager Shirey, Mayor Luken, FOP President Fangman and Police Chief Streicher
From: Your Negro Tour Guide
Re: Let My People Know
Gentlemen:
You had to see this coming.

Knowing, as surely you did, that Negroes here had been in a deep, languorous and stupefying sleep since we burned Avondale in the 1960s, you must have known that, once we woke up, we'd be irritable.

I am confident you knew we'd be hostile, and we'd wake up swinging. Surely you were not—collectively nor individually—so ensconced in your own white sale slumber that you were blind to our storm front thundering down Vine Street like a twister across a Kansas plain.

You must have at least smelled its very nearness.

I will afford you each the benefit of the doubt when I tell you that perhaps, well, just maybe, you thought you could pass off another incident of police misconduct, City Hall's nonchalance and infighting, the Mayor's fear and denial and everybody's general malaise as just another day at the office.

But black folks, see, we've got sore faces. Both our cheeks are bruised, we've turned them so often. There are no more House Negroes, and we no longer subscribe to plantation thinking gleaned from years of listening to your plantation lullabies.

We want answers. We demand them.

Oh, I am sure you'd like a few answers of your own.

Like I am sure you'd like to know why seemingly innocent people—hot dog vendors, store and bar owners, motorists—were snatched up, abused and trampled during the ensuing melee after Officer Stephen Roach shot and killed Timothy Thomas.

You're wondering why you had to resort to curfews and talk of bringing in the National Guard. You want to know why all the attention from national and international media?

Your answers are in the disenfranchisement, the centuries-old layering of class, race and gender, the racial profiling, myopic attitudes and sub-standard training of police and the paternalistic society you've masturbated into a foaming-at-the-mouth monster.

This is what you have seen: Rock-throwing, name-calling, vandalism, hatred, depression, oppression and stereotyping are your crop.

And we've reaped it.

And now, sirs, where are our answers? And let me tell you that we do not want to be placated, patronized or demeaned. Tell us the truth. We yearn for truth **like water for chocolate**, because rioting and looting is the worst of us. It is the least of who we are, and it negates and shames our legacy.

I did not attend or participate in any of the rallies, marches, prayer circles or rioting. I did not trust myself. I did not want to be shoulder-to-shoulder with other like-minded black people, inhaling identical anger and exhaling twinned frustration.

For me, your curfew was an opportunity to embrace myself with reasonable calm, away from the yelling, cameras, hysteria and histrionics. During that time I turned to two of my favorite men—God and James Baldwin.

In *The Fire Next Time*, Baldwin quotes W.E.B. Du Bois: "The problem of the 20th century is the problem of the color line. A fearful and delicate problem, which compromises, when it does not corrupt, all the American efforts to build a better world—here, there, or anywhere. It is for this reason that everything white Americans think they believe in must now be reexamined."

"Color is not a human or a personal reality," Baldwin wrote 29 years ago. "It is a political reality."

And God, in his faithfulness, made a covenant with Noah and promised no more flooding. Genesis 9:15-16 reads: "Never again will the waters become a flood to destroy all life. Whenever the rainbow appears in the clouds, I will see it and remember the everlasting covenant I have established between God and all living creatures of every kind on the earth."

An old Negro aphorism sums it up. "God gave Noah the rainbow sign, no more water, the fire next time!"

Let us know something, gentlemen. We need more than Monday through Friday/nine-to-five/water cooler healing. We need faith. We crave truth. We demand justice.

Show us a sign.

Respectfully,

Kathy Y. Wilson, Your Negro Tour Guide

cc: Cincinnati city residents

The Son Also Rises

while they could

they held him down and

chopped him, held him up

my little fish, my blueness

swallowed in the air

turned pink

and wailed.

—NATURAL BIRTH, TOI DERRICOTTE

Dear Angela:
You don't know me, and it's just as well.
But I know you.
I know you're guilty.
You're guilty of being just another unwed young black mother and it's a past you can't outrun. No matter how far you've come or how old your baby boy was when he died.
Plus, you're a sociological convenient store.
We like runnin' blame on young colored girls; ones like you were when you had Timothy.
In and out and in, you're always open for it.
When whites cop to blaming you, they're racist; but when blacks don't take the initiative to help change your cultural circumstances, we're complicit because really we don't like black women.
I'm trying to love you.

Should we to meet I'd be one in the swell of people in your face, hugging you and whispering to your ear that it'll "be all right."

That's a lie.

So far it is not. We're a long ways from all right.

Each time I see you on television I wither.

I share your fatigue. Although you've called for calm your face betrays you.

You battle martydom with your swollen yes, chapped lips and rounded shoulders.

In my sanctified imagination I think Mary, the mother of us all, probably did the same thing as you. I think, after they crucified Jesus, she told her people to lay low and be cool.

"God's gonna work it out," she said.

Think on these things:

"If Timothy comes, see to it that he has nothing to fear while he is with you...No one, then, should refuse to accept him Send him on his way in peace so that he may return to me." —I Corinthians 16:10-11

Timothy as the sacrifice? Starring you as Mary?

Too much pressure.

Here's what's real: Timothy's murder was unjustifiable; wasn't right.

And here comes Mother's Day. Dat bitch.

Knowing how my mother is when one of us four don't regularly call is nothing compared to you knowing Timothy won't ever call again.

Press conferences, indictments, federal investigations, looting, curfews and confusion won't resurrect Timothy. Nor will it untangle for us your relationship with your son.

See, I think the relationship has gotten lost. We're wrapped up in examining race relations, pointing fingers, naming the next to be fired and predicting the next riot that we've overlooked your relationship with your son.

Since Timothy's death, I have really been looking at black men.

I mean, really looking.

I see his black youthful arrogance in the swagger of his brothers walking around—'do rags, sagging jeans and expensive gym shoes. Timothy's fragile freedom is in the way they jaywalk through moving traffic; life-sized pigeons. There's Timothy's grace in the way these young, unwed fathers cradle their babies on the bus, push strollers down the sidewalk in full urban armor: diaper bags thrown over one shoulder and earphones hanging off their necks.

And I say to myself: It's a wonder-filled world.

Why can't everyone understand these men?

I wanna know why, even when they do wrong and do time, why can't everyone see these men for what they are, for the scared boys they are?

I've checked the way white people avoid their eyes, the way white women still switchin' their purse from one arm to the other, the way self-respecting/self-loathing black businessmen revolve around and separate themselves from young men like Timothy.

But we need somebody to blame for young black men like Timothy, the ones with multiple petty offenses which ultimately fashion nooses and they swing from the halls of just us.

Then came you. We blame you.

Who raises their kid to be running from some dumb shit, to be running for his life through the night from the police?

You didn't raise your son to be trapped in an alley, his last thoughts maybe of you, maybe of home, maybe of his child.

That's not who you saw when the nurse brought him to you and laid him on your breast.

Sorry it's come to this. I'm sorry your son's life is a cause.

Somebody's life had to turn us around.

Wake us up.

Somebody was gonna bring us to our knees.

Your son was the lamb, after all.

On Mother's Day, I'll be silent for a time. I'll think of you and the son you lost and the children you still hold close. And I'll say thank you for giving us Timothy.

Love,

Kathy Y. Wilson

Mo' Money, Mo' Problems

❖❖❖❖❖

*"I don't know what they want from me.
It's like the more money we come across, the more problems we see."*
—"MO' MONEY, MO' PROBLEMS," NOTORIOUS B.I.G.

Mayor Luken waited to cross Race Street.

He was on his way to duck into and out of the Unity Rally—aka the Courtis Fuller Show—on Fountain Square.

Fuller is a once and again local news anchor and former Luken colleague when both men anchored at the same station.

He's mounted his mayoral campaign to try to wrestle the city from Luken's frat-boy grasp.

Two black people flanked Luken.

The black lady on his left talked to him and as she did he looked, well, bothered.

I yelled "Luken!" from my open car window in that scary boom like my daddy used to when he caught me sneaking Ho-Ho's off the kitchen counter.

The mayor looked, well, startled.

Like he'd been asleep and slapped awake.

I was trying to wake him up.

And the way to do that is to hit this tired city in its fat wallet.

People will suffer, others will complain and still more will question why an economic boycott of Cincinnati has been called by local protest groups.

The answer?

In two words: Timothy Thomas.

His shooting death by Officer Stephen Roach didn't start this sore to festering. We've been infected for decades. And pissed-off Negroes in April picked at that sore until it started bleeding.

But Thomas should not or cannot simply be relegated to dead martyrdom or elevated to a cause célèbre.

Al Sharpton's come and gone, and Jesse Jackson never came.

121

This is our problem now.

Thomas was a flashpoint, the starting line for change—real change.

Likewise, City Hall cannot or should not get off so easily as to be allowed to keep portraying Cincinnati as a place where vendors will want to bring their wares.

The mayor's nobody's ambassador.

Change is our ambassador.

The only way out-of-touch law enforcement, politically ineffective City Council members and Luken—strong mayor wannabe himself—will take seriously any of these rallies, prayer fests, marches, meetings and forums is if we back that thang up with a show of hands—in our pockets during an all-out economic boycott.

Rah-rah folks might think, "Aw, it'll hurt the city. We won't be 'big league.'" "Yeah, it will hurt the city—and that's the point.

We will remain "bush league" as long as we keep killing one another and ignoring the reasons why.

We never speak to our issues.

Cincinnati needs a good, old-fashioned time out.

We need to be left alone, sent to our rooms without dinner and sat down facing the corner, so we can think about what we've done. We need to emerge with a mouthful of apologies and acting on our best behavior.

Black folks might balk at a boycott. We'll be wondering, "But, what about the JazzFest? I already bought my outfit."

To that I say this: We pretty much stayed home when City Hall trotted out James Brown for the dog-and-pony show that was the (Dis)Taste of Cincinnati. So stay home this weekend and listen to CDs. Besides, Frankie Beverly hasn't released a new album in almost 20 years. How exciting could it be to sweat through a silk short set to his tired act?

Let the out-of-towners—those detached from the emotional heft of our mess—come here and leave feeling embarrassed and unwelcomed by the doors of downtown merchants historically closed during this hysterical time.

Let them walk the streets left vacant by us.

Let the performers play to near-empty seats. Let their canned rhetorical question—"How y'all doin', Cincinnati?"—resound and hang in the air like the pall of our own fatigue and confusion.

Maybe, through the silence, the answer will come back: "Not so good."

By keeping our hands in our pockets and by telling performers and conventioneers to bypass us, Luken will see that the result of his ineffectiveness is an economically emaciated city.

I know it's harsh to personalize this thing. I've got nothing against Luken; but I've got nothing for Luken, the mayor who flippantly called the boycott "economic terrorism."

No, Mayor, terrorism looks more like endless racism and constant police misconduct ending in suspects' deaths.

Such a flippant response to a progressive idea is telling of the mayor's frustration.

Further, his lack of ideas stick out like me at a Klan rally.

Wanna be strong mayor? First, you gotta be strong. You gotta work. Status quo, ain't working for everybody.

And this is what happens when disenfranchised people get serious.

Now I know none of this will happen. I know black folks won't stay home this weekend. Buildings will go up, conventioneers will convene and Luken, looking at turns bothered and startled, will keep telling us to ignore the rebels and just maintain.

If voters don't return Luken to office, we won't be listening to his bad advice much longer. Meantime, keep your hands where I can't see 'em.

The Unbearable Whiteness of Being (A Postlude)

❖❖❖❖❖❖

"This is a song that makes me spill out all my guts."

—"SOMETIMES," BILAL

Just when you thought it was safe to return to your life ...

With terrorist-sized holes in the world it might seem a bit trifling to be regurgitating/ruminating/marinating over the outcome of the trial of Officer Stephen Roach. What nerve.

Sweeping Timothy Thomas/Stephen Roach aside is like saying we've heard enough about AIDS.

That can never be.

What is apparent, however, is that where Cincinnati-style justice is concerned, nothing's shocking. What did we expect? I mean, really.

Whether Righteous Caucasian or Marginalized Negro, surely we didn't expect the system that gave us Roach, Judge Winkler, Police Chief Streicher, FOP Propaganda Man Fangman and Mayor Mister Luken could also create someone with the balls to rise up like Jesus—the other white meat—and do the right(eous) thing.

After stomaching part of the trial in person, I walked away secure that Roach would walk on both charges. It was something in Winkler's Invisible Man demeanor that screamed, "Not on my watch!"

My mother's DNA gave me good intuition.

After sensing Roach's "innocence," I feebly warned folks of the trial's outcome. But they either overintellectualized the law, race and justice or they ranted like street corner prophets. Temporarily insane, they were.

What else besides lunacy could explain the assumption that a white, German Zinzinnatian society and culture such as this would reverse itself and participate in a self-imposed click/drag/delete?

I'm talking now about not just a reversal of history but a reversal of fortune.

What we have here is a failure to communicate.

Somewhere along the line, we neglected to wrap our minds around the fact that ours is systemic racism.

This is not a situation where flashpoints of racist behavior flare up out of nowhere.

(Does it ever?)

No, our system — judicial, educational, economic, housing, health care and political — is rotten all the way to its roots.

The dirt is dirty.

Everywhere I went after Winkler's mid-morning pantomime of the verdict, folks were aghast. As a coping mechanism, many suffered diarrhea of the mouth.

Those who ran on about the miscarriage of justice, who sang in the "here we go again" chorus or who anticipated that Roach would've at least gotten a good-faith slap on the wrist are beggars in the marketplace, as Bug, my friend and barber calls them.

And it ain't even our marketplace.

Negroes here aren't *thriving* or represented on a level commensurate with our talents and our sheer numbers.

According to the 2000 U.S. Census, 43 percent of Cincinnatians are Negroes. But something's amiss when the only time you see an all-out black "presence" is if and when you're in a severely economically depressed area.

That's because the main girder holding racism aloft is economic disparity.

Negroes flock to Atlanta because of its saturation of all things black. Atlanta is a collective reparation. After the Civil Rights Movement, black leaders with heft and name recognition helped shape Atlanta into a modern-day black Mecca.

And they did so with the cooperation and blessing of white folks. Aye, there's the rub.

Like Atlanta, this, too, is a Southern city. The difference is our whites are none too interested in giving up any of that tasty economic pie they've been scarfing down. And that's because ending (or at least greatly easing) racism has little to do with leveling off *human* inequality and everything to do with leveling off *economic* inequality.

And so, Whites in Most Power (WIMPs), it's up to you to turn the corner. We're in the car, but the WIMPs are driving. In essence, we're still beggars in the marketplace, and what an evil, surreal marketplace it is.

The afternoon before the verdict I was in Over-the-Rhine at the window of Bambino's Pizzeria ordering a slice for lunch. Sheriff Simon Leis' ghetto bird helicopters buzzed overhead.

Police overseers were checking to see if Negroes were meetin' to scheme behind the slave quarters.

We weren't.

Following the verdict, the mayor instituted a citywide curfew.

He was fearful we'd again take to the streets like we did the night Roach shot Thomas.

On the second night, I ventured up to tony, predominantly blond Mount Adams to see for myself if those privileged few were abiding by the curfew they'd blatantly ignored in April. The only people on Mount Adams' streets were me and a black male news reporter doing a live feed for ABC affiliate Channel 9.

Finally, a lockdown we could all enjoy.

How ironic: Two free Negroes allowed out to do our jobs.

Dead Nigga Blvd.

❖❖❖❖❖❖

The air is different there.

I finally walked to Republic Street near 13th Street.

On Good Friday afternoon, I saw for myself the fading shrine marking the spot where Timothy Thomas, 19, scared and running for what would be his life, died of gunshot wounds and too many traffic tickets.

Like a crystal, we've held Thomas' life up to the light and turned it every which way, hoping the prisms would refract and give us Magic 8 Ball style answers.

Whose fault was it: the runner or the shooter, the system or the oft-arrested delinquent, the mother or the son, the media or the reader?

The homeless call it home.

So do strained families, crack addicts and slingers, manic street preachers, doomed and transcendent children, lives in decline and those on a twisting track to Nowhere.

No one really belongs there.

Yet they all do.

Their predicament is ours.

There's no place for pitying. There is room for consideration.

There are places where, *especially* as a black person, blackness doesn't guarantee carte blanche.

Rather, it's how the Negro navigates the terrain that gains her entree.

Regularity helps.

Residents of places like Republic Street know immediately who does and doesn't live, work or do business there.

I was the Tour Guide in need of a tour guide.

With April, a fledgling documentary filmmaker, I walked some of the neighborhood. I've known it as a passenger during drive-bys of bottom-feeding Negrodom. I've seen it early in the morning and late at night from car windows. I've passed through on its main streets, and as a pedestrian I've come up against its borders.

Passers-by take a whiff of us and alter their behavior.

As a journalist, I've seen and respect that distrust. But I get to leave so distrust matters little.

As we turned north on Republic, we entered what appears to be a movie set, like the crumbling buildings were held upright by stilts and made of fake facades. Before we reached the U-shaped alcove of the shrine to Thomas, a man, mouthing something without speaking, slumped on concrete steps and sucked wildly on a cigarette.

Farther along, a woman leaned on a tricked-out car.

There is a three-story-high tenement. In my sanctified imagination, I saw German immigrants chasing children out to play, hanging laundry over its railings and throwing dirty wash water onto the street.

Several people leaned over the railings. They observed us, neither warily nor with familiarity.

As we drew closer to the shrine, hidden from the street by narrow walkways formed by a low brick wall and an abandoned building, an effeminate older black man wearing large glasses, dentures and a baseball cap grasped a wire fence with one hand.

He leaned lazily across the sidewalk and said a friendly "Hello" as we passed. I glanced back at him and realized, with the slight nod of his head and arch of an eyebrow, he was sending signals to someone somewhere.

"Here it is," April said abruptly.

I almost walked past it.

There was no more anxiety.

I relaxed.

It's cooler in the U of the killing ground.

It feels like a sanctuary.

I understand why a desperate someone running for his life would run to this spot.

In distilled darkness it is a perfect hiding place.

In a corner where two low walls intersect, there's a rusted shed. Along these walls there are messages from mourners, street artists, well-wishers, insiders and inciters.

RIP Tim, then an arrow pointing to: *13th cop's killed my friend*.

"Please place rubbish in cans," reads a sign above it.

Against the shed sits a weathered and tattered makeshift shrine, similar to those at sites of car accidents.

Let's keep this clean for Tim.

God was hear that night with him

they left together (Be safe)

There is a child's shoe, bricks, toys, faded and broken plastic flower arrangements and a copy of *Revolutionary Worker* with the headline, "The

New Situation and the New Challenges."

How prophetic.

Three wreaths and several burned-down candles adorn the shrine.

To the right there's a large watercolor of horses romping in water.

Handwritten messages have been scribbled across it.

Show them you love them

To the Mother's whose son's are still living you are D-vine

13th RIP Tim Miy Nigga much love

And on a far wall by itself: You pigs. An arrow points downward to the message: Fire kills

We spent enough time in the alcove for us both to get pictures — mine mental, April's on videotape.

Backtracking, we ended up on 12th Street at Vine.

The block was hot.

The warm weather agitated and excited. Throngs of mostly black men paced, gathered, shouted obscenities and greeted one another in the bombastic language of black love that's really the black size-up.

Some of them leered, some spoke and others locked gazes with us.

Trudging north on Vine Street, odors and sounds rose and fell.

Noisy.

Pissy.

Busy.

A police helicopter buzzed overhead.

I looked up, like I could make eye contact with its inhabitants.

We walked on, making our way to Main Street. The natural electricity dissipated, and the anticipation of happy hour, Final Friday and hobo-dodging Yuppies made for a more easily digestible environment.

I left the shrine with no deeper understanding of anything — of boycotts, cowboylike cops, fleeing black teen-agers, the ghetto or poverty.

The shrine will soon go the way of Timothy Thomas' blood.

Then where will we be?

Looking for Easy Street?

Got Justice?

During the March for Justice observing the one-year anniversary of the police shooting death of Timothy Thomas I wasn't in the number as a reporter or writer.

I went to mend my splintered humanity.

I'm also not a member of New Prospect Baptist Church.

I have disagreed publicly and privately with Black United Front leader and New Prospect's pastor, the Rev. Damon Lynch III.

But I went there Sunday afternoon to walk with him and his congregants because I wanted to be in the presence of peace.

We embraced before the march. Bygones went that way.

I'm not a joiner. But as we walked south on Elm Street to Fountain Square, I belonged to something. Uninhibited, I sang, clapped and connected with strangers.

I changed the words of "We Shall Overcome" from "someday" to " this day."

With Findlay Market at our backs, we cut a swath through the neighborhood that symbolizes every wrong and right thing about Cincinnati. I watched as the black men in our procession extended their hands and engaged the idle black men in the neighborhood. "Come join us, brother," the men said.

By the time we neared the commercial center of downtown, Lynch's demeanor, posture and gait changed. He went from singing, joking and laughing to a solemn, almost meditative state. His shoulders rounded, and his stride turned to a slow lope.

He was walking into a moment.

We walked onto the square, and the crowd parted a path. We squeezed in at the foot of the steps. An African drum ensemble drummed and, as if they'd rehearsed, perfectly picked up the rhythm of the call-and-response song we'd been singing along our route.

Some of the Jazz musicians onstage also picked it up, and we made a joyful noise. It was like the Freedom Singers, John Coltrane and several Art Blakeys all jammed together.

I was transformed.

I promised my friend and Timothy Thomas' mother, Angela Leisure, that I'd be down front for her speech. I told her I'd send her love daggers.

As she sat in her chair waiting her turn to speak, she looked twisted. Her eyes were small, her face was anguished.

We locked gazes.

I smiled and pointed to the message on my T-shirt.

"Got Oxygen?"

She mouthed the words and smiled quickly.

"Breathe," I said. "Breathe in and out." She did, and it calmed her a little, but the weight of the day, of Timothy's absence and of the past year pulled her shoulders down.

She looked vacant and pained. Like: Anywhere but here.

I wanted it over for her, ebullience be damned.

Leisure spoke about mandatory calm and peace. She told us she finds solace in the grace, mercy and faithfulness of God.

Her voice was steady, almost monotone, and she never looked up from her prepared speech. I think if she had, she would've disintegrated.

As she read from her paper, I imagined the entire city was still and leaning in to hear.

Afterward, the mass of people on Fountain Square heaved itself onto Vine Street, then Ninth Street, finally stopping in front of City Hall.

The organizational component of our quest for justice unraveled.

We rallied a little more. And as we struggled to keep the energy high, it dawned on me that the people most in need of the humanity were absent.

They know who they are, because they know how they felt wherever they were that day.

Some of the marchers then converged on District 1. Throughout, the police were uncharacteristically restrained.

They were present, yet shadowy, hovering like good overseers.

Finally, the most manic and resolute among us ended up on Republic Street.

On the street in front of the alcove where Timothy Thomas and Stephen Roach met and decided our fates, the Bucket Boyz turned what could have been a morose interlude into an old-fashioned, New Orleans style wake and funeral march.

Members of the Human Relations Commission made sure we didn't block the intersection. That kept the police from engaging us.

The Bucket Boyz' dance corps, a ragtag group of young black girls, stood in formation.

"This is for Timothy Thomas!" one said.

And in a way only black people can and are sometimes singularly able to understand, they danced and beat the blues down. Beating their drums, dancing and chanting, they led a processional through the shrine.

It felt like church, like an exorcism, like Mardi Gras, like the saints were marching in.

There wasn't any violence.

The police weren't welcomed or regarded.

It was a fellowship of people traumatized by a year of violence, lies, misplaced accountability and of hangers-on emerging from the ashes to forge careers from tragedy.

We sang, yelled, screamed and danced.

Who knows if, from the heaps of paperwork of collaborative agreements or from behind the closed doors of covert meetings, justice will ever emerge in this city?

Who knows?

Last Sunday, we laid our burdens down.

And, in that way, justice was served.

Mr. Livingston, I Presume?

◇◇◇◇◇◇

I was in the studio one morning at black talk radio station WDBZ (1230 AM) "The Buzz" when Nate Livingston was offered a regular on-air talk show gig by Program Director Lincoln Ware.

The offer was made live, on the air.

It also was made hesitantly and with provisions.

Can you say *paternalism*?

It was like watching a reckless teenager get the car keys.

Then we all waited around for news of the impending wreck.

And wreck, Livingston has.

You get what you pay for with Livingston.

That is, if you want a bombastic personality, a confrontational air and half-cocked, look-at-me tactics, he's your man.

He's the "I" in the IGA of "I Get Attention."

Don't lie.

That package is precisely what Ware and "Buzz" owner and Blue Chip Broadcasting Chairman and CEO Ross Love wanted when they hired the man.

But now, suddenly, Livingston is *Negro non grata*.

I was on "The Buzz" once, appearing on Livingston's short-lived show to talk about this column.

Livingston was his typical self—trying to bait me into a debate over my choice of "Negro" in the column's title. Also there was an underlying current of envy, as in, "Who's this black girl with all this freedom in a white newspaper?"

That again?

He seemed taken aback that I say what I say.

I understood where he was coming from, though.

Because even though he was at a black-owned and -operated station, I could almost see his short leash. It was like Love was somewhere with his finger poised just above the button that would snatch open the trapdoor to swallow Livingston whole.

However true that might be, Livingston must own up to his current wardrobe choice of the orange Hamilton County Justice Center jump-suit.

A few weeks after my initial appearance at the station I was asked back to co-host a show.

By this time Livingston had publicly promised to go downtown and protest with his "brothers on the front line" over the treatment of black patrons of the JazzFest.

This was at the onset of the formation of the Cincinnati Black United Front, a grassroots group that later emerged as boycott leaders and lawsuit plaintiffs.

Members were outraged that several downtown businesses closed during peak festival hours.

Back then, Livingston brazenly *promised* to get arrested.

It seemed like an unintentional inside joke, punctuated with a personal punchline.

Only Livingston could hear it.

Livingston got arrested for taking the stage while Mayor Luken made a spiel during opening ceremonies for Oktoberfest.

I applauded Livingston's tactics back then—sort of a *bullshitus interruptus*.

But his lighthearted wink-wink manner didn't just backfire.

It diminished the seriousness of the festival issue and demeaned the efforts of the "professional" protesters who burned up shoe rubber for that cause.

After that, Livingston was a fool if he didn't know his bosses had started a growing list of his embarrassments to the station. These are new-money black businessmen backed by smart-money white businessmen who are as interested in being a valid voice for the community as I am in being the mayor of Cincinnati.

Not.

Livingston was fired because he was arrested.

But an orgy of other issues dangled from the firing—including Ware's outrageous (if not probable) allegations that Love brokered some kind of a deal with Luken and his protest of the Taste of Cincinnati during a "Buzz" broadcast.

Ware has publicly expressed disbelief over Livingston's "disrespect for management and ownership."

Love is mute.

Station management is obviously humiliated.

Upstaged.

Mastered by the servant.

If you ask me, the three are a triumvirate of dunces who should be forced to kiss and make up.

Ware is suffering more a blow to his ego than anything else. Back in the day when he was a volunteer renegade, Livingston was remaking himself in a Mini-Me image of a louder, more hostile yet more informed and more street-savvy Lincoln Ware.

It's gotta hurt when the monster you've built goes off and embarrasses the hell out of you.

Once the king of WCIN (1480 AM), the always-struggling bastard stepchild of local black radio, Ware is now fat, comfortable and operating on cruise control at "The Buzz." He's forgotten what it was like to be new at something. He could've gone to bat for Livingston.

Oh, the perils of damage control.

Livingston, who wasn't violent when he commandeered the Oktoberfest stage, is serving a whopping 60-day sentence—a final, rusty nail in his self-constructed coffin.

The sentence is too stiff.

What would've been much more appropriate is if Livingston had been sentenced to community service, something like presenting a reasonable, literate point of view on the radio for 60 days and holding his bosses accountable for their collective ineffectiveness.

Now *that's* community service.

Same Ol' Song

❖❖❖❖❖❖

*"Each day I say today won't be like yesterday,
but it stays this way today and everyday."*

—ALANA DAVIS

There are some worth singing.

Some Negroes headed south the afternoon of July 20, 2001.

Judging by their dress, they were soon to take their places at the JazzFest, a formally annual festival packed with three nights of r&b and soul.

Unable to sustain itself against rising production costs, political trickery and boycott fallout, promoters took the package to Detroit, home of a great majority of out-of-towners who religiously descened on Cincinnati for festival weekend.

There is new-money gaudiness to the uniforms donned by Negroes who go to the festival, its after-parties and events.

Apathy requires a look.

It begs for a soundtrack.

The bass line holding down the bottom is the surreal juxtaposition, in mainstream media, of surges of turmoil and splashy spreads on the U.S. Olympic Committee (USOC) touring the city.

It is the dry-docked nightmare of bullet-ridden black lives competing for space against a white man's wet dream of honor, money and patriotic glory.

Carmaleetta Rose, the latest to star in a recent episode of "Black Mamma Drama," keeps vigil over Devonte Williams, her 2-year-old son caught in the crossfire of another chapter of Wild West gunfire.

The street keeps percolating—like acid reflux.

Seventy-eight gunfire victims in 60 violent episodes.

It makes little sense to therefore be luring and touring the five white guys of the USOC Evaluation Team to and through Cincinnapathy.

But the motions must be gone through: Charts and packets have already been printed up and paid for.

Despite the glaring absence of diversity in their midst, the USOC delegates should still see us in real time—wilting in our inability to live peacefully in this broken-down jalopy version of diversity.

We've got a race problem.

We don't deserve to host the Olympics.

Growing up, we couldn't have company when we misbehaved.

The fracas has left us guiltily mumbling and stumbling around.

During the weekend many of the white folks I encountered made great strides to let it be known they are not racists and that racism sucks.

Such confessions feel disengenuous no, stilted...no, overwrought and bought with overly apologetic well-meaningness.

And someone keeps turning up that damned music.

I was one of three panelists Saturday at the Contemporary Arts Center (CAC) discussing race, identity and nearly everything else in and out of conjunction with "Adrian Piper: A Retrospective."

I navigated Ujima revelers to get to the CAC.

In the street I ignored the Gap Band's "Burn Rubber" blasting from speakers.

I fought the urge to splurge on a fish dinner.

By the time I stepped inside the cool interior of the CAC, joining the 30 or so others who'd shown up, I felt weighted down. I looked out a large window overlooking Government Square, converted then to the faux busy-ness of an African market.

Beside the window are Piper's enlarged and grainy photos of smiling black faces covered by her ticker tape, stream-of-consciousness phrases typewritten in red spilling across countless grids.

On the street below us, words distorted inside the thundering music.

I stood there.

Silent.

I felt separated and alienated from those black people, like one of us was a traitor.

And the same "Apathy Anthem" kept playing, its needle stuck on the chorus of "What do you want from us? It's somebody else's problem."

Meanwhile, mainstream media kept spoon-feeding us images of shiny, happy Negroes (though noticeably fewer than in years past). Even the decreased attendance numbers was explained away.

As I tried to catch the tune of the song, it dawned on me that Cincinnapathy has morphed into one big groaning public relations machine.

We've slipped into damage control at warp speed.

Judge this: from the banner in the window of the extended-stay hotel Garfield Suites chirping: "We're glad you're here!" to Ujima-Cincibration Event Coordinator LaJuana Miller's on-like-make-up, face-aching smile squeezing out subliminal messages, all the way to placid, greeting-card editorials attempting to shush the malcontents.

The Apathy Singers joined voices in a refrain of "What's the big deal?"

Out-of-town Negroes were quoted saying they didn't know about the economic boycott enacted in the aftermath of the police shooting of Timothy Thomas.

Either that or they weren't about to be kept away from their Aunt 'Re 'Re.

One Detroit woman—count on the Motor City—said, yeah, she'd heard about our mishaps.

She ticked them off like a grocery list.

Riots.

Police shootings.

Curfews.

Now "something about a boycott," she said.

"But all we're really trying to hear is Aretha," she told a *Cincinnati Enquirer* reporter.

A big chicken wing to you too, lady.

Finally, the weekend was over.

Visitors went home.

Streets were swept and barricades were removed.

From the silence the song deafened.

But maybe it's a sound only dogs can hear.

Black on Both Sides

❖❖❖❖❖❖

Just in time for Black History Month.

Negroes we can be proud of.

Comedian Bill Cosby is every white person's favorite and safe comedian: the elder Will Smith without all the nervous laughter.

Smokey Robinson is Motown's brown Dick Clark: ageless and somehow relevant.

The two threw a one-two economic punch that's got some among us reeling and dazed and others madly strategizing.

In one corner, Vice Mayor Alicia Reece is waving smelling salts under Mayor Charlie Luken's nose: "Wake up, Mister Charlie! Wake up! They ain't comin'! They been listening to the wrong people!"

Point is, they're listening.

And here comes the damage control.

But before we hear a word from black sponsors á la white bankrolls, a little housekeeping.

First, I proudly return Cosby's Negro Membership Card and gladly renew Robinson's. Cosby's had been yanked after he'd forgotten how much weight his status and name recognition yielded during countless and shameless appearances at college graduations in exchange for fat checks and honorary degrees.

I'd forgotten that Heathcliff Huxtable knew how to keep it real, that everybody doesn't own a brownstone.

Robinson's membership had, well, just lapsed.

Meantime, our mayor has returned to his part-time job of promoting concerts, a job I thought he'd quit after his love fest with James Brown at the (Dis)Taste of Cincinnati.

Speaking of Sold Out Brother No. 1, apparently Cosby and Robinson aren't as strapped for cash as Brown was and therefore have no need to help Cincinnatians get our minds off our problems.

Good for them.

Battle lines are drawn.

Robinson and Cosby are people whites know and even like. Cosby's upcoming Cincinnati show was close to a sell-out, and tickets weren't cheap.

By not coming, the two entertainers have heralded a message many of us knew all along: Cincinnati's racial tension is neither "their problem" nor a "black thang."

It's now a serious economic issue, which makes it an equal opportunity problem.

Why?

Because the city's pocketbooks have been threatened with deflation.

What's that?

The sound of white people pricking up their ears.

Two things intrigue me.

For one, backers of an all-out economic boycott like the Coalition for a Just Cincinnati probably weren't taken seriously before.

Before Cosby and Robinson pulled out, the effort to get the attention of city officials—and the world—by soliciting support of a boycott was like a game of hoops between the Harlem Globetrotters and a girls high school squad. The city had a lot of flash, power and hand jive.

Then the underdogs drafted Kobe Bryant and Allan Iverson.

Now we got us a game, folks.

And Reece is begging: "Put me in, coach! I'm ready to play!"

Ads touting our supposed racial progress will appear across the country specifically targeting black audiences.

So, in-between stories in *Ebony* about how a reunited Destiny's Child spends their down time rollerblading, going to church and caring for sick babies, look for ads espousing how Cincinnati hired a black female city manager and how we've set deadlines to do what the Justice Department told us to do about our police department.

They're comin' for us. Suddenly, people who could've cared less about how we live will spend money to convince outsiders we're living more harmoniously.

Be careful, and do not be fooled.

Outreach in the name of strategically placed advertisements is little more than damage control.

It's all about the Benjamins, baby.

In whitespeak, money matters, and there's lots to be lost if big-name Negroes start whispering among themselves. The truth is that money is power, and black folks have more of both than even we realize.

All told, innocents will get hurt.

That's the fallout when people are held accountable for their injustices by the ones who've been oppressed and ignored for so long.

It's time to get served.

It bears repeating: Innocents will be hurt. Several small downtown and Over-the-Rhine businesses are already limping, and some will expire.

But we cannot laugh this away, and we cannot sing this away.

We must live it away.

And we've got to live through it one day, one concert and one ad at a time.

See you on the other side.

Now go home.

The Cosby (No-)Show

❖❖❖❖❖❖

Cosby, Smokey, Prince and Marsalis.

It sounds like a low-rent, late-night, off-channel law firm.

We know them as the growing contingent of black men who've disallowed us the pleasure of their company.

This boycott sucks. It sucks when your old favorites get conscious.

But it's grist—tasty grist.

I'm sitting in strange seats at the boycott.

I got front-row seats in the Torn Section.

In theory, I'm a supporter.

But, as a member of the media I infiltrate the camps of famous people for interviews.

Resulting preview stories entice readers to attend concerts, etc.

Jazz and classical trumpeter/arranger Wynton Marsalis was one such subject looming on my professional landscape.

But it wasn't to be.

Marsalis is the most recent among black male artists in a thickening list to cancel their Cincinnati engagements, each in a different language (tour snafus, illness, scheduling, etc.) but for the same ultimate reason.

First, comedian Bill Cosby cancelled his gig at the Aronoff Center for the Arts. Then Motown legend Smokey Robinson vetoed his appearance at the Taft Theater.

Both are represented by the William Morris Agency.

Next, rock's morphing glyph Prince, citing 'technical difficulties,' backed out of his appearance at Music Hall.

Most recently, Marsalis said, 'Thanks, but no,' to his upcoming Aronoff gig.

Frankly, I am surprised these big-name brothas are showing this shoulder-to-shoulder solidarity. I am just old enough that the civil rights movement isn't some musty footnote. However, I'm young enough to have come into my own consciousness during the illest killing fields of the blin-bling bank-bank hip-hop era.

I long ago stopped being surprised and disappointed when black celebrities, causes be damned, took the money and ran all the way to an off-shore account.

This surpise is pleasant.

National Black Chamber of Commerce member Prince contacted the group requesting the organization gather facts about Cincinnati. There certainly were going to be 'technical difficulties' if local promoters failed to disclose economic and social truths to the artist who, not long ago, wriggled himself free of a hellish Warner Bros. contract and appeared in public with 'slave' stenciled on his cheek while the lawyers duked it out.

Who among us is willing to write 'slave' on our faces?

Artists like these do the conscious dirty work for us and we know it.

We just like to ignore it by belly-aching about a missed concert.

So far, boycott demonizers have underestimated boycott organizers at every turn.

Naysayers will not take their hands off the boycott death knell. It's like a car alarm with a short—it keeps blowing and nobody believes it 'cause it's constantly sounding.

And the groups, Coalition for a Just Cincinnati among them, have proven not just their seriousness but their sociopolitical mightiness.

But thus far it's been a forest mighty black.

It's great all these black men are flexing power and intellect.

And while this blacks-out makes big-name Negroes look and feel all good and righteous, it lets big-name white performers off the hook.

And in this way, the economic boycott changes hands from money to race.

We all know we need white people to get it done.

What about Jimmy Buffett? *Please* ask him not to come.

Until the comfortable are afflicted, the boycott won't amount to anything more than a heaping pile of smoldering black singers, dancers and comedians.

And the comfortable are privileged white people, whatever their privelege amounts to.

If boycott organizers hit up someone with (white) name-brand recognition, I guarantee legions of put-upon white citizens will be calling for a truce.

Boycott organizers have only been targeting the big-fish Negroes when all acts amount to fair gain/game.

As it stands there are class issues at work.

And, ultimately, isn't that what all this is really about?

It's underpinnings are classist because there are blacks who do not support the economic boycott.

The Cincinnati Arts Association (CAA) is threatening a lawsuit against boycott organizers, claiming 'tortuous interference.' In short, that means, 'Stop crashing our parties and let us make money.' The CAA is so far seeking $77,000 in lost ticket sales and a promise from boycotters to cease contacting scheduled performers.

I'm wondering aloud now:

How's it feel to be in the seat of the reactionary?

Aloud again: I'm kissing all future media/comp tickets good-buy.

If whites stood up, they'd see this for what it is.

They're nervous now because the boycott game has turned into a power play and they feel power slipping. And the rope burns must feel like they do in a losing game of tug-of-war. The losing itself burns deeper when you show up, cocky, assuming your underdog foes can't possibly win. Why, look at their uniforms. You were right not to even practice.

Look, the boycott is divisive.

And such divisiveness works against the unity of humanity.

And neither battle is humane.

Be certain: It is a battle.

Race-baiting boycotters have played on the (black) guilt of black performers when, instead, *everyone* considering Cincinnati as a tour or convention stop should feel twinges of guilt or, at the very least, some concern.

Whether black, white, Asian, comedian, rhythm & blues, jazz and bluegrass, they should be appalled by our behavior. How we handle ourselves and the lessons we'll take away are morality tales even the Huxtable kids could appreciate.

But that *Cosby Show* was just television. It wasn't real.

Cosby and his band of sepia no-shows know the difference between fantasy and reality. And they're all somewhere else wondering why we can't figure out the differences for ourselves.

Cincinnati: Negroes 'R Us

❖❖❖❖❖❖

In their feeble attempts to paint Cincinnati in diverse brush strokes, the mayor and vice mayor (the "black back-up") have mounted a media juggernaut.

They call it cheerleading. I call it damage control.

If you haven't seen the "Cincinnati ... We're on the Move!" pamphlet touting this as a "diverse and proud city" get ready to guffaw.

In it, an anonymous "we" are "working hard to make our city a model for urban communities."

I worked briefly in advertising and that's baaaad copy for: "*Nobody* will know the troubles we've seen."

Riots? What riots?

We're not rebounding from any misunderstandings, there's no talk of regaining any footholds.

It's all pie in your eye by and by.

And it's a black-out. Blink and you'll think you're reading a promotional pamphlet for Baltimore or Washington, D.C.

With this sepia cheese-fest, City Hall makes it clear that Cincinnati has its share of Negroes and, no, they don't all live in Over-the-Rhine, throw rocks at the cops or require a curfew.

Jump back, Miss Liza! Some of dem darkies is happy!

The cover is splashed with adorable black children smiling widely, black Bengals crouching at the scrimmage line, a middle-aged black couple in repose and even a high-kicking black drum major from a historically black college.

It gets darker.

Inside it's a veritable dog-and-Negro show of black vendors, black entrepreneurs and Negroes at play.

With all these Negroes, the campaign should have been titled: "Cincinnati ... Negroes 'R Us!" Or "Cincinnati ... Negroes? You Want 'Em? We've Got 'Em!" Or how about "Cincinnati .... Our Negroes Ain't Just For Killin' Anymore!"

Flip the Kinko's-calibre pamphlet open one, two, three turns and you'll a hastily inserted image of Valerie Lemmie, Your New City Manager, superimposed like a paper doll leaning on the roof of City Hall.

(Let's hope she'll actually lean on City Hall when she gets here.)

The back page is a perfect kiss-off.

There are four photos arranged at jaunty angles of famous, once-famous and "who's that?" black athletes. Aaaah, now that's more like it, Negroes as we know them: athletes.

This campaign, with its whispery have-you-heard-about-April-please-ignore-the-boycott undertones and its off-the-scale laugh factor, is officially surreal.

It's a comedian's wet dream.

Can you imagine what David Letterman or Conan O'Brien would do with this material?

But let's get real. Please.

City government types are trying to feed us literature dipped in shiny, happy Negroes when, for more than the past year, the Negroes I know have been walking around in a numbed state of post-traumatic stress disorder.

We ain't smilin.'

We's depressed.

See, the Negroes I know and observe are trying to figure out just how much of the April rebellion they want to own. They want to know their culpability. And they know, regardless of zip codes, social memberships and cultural alliances, what it really means to be black here.

Do you know?

I do.

Pull up a seat.

To be black in Cincinnati is to be in a constant and conflicted state of identity, as in, "Am I a target and, if not, why not and when will I be?"

To be a black Cincinnatian means being defensive while keeping your hostility in check. It means making your way but having an explanation at the ready for your position.

It *should* mean being honest about your blackness, and that's only part of what's troubling about this chirpy campaign. We can expect the "black back-up" to play politician, because that's what she is.

Don't be mad if you're black and you voted for her and now she's not acting black enough, whatever that means. Regardless of race, politicians are self-serving. She's in turmoil like the rest of us, only she's gotta smile through it.

I don't.

I heard the public relations brain trust behind the pamphlet is a black man.

You should be mad at *him*.

Maybe he feels like he's doing some good. Well, he can figure out just *how* good after the check clears.

Finally, though, being black in Cincinnati means being disposable.

And if you're a black Cincinnatian and you haven't been in some way disposed of properly, then you're fresh for the exploiting.

We all are.

We're Pop 'N Fresh Negroes, stored in a clean, dry place until it's time to rise and shine for the imagemakers and image manipulators.

They call on, quote, display, depict, profile and point at us only when there's an agenda to advance. Ain't nothin' wrong with that, even. Black folks simply need to wake up and know it when we're getting played.

Then when it's time we can one day call that loan due and be a player.

There's little difference between the politicians' brand of exploitation and that of the auctioneers who used to pull back the lips of slaves to show off their strong teeth to prospective owners.

And Cincinnati employs countless such postmodern auction blocks.

Luken and Reece stand back-to-back on the pamphlet's opening flap like a Peaches and Herb Reunion Tour photo.

While they're trumpeting all of our attempts, accomplishments and successes, we're left to cluck our teeth, roll our eyes and try to laugh it off.

Ain't shit funny, as we say in Hamilton where I grew up.

Beneath the surface of the flimsy cheap paper stock comes another body blow.

You know when someone in charge of you thinks they're doing you some good and it ends up doing more harm?

This pamphlet is it.

It's half-baked. Schmarmy. Offensive. Untruthful.

This sorry pamphlet is like a hot gun winding its way through the streets.

Hustlers wonder how many bodies are attached to the gun.

So it is that we must ask ourselves: How many bodies are on this pamphlet?

Carpenter? Owensby? Thomas?

If you get your hands on one of these pamphlets before April 7, drop it back off at City Hall.

Let them account for the body count.

Assume the Position

Despite counting a handful of independent retailers among safe spots to drop my cash, I have supported the economic and human rights boycott of downtown.

When Bill Cosby, Whoopi Goldberg, Wynton Marsalis, the O'Jays, Prince and Smokey Robinson all separately backed outta Cincinnati, I was thrilled.

I sat back and made mental notes: Which ones had character and which ones were renting out for a paycheck?

Folks have tried to discredit the boycott's frontline lieutenants like the Rev. Damon Lynch III of Cincinnati Black United Front (BUF) and Coalition for a Just Cincinnati (CJC) Co-Chair Nathaniel Livingston Jr. as the 14-month-old boycott wears on.

Boycott skeptics and haters wanna know where these picketers, yellers and bullies get their money.

Why can't they just let us drink beer and go to concerts in peace?

Boycott naysayers have repeatedly sounded the movement's death knell.

The boycott, however, has been like a city bus—it's not always on time, but eventually it shows up.

Tick off the list of arrests, media stunts and Livingston's judicial back talk, and it's apparent the boycott morphed from a rag-tag group of noisy Negroes to a reasonably organized social movement defined more by class than race.

Two Oktoberfests ago, Livingston was arrested for interrupting Mayor Charlie Luken's speech. Hamilton County Municipal Court Judge Ted Winkler fined him $100 and slapped him with a 60-day sentence. After he served 37 days, an appeals court upheld the original sentence and Livingston returned briefly to jail to serve the remaining time.

But not before having a word with Winkler.

"I consider you to be part of the problem, not part of the solution," Winkler told Livingston in June 2001. "I was actually hoping you'd apologize for embarrassing the mayor."

"I have no apologies for the mayor," Livingston told the judge then. "I think *you* are part of the problem."

Talk about a Jack Nicholson-inspired "You can't haaaandle the truth" slapshot.

Ten days earlier, Livingston had been fired from black talk station WDBZ 1230 AM "The Buzz" for claiming the mayor bribed his boss, Ross Love, with a high-post Cincinnati Community Action Now (CAN) appointment to keep on-air talent from criticizing Luken during the 2001 election.

Livingston weathered a 1997 firestorm when he told callers to his guest spot on WLW-AM to "Go kill Deters," referring to then-Hamilton County Prosecutor Joseph Deters.

Last fall Livingston again zipped on his pesky sweat bee costume, demanding the city stop Chief Thomas Streicher from wearing his police uniform while campaigning against charter amendment Issue 5, a ballot initiative to stop outside job searches when hiring high-ranking city officials.

If you think Livingston just recently came by his necessary evilness, he's been at it longer than you can say "fire Streicher" 10 times.

Five years ago as part of the Black Marchers, Livingston was the loud mouth demanding answers about the shooting of Lorenzo Collins, the no-caliber brick-wielding escaped mental patient cornered by and shot to death by Cincinnati cops in a Clifton Heights yard.

Livingston rarely misses a city council meeting, and he and coalition co-chair Amanda Mayes maintain contact with activist leaders in other cities. They often head off potential visitors by taking sit-down meetings to explain the economic apartheid in these parts.

On a situation-by-situation basis, I've struggled with whether to attend concerts, ballets and operas. I have decided against eating at certain places and refrained from going to street festivals, averse as I am to swelling, beer-swilling crowds anyway.

These tactics worked for me.

I didn't push my choices and opinions off on anyone else.

They were private.

That way, I didn't have to validate to anyone else's satisfaction or argue up or down what I was doing.

But something's turning. I want answers.

Lynch, Livingston and the rest have our attention.

In so doing, they've weakened the status quo by slicing a fine slit in city coffers so the money city officials were accustomed to earning drizzles away.

What's missing from the boycott, though, is the other hand.

What now, my love?

Where you tear down, you must rebuild.

Rebuilding is the fundamental tenet of decades-long tactics honed by historical black masters of the economic boycott.

Fourteen months is long enough.

There should be more clutched in your free hand than a lists of do-or-die demands and no-show black entertainers you swayed from touring here.

What's the future and what's your role in it?

If you expect us to keep making choices as a result of the piñata you've poked to exploding, where's the return on our faithfulness?

Use this time not to make careers.

Rather, make leaders.

Demand inclusion, create social programs and build so there will exist a legacy to your labor.

Don't squander the city's — and the nation's — attention.

You've been arrested enough to know that spread-eagle position.

Now turn and face another one.

Boycott This

The stale-ass economic boycott of Cincinnati ain't never been about race

Two years on and we're poised at the threshold of a class war.

The boycott's acid-refluxed up our classism.

Some blacks don't wanna be black-by-association, because siding with (mostly) black thugs bullying the city is some black shit. Not-so-black blacks move north or east, get comfy with *The Enquirer* and recycle the scary parts.

Who cares or accurately reports how much money is denied white pocketbooks at the behest of Prince, Bill Cosby, Whoopi Goldberg and other beings of supreme leisure? Meanwhile, the underclasses overstand the gimmicks of poverty and the privileged few are threatened by the impending exclusion. Yeah, it sucks thinking about one day not having it all.

Hence, boycotts are designed and exist to make topsy-turvy turns of the ruling (capitalist) classes. No more more-for-us-less-for-them status quo.

Tectonic plates shift. Preexisting imbalances in opportunity, money, power, access and privilege level off a little.

The job description reads thus: *Wanted immediately for life-changing work! Must be energetic, enthusiastic, wily and able to leap short mayors in a single bound. Enjoy chess-like maneuvers of community organizing, have little to no ego and nothing better to do than fire off e-mails, paint posters and get arrested? Then this job's for you! No pay.*

Who wants to mess with that? Ask the so-called "leaders" who've mis-stepped and otherwise led us into the crapper by tangential character assassinations aimed at one another. They're in over their heads.

The one thing that must emerge from this debacle is new blood.

We demand a new faction of progressive, proactive and intelligent folks not mired in politics clutching paid-in-full first class tickets to ego trips.

We require people who'll know that divisiveness in and of itself is mean and little but powerful is divisiveness shrewdly executed to eradicate life-threatening economic inequities.

Dear reader, stop believing the hype administered by mainstream media dripping into your apathy IV.

People are confused by the boycott. People are divided over the boycott. People are tired of the boycott. People are empowered by the boycott. People are egomaniacal because of the boycott.

Egomania Avenue is a two-way street traveled by boycott opponents and supporters alike. Under the influence of truth serum, Nathaniel Livingston, Amanda Mayes, the Rev. Damon Lynch III, Juleana Frierson, Mayor Charlie Luken, David Pepper, John Cranley and the entire wacky cast would cop to schizophrenia over this boycott.

To varying degrees they're discredited. They're alienated from negotiating with the other and we're awash in the jism of stalemate.

The basic tenet of the economic boycott is the demonstration of previously overlooked economic might by withholding said might. Once underway, a boycott must replace what it's swept away.

We've got the "swept away" concept down, but we're looking at a scorched earth partially because even boycott backers aren't entirely convinced.

The air was weary at the lackluster April 7 Sanctions Summit II at Lynch's New Prospect Baptist Church. Outside, Livingston, Mayes and their militant minions frothed at Lynch and Frierson through an occasionally opening door. Boycotters boycotting boycotters. How cannibalistic.

Inside, the gathered could barely get it up as demands were ticked off in a (yawn) same place/same time rewound tape.

Here's one problem: the demands. Fuhgedaboudit.

Speak to and solve the systemic issues that bled like Timothy Thomas and dropped us off here in the first place.

Second, try truth-telling. It's wintry fresh.

Blacks, make choices. Choices cannot be predicated on intra-racial classism or on our unsuccessful subjugation of other minorities. No Jew-hating, and no Jew-hating on behalf of "the cause."

Was Mayes' perceived anti-Semitism on Fountain Square in fact the real-deal Holyfield or just a half-baked attempt to lance a bigger boil? Yep. Nope.

When you're not smart enough to pull off a fete of that magnitude, attempt it first at home. That move laid bare the ineptitude and divisiveness driving the boycott.

It failed because it didn't galvanize boycott detractors or supporters armed with other strategies. Instead, we all chortled and brayed.

(Bear down here for onslaught of electronic vitriolic vomit from Livingston.)

Whites, stop making the same choices. You don't get to keep enjoying lap dances to the hit, "Ain't No Black Leadership."

Get up offa that thang and do some work. Whomever "wins" or "loses" this by blinking first won't negate Cincinnati's segregation.

Our lives, jobs, children and deeds are sprinkled with the residue of Reconstruction. There's no weekend visitation on racial and cultural responsibility. It's yours as much as it's ours.

If your mayor keeps snorting he won't talk to "those people" and you— as white taxpayers, council members, lawmakers, police brass and big-ticket business owners—don't put a full-court press on his ass/ego, then you're all equally complicit in this city's racist and classist stagnation.

Congratulations. It's our anniversary.

Still Dickless After All These Years

❖❖❖❖❖❖

"The city's gotta unify and come together."

—MAYOR CHARLIE LUKEN ON NOV. 6

Our once and future mayor is stuck on stupid.

Mayor Charlie Luken greeted a *CityBeat* reporter on the night of the biggest political win of his lackluster career by saying he was still waiting for his endorsement (we endorsed his foe Courtis Fuller) and that at least we hadn't criticized his anatomy.

The mayor's holding a grudge.

It's soooo Cincinnati.

So's his obviously hostile and paternalistic behavior.

Luken seethed with a "because I said so" vibe during an onslaught of damage-control soundbytes.

You know the ones.

In some he explained away the initiation of two citywide curfews.

In others he didn't address his testicular-in-absentia when he didn't have the cajones to fire City Manager John Shirey for not firing Police Chief Thomas Streicher.

On election night, however, it all surfaced.

He bore his teeth.

He's mayor! He's back! He can hide the hostility no longer! And why should he?

Luken's snide aside refers to the *CityBeat* headline, "Roxanne Is Gone, So Why Is Our Mayor Still Dickless?"

The headline accompanied a Dec. 7-13, 2000, story questioning the mayor's inability or disinterest in stopping the Ku Klux Klan from erecting its annual holiday cross on Fountain Square.

Back then, *CityBeat* took Luken to task for his lack of moral indignation and his inaction. On Nov. 6, you awarded him for the same condition.

His 55-45 percent victory over Fuller isn't a reason to breathe a sigh of relief.

We're all tired.

We all could use a sigh.

But hold your breath. This is only the beginning.

You see, the lack of ideas, the hostility, the myopia and the sidestepping—remember when Luken ducked out of a City Hall meeting after Timothy Thomas was shot?—are part and parcel of what got us here in a sinking ship with a distracted captian.

Watching Luken in (in)action is like watching videotape of a drunken captain steering a ship full of sleeping passengers into an iceberg. Can you say Titanic?

But who's gonna save us from ourselves? Individually, we must.

The outcome of Cincinnati's first direct election in 76 years doesn't prove Luken is the strongest.

It proves voters are afraid and in love. With status quo.

It could've been a new road, but instead it's the same cow on a long stretch of Kansas freeway. And when we finally come to rest after this anxious journey that could've been our trip to bountiful, we'll see we're actually at the beginning.

Again.

Yeah, this is the beginning. It's the start of something new, of a new set of tests.

And I don't envy Luken, a man so concerned with proving his opponent's inexperience for the mayor's job he neglected to convince us he wanted or even deserved the job.

That goes for the others who badmouthed Fuller.

Sure, he was Fuller Lite when it came time for political-speak.

But at least he wasn't afraid to walk among the people he wanted to lead.

So with four years looming, Luken has his work not just cut out for him—it's sitting in a big heaping pile of parts like a bicycle on Christmas Eve.

He's gotta convince us he likes us, and then he's gotta prove he's not annoyed by us.

And I ain't just talking about *CityBeat*.

Hell, as far as this paper is concerned, Luken doesn't have to ever speak to another *CityBeat* staffer again. In fact, he'd prove himself a stronger man if he came out and said so and ceased with the passive-aggressive frat boy behavior.

Instead, he tosses off biting asides in front of other media members to embarrass a *CityBeat* reporter when he could've been leading the charge to "unify and come together."

Maybe he was trying to dish it out like it was served.

I know what you're thinking: What's the big deal?

Well, it's this kind of Homer Simpson behavior that keeps Cincinnati mired in the National Hall of Shame.

D'oh!

We can't ever seem to clear away the early-morning eye boogers and see life for what it is.

Character is who you are when no one's looking.

Therefore, I think we've got a petty mayor who thinks he's supposed to be mayor because of some name-brand recognition, family pedigree and even because of boredom.

Either that or he's got *egous humungus* and it restricts him from getting out of the way of change.

Apparently you don't think so.

You invited him back.

As for saying something about his anatomy, at least we know Fuller's shoes are bigger.

LUKEN

How Does It Feel?

❖❖❖❖❖❖

Insulting the white male penis metaphorically castrates power, privilege, authority and entitlement at the very root of their orgiastic entanglement.

Want proof?

Responding readers most insulted by "Still Dickless After All These Years"—my rant exposing Mayor Charlie Luken as a grudge-holding frat boy—are those who took my discussion of Luken's tool literally and not figuratively.

I've always said that offending white men guarantees the loudest chorus of response.

Bad mouth their women, children and even their mamas.

But you'd better never come gunning for them.

Generally, white men are harmless so long as you don't flick the light on at their parties.

A good negress tattletales to the overseer about everything else. But as soon as said negress tells the overseer he's mad with power and that it's not sitting well with the minions, the negress is then punished in the only remaining manner the now-castrated overseer knows.

She's punished emotionally and intellectually.

And repeatedly.

Readers hurl venom through cyberspace under the pretense they're spoon-feeding me my own medicine. In the past weeks I received about 100 "Still Dickless" e-mails.

It proves people are reading *CityBeat*—even people who preface their tirades with, "I don't usually read *CityBeat*."

Like the one that began, "First of all an admission—I don't normally read the rag for which you write." That reader's letting me know he's above me.

(Not the mission position again.)

I know a typically Cincinnati-style, paternalistic tongue-lashing when I read one. The writer goes on to say that he was on his way to the bathroom in a bar and, failing all else, could've used *CityBeat* as toilet paper.

He does congratulate me for finding a home for "my inane brand of journalism."

Later he makes a sideways analogy among mayoral incumbent Courtis Fuller, Jesse Jackson and Al Sharpton, connecting them as "racist grifters."

I like that phrase. But the analogy is skewed.

He hints that he "knows the man" (Luken) and says I clearly do not.

He closes with "Titless After All These Years."

I'm uncertain whether he's referring to himself or me.

Despite the outpouring of pro-Luken e-mails, I don't think this is an organized effort. Surely the mayor's supporters aren't holding covert meetings wherein they strategize to stamp out anyone who would dare criticize him. It merely demonstrates Luken's people not only showed up at the polls—they're closing ranks around their boy.

Another reader told me I was pissed off "my candidate" didn't win.

And what's wrong with that?

The same reader asked why I hadn't commented on the increase in crime among blacks since riots erupted in April after Officer Stephen Roach shot Timothy Thomas.

I have.

To recap: The increase is due to the cops' new-school "no contact/no arrest" brand of de-policing and the flood of stolen guns in poor black neighborhoods where rioters looted pawn shops.

My favorite is the e-mail where the guy is "impressed" that a high school freshman got her work published in a "professional" paper.

But for its seething undercurrent, the quantity of "Still Dickless" bashing is nonetheless impressive. Read between the lines, though, and what's really at work is paternalism, sexism and racism.

No one will come out and say what it is.

And that is: Nigger, who the hell do you think you are?

Moreover, everything my critics accuse me of misses the point. I wasn't pretending to portray myself—angry, disgruntled, agitated and even hostile—as anything other than what they perceived coming off the page.

Further, I love the way readers criticize feelings but rarely facts.

They try to make a negress columnist feel inadequate.

That stinks of oppression.

I'll flip the script on one reader's advice to me and say to the venomous: Get over it. Columnists are opinionated.

Duh.

Besides, fodder from the Luken/*CityBeat* relationship is endless.

We've got four more years with the mayor, and just as sure as we've been critical we'll give him his props when it's apropos.

He gets starter points by appointing as vice mayor Alicia Reece, a young black.

See, he does have ideas after all.

Either that, or he's cunning enough to set up a black back-up.

And speaking of black women backing up, this e-mail barrage boils down to thin-skinned white guys assuming their staus quo feels good draped all over everyone.

It's shocking when a black woman lashes out against their self-made power structure.

I'll end this debacle by answering Dave Ginter.

In his published letter to the editor, "Move on With Your Life," Ginter said he "sniffed envy" amidst my talk of Luken's metaphorical anatomical deficiencies.

You're wrong, Dave.

I don't require or envy the white male penis in order to feel all the power white men assume they hoard.

Rather, I've got what you think you've snatched in a post-castration sissy fit.

I've got intellect.

And mine's bigger.

Do as I Say, Not as I Do

❖❖❖❖❖❖

Mayor Charlie Luken's first official order of business as "strong mayor" is fraught with double standards.

Luken appointed the Rev. Damon Lynch III to Cincinnati Community Action Now (CAN) for political reasons. Lynch is intelligent, articulate and connected to a faction of Negroes—namely the Black United Front—who'll never orbit Luken. And Lynch is outspoken.

Those are the same reasons Luken kicked Lynch off CAN.

It's almost as if the luxury car in the showroom turned into a hooptie as soon as Luken drove it off the lot. All the while, Lynch was wearing an "As is, no warranty" sticker.

Luken's appointment of Lynch looked good back in the hazy post-riot days. Probably felt good, too, seeing as how we were reeling from the shooting death of Timothy Thomas and Luken didn't know what to do with his mayoral muscles.

Lynch is intelligent because he knows the only way to the heart of powerbrokers is through their pocketbooks. He's articulate and outspoken because he's let it be known he never asked for the "officialness" of the CAN appointment and he's never copped to being a team player in the city's brand of racial and economic balling. He never asked for a seat at the cool table in the lunchroom.

The Black United Front—the Sweat Hogs of local activism—stayed the course, regardless of waning media interest and protest fatigue, by picketing and/or boycotting downtown businesses suspected of snubbing Negroes during the JazzFest weekends. Luken rarely came into contact with these folks except to have them ejected from council meetings.

So now Luken is bitter that the man he chose for his team is strategizing new rules for the same game.

"The level of racism, discrimination, tyranny and general oppression in every area of life here in Cincinnati has grown to such a level that only national and international economic sanctions may get the attention of the corporate leaders and their political servants," says a letter on Black United Front letterhead signed by its president, Lynch, that was sent to an undisclosed number of potential Cincinnati-bound conventioneers. The letter made its way to City Hall.

"Think of the irony of living in the city where the centerpiece of the National Underground Freedom Railroad network is being built, and we are struggling through the highest state of Apartheid," the letter continues.

That's probably the point where Luken started feeling betrayed and perturbed.

"You are hereby dismissed from further involvement of any kind with Cincinnati Community Action Now," Luken said in his terse, one-line statement to Lynch.

Luken's pissed off, and rightfully so. Who does Lynch think he is, disrupting the city's progress?

We are progressing, aren't we?

Think about it. If CAN's mission is to help restore the racial and economic order in Cincinnati and to alleviate disparity in those same areas, shouldn't the group also be shoring up the stability of the city's foundation that fell to disrepair and got us here in the first place?

Lynch is a minister, so he undoubtedly believes in penance. Perhaps with his back against the brick wall of atonement, Lynch poked and sabotaged the flowery outer coating of CAN's sugary shell and its alleged mission so he'd be ousted from a job he probably never wanted in the first place.

Confused, betrayed and embattled, Luken has excommunicated the man for the same reasons he courted him. All the while he's blasting Lynch for some of the very same things he's guilty of himself.

"He has been counseled time and time again to cooperate for some · good results and he throws it all away because he seems unable to resist name calling," Luken told the press.. There's that infamous Mister Charlie paternalism again.

Luken is calling for Lynch's apology to the city and the cops. To that, I say: We're still waiting for our apology from Luken.

All this political leap-frogging reminds me of the lunch-line tango we used to do in junior high called "cuts/cuts back." It was an exercise in futility wherein someone from the back of the line, upon spotting a buddy further up in line, would cut in front of that friend. The person they cut in front of would then cut back in front of the line jumper.

People at the tail end of the line were mad they'd all been pawns — dissed by interlopers and manipulators.

It's a long-forgotten game replayed and recast by Luken and Lynch. And don't you feel like you're at the tail end?

If You Book Us, We'll Come ... Not

❖❖❖❖❖❖

White people in Cincinnati can't live with Negroes, and they can't live without us.

We all know majority-sponsored street festivals in Cincinnati are excuses for white people to get drunk in public. Someone was afraid some black folks with nothing to lose—and isn't that most of us lately?—would show up at Taste of Cincinnati and literally crash the party.

In a call for "peace," y'all wanted us to lazily stroll the Taste midway so bad you scrambled around booking black musical acts faster than you booked us on those one-way trips on the slave ships. And you wanted more than the few chosen local Negroes both safe enough to entertain and desperate enough for inclusion in your white-boy reindeer games.

Nah, you wanted those singin' and dancin' Negroes who would, you hoped, make us drop everything and boogie on down to Taste of Cincinnati. Was it really the entertainment you were concerned with nailing down, or a last-ditch effort to appease us?

After all, music soothes the savage beast, doesn't it?

We all know the drill. First were the Isley Brothers. Smart move. They grew up in Lincoln Heights, and Negroes love that old-school stuff. It reminds us of simpler times when Negroes all pretty much lived in the same neighborhoods and our only worries were what to wear to church and how to keep our white-walled tires spotless.

But shame on y'all. I didn't see this same effort to get the Isleys or Midnight Star or other local, nationally known Negroes for Pepsi Jammin' on Main. That lineup was purely whitebread rock & roll.

Oh, that's right. I forgot. WEBN runs that show.

(Note to anyone who cares: For a successful, reasonably integrated lineup for a music-based street fair, check out the Third Annual Indy Jazz Fest this coming July.)

Then the Isleys backed out. Sorta smacked of apartheid and Sun City in South Africa, eh?

Hmmm. Let's see. Who else is sorta local and on the who's-gonna-save-our-asses-and-show-the-Negroes-we-ain't-so-bad speed dial?

The O'Jays? Still too relevant, maybe too expensive and waaaay too Negro specific.

Nancy Wilson? Jazz. That's out.

Hey! Who's that old black guy who could do the splits really well? You know, the one with the bad home perm who used to record here a long time ago? Charlie Brown? James Taylor?

James Brown! Yeah, he'll do it. He needs the money. He'll play anywhere.

So while a few, scattered non-protesting blacks and a whole lot of whites waited for the Godfather of Old around noon on May 26, the Taste of Cincinnati could be summed up in two separate freeze-frames.

First, a white yuppie—in a move to call attention to himself, prove he was down for the cause or work out white guilt—wore a T-shirt with George Clinton's P-Funk manifesto, "Paint the White House Black."

Nearby, a white police officer loudly and deliberately explained the mysteries of equestrian behavior to two young black boys petting the nose of a police horse.

Everyone tried too hard. Each scenario was a photo op. Each illustrated how schizophrenic this city is.

Speaking of schizophrenic, it's funny that Mayor Charlie Luken heretofore turned a deaf ear to what precipitated Officer Stephen Roach's shooting of Timothy Thomas but could figure out what James Brown was saying.

Luken says he spoke directly with the Godfather of Mold before and during Brown's in-and-out visit. Whatever was said between the two strange bedfellows, it worked, and Brown came.

The media was reporting attendance figures during Taste of Cincinnati like this was some sort of competition, like someone was going to "win."

There was a winner, all right. It was the Godfather of Stole, who shimmied off with 15 grand after one, weak karaoke song and a brief, indiscernible speech.

Peace is a mutha'. But like James Brown says, "You got to have a mutha' fuh me."

Talk Up Not Down

❖❖❖❖❖❖

I was looking for an average, work-a-day black cop.

Nobody extraordinary, just a black officer looking to talk about what it's like standing on that side of the law.

What about divided loyalties, being an overseer among massahs, a uniformed black man divvying out white authority to the uncoiled black rage of these days?

When a black cop buttons his uniform in a divided city, does he compromise some fundamental part of himself or seal in his identity? What separates him from the black men he apprehends or protects?

Where's his membership?

"I know where I belong," says District 1 Sgt. Andre Smith, a 36-year-old black officer.

"I belong on the side of truth."

Torn loyalties

Cincinnati didn't just arrive at bubbled-over, untethered frustration in the wake of the shooting death of Timothy Thomas by Poilice Officer Stephen Roach.

We've been a covered pot left boiling too long.

"Based on the circumstances, I'd be hard-pressed to justify why he was shot," Smith says of Thomas. "Can I forgive an officer for making a mistake? Yes, I can. But we have a responsibility to be forthright and to acknowledge when we're wrong."

Riot fallout for Smith was bittersweet. It's been a time of self-realization and undeniable blackness.

"I can honestly say I never really felt torn until the time of the riots," he says. "On the front lines, all I saw was brothers and police squaring off. I pulled up to a group of brothers holding signs saying, 'Honk for justice,' and I honked. I also told them to be careful. For the first time with the young brothers, I saw a man looking at me who just looked right through me."

Smith says blacks question his loyalties and his sensibilities as a black man.

"With me, I have two strikes against me," he says. "They'll see me and see me as a police officer. They'll see my black face. They may see me as a sell-out, but inside they're hoping I'm a black man, so they'll give me a shot.

"(The riots) gave me an opportunity to talk with them, to dialogue with them. It's unfortunate, because there are a lot of good white cops out there who don't get that shot because of the actions of others."

Smith is confident and outspoken, a barrel-chested, fire hydrant of a man, a 14-year veteran of the Cincinnati Police Division and a native of Chicago's south side.

He's shot his gun once in 14 years.

'Black men do wrong sometimes'

A 1997 shooting stemmed from a traffic stop of Calvin Way, who was driving erratically. Way crashed his car and fled on foot carrying a .9-mm pistol. Shots were exchanged. Smith shot Way in the leg. Pretty routine work for a cop in a city this size.

"I've been in the highest of intense circumstances that you can be in as a cop," Smith says, "but I still think you should be expected to perform as a professional in those situations or you're in the wrong field."

"In those situations" refers to incidents more life-altering than he lets on, some of which occurred within the department. Smith has been a flashpoint since he left Chicago State University his senior year to sign on as a Cincinnati cop.

Also in 1997, Smith circulated a petition critical of police investigations following the shooting of Lorenzo Collins, the brick-wielding, escaped mental patient gunned down in Clifton near the University of Cincinnati.

His superiors slapped Smith with a "failure of good behavior" charge.

Smith refused to sign the reprimand.

He's been suspended, fired, rehired, ostracized, demonized, inspected, investigated, grilled and suspected. The string of incidents could be considered professional recklessness if it hadn't all been capped and defined by one word. Nigger. It stomped his identity like a roach.

Remember Smith now? He's that black cop who filed a complaint last year against Chief Streicher claiming Streicher called him a nigger during a training session.

He's also that black cop who resigned in April from the local Fraternal Order of Police (FOP) chapter to protest racism within the force and his dissatisfaction with police leadership.

Smith says across-the-board ramshackle city leadership is deeper than any racism within the force, more detrimental than the repercussions of his allegations against Streicher and more damaging than rubble left by the April riots.

"I think the structure needs to change, and that would be a testament to whether or not the leadership needs to change," he says. "We've got a city council that doesn't have to be accountable to anyone. The system we have right now does not allow the community to control the police division, and they should. We work for them."

Smith says city leaders were rocked to their collective core by national attention from the rioting and by the fact that blacks rioted at all.

Worse still, Smith says, city officials are stunned by the degree to which the rioting has turned into protracted protests.

Ironically, he says, the rioting legitimized blacks' long-standing claims of racism and disenfranchisement.

The irony for Smith?

Being a black cop during these times.

Beneath the politics of race, he's a black man doing a job he loves.

"I'm a black police officer, but I'm a black man first and I know black men get stopped and arrested," Smith says.

"My blackness causes me problems and I accept that, but I know (black men) do wrong sometimes."

"Fuck Fangman" is scribbled graffiti-style on an Auto Mart circular box on Ninth Street downtown. A hand-drawn sticker depicting a bitten donut with the words "Less beatin', more eatin, stop police brutality" (sic) is stuck to the side of a public pay telephone on Vine Street, the city's main artery.

FOP President Keith Fangman, with his unflinching pro-police stance, embodies most of what many folks find faulty about our cops.

Anti-police sentiments, once only perceived and rarely spoken in mixed company, are now obvious and pervasive around town.

Smith knows this.

He knows not only because he's a 14-year veteran of the police department but also because he's felt estrangement within the department for being outspoken against inter-departmental racism, lackluster leadership, shoddy police practices and substandard police/community relations.

Nigger in training

Smith has a reputation. He's been called names. He's a whistleblower.

"I've been called many things," he says. "I've had more bumps and bruises with the police force 'cause I was battling other people's issues that had nothing to do with me. I'm an emotional person who sometimes acts with emotion. I have a need to see people treated right. We, as cops, have a responsibility to see people treated right, and we abuse it."

Smith also wants to be "treated right."

He's not a martyr.

He's not passive-aggressive.

If he feels slighted, he makes it known.

When his career ends, his deeds as an officer might be overshadowed by his actions as a man.

His supervisors might know Smith as dependable, arrogant and professional, and even as a troublemaker. To the general public, he's that black cop who gained infamy and status when he accused Chief Streicher last year of calling him a nigger during a training session.

In April, disgruntled by racism in the department, Smith and several other black cops seceded from the local chapter of the FOP.

Despite popular belief, Smith's and Streicher's tango didn't begin or end at the allegations. Their relationship goes back to Smith's days as a new recruit when Streicher was a District 4 lieutenant.

An evil boomerang, a tug-of-war

"Streicher likes to tell this story," Smith recalls, " 'When I first met Andre, I told him he could go as far as he wanted.'

"I say the first time I saw Streicher, common sense said stay away from him. It wasn't fear or intimidation. It was just his presence. When Streicher was lieutenant, the role call room was so racist, white cops sat on one side and black cops on the other."

That palpable racism within the department spills into the communities the police are hired to protect and serve, Smith says. Like an evil boomerang, it returns to the department, landing squarely on officers' shoulders.

"A lot of officers are scared," Smith says of police morale. "Fangman and the FOP have done a good job of scaring officers."

Because he's been so boisterous in publicly recounting police activities, Smith knows the cold shoulder of ostracization within the department.

"A lot of white cops think I'm a racist," he says. "But when they get to know me ... you either like me or you hate me. I treat people like I want to be treated."

That's the truth and an oversimplification.

Smith is equally bound by two responsibilities: his blackness and his uniform.

It's not always clean or easy. But there's honor in the attempt.

He's shed the frustration of the training incident with Streicher.

As a black man, Smith says his first inclination was to settle the incident old-school, Southside Chicago-style.

But a cop has channels to follow.

Beneath that tug-of-war beats the heart of a cop.

'Always a yearning'

"I don't have anything personal against him," Smith says of Streicher.

"I'm a sergeant. I wrote the chief up for rule violations. When the city tried to shut me up, I screamed as loud as I could. I did what I thought was right, and it's not my problem anymore. If the man gave me an order right now, I'd follow it. I see him, I salute him.

"I gave him a lesson in racial diversity he'll never forget. I trained the whole police department with that shit."

Sound arrogant?

Actually, set aside the drama swirling around Smith, and at bedrock is his lifelong desire to be a cop.

"It was always a yearning," he says. "I couldn't tell you why, especially with my experiences with police officers. Maybe I should've listened to my philosophy teacher, who told me I wouldn't make a good cop. He said my frame of mind was not that 'of the system.'

"Actually, I think there's room for everyone. I think we're all committed to the truth and there's room for everybody."

Even Officer Stephen Roach?

"It all depends on what really happened," Smith says. "I don't think a cop should necessarily be fired because he caused somebody to die. If he made a mistake, then no. If he called (Thomas) a name and point-blank shot him, I think (Roach) should die.

We need to look at the issues."

Those issues aren't limited to doling out responsibility, but that's the crux of it, Smith says.

"I don't know Timothy Thomas. Did he have some responsibility?" Smith asks. "Yes, he did. He shouldn't have run. Did he have to die? No, he didn't. Timothy Thomas should've accepted his responsibility and he'd still be alive. This whole thing is just a big pot of irresponsibility."

Many agree.

Many more place responsibility solely on one person while others, like Smith, dole it out to groups of people.

Smith, love him or hate him, maintains his responsibility to the truth—

as a man, a black man, a cop and a black cop.

Smith says he'd still encourage blacks—especially black men—to join the department.

And he'd do it with the hushed truth of three words: "We need you," he says, leaning in.

"We need you."

Nigga

"Peace/Sucka nigga
Whoever you are/whoever you are/whoever you are."

—"SUCKA NIGGA," TRIBE CALLED QUEST

This is what *The Cincinnati N-quirer* should have said in its quasi-socio-logical dissemination of nigga/nigger.

First, just come out with it.

Using the played-out tactic of dropping letters from the word—check the headline, "The Evolving N-Word"—and keeping it up throughout the piece isn't just corny, it's thin-skinned and demeaning.

"The Evolving N-Word" is disguised as an article.

Worse, it's dressed up in the clothes of a public service.

It's Huxtable when it should've been Baraka.

Its sources are stale, its editors visionless and its reporters afraid.

N-quirer reporters should have talked to some experts, *real* experts.

Real niggas.

Not to negate the histories and experiences of the quoted reverends and the rest of the cast of characters, but c'mon.

There's little besides polite responses to supposedly impolite subject matter.

You mean to tell me that the Rev. Fred Shuttlesworth, who marched with King, can't summon the rage and fear he felt when he was pelted with "Nigger!"

It's either boring or sad that Shuttlesworth is soft on retracing the fam-ily tree of our raciial identity from Negro to colored to nigger to niggra to Negro to black to Afro-American to nigger to African-American and back to nigga/nigger.

With few exceptions, reporters at *The Cincinnati Enquirer* write like they're afraid to brush against real people, like reality might rub off on them

This article's "shhhh" tone is perfect for libraries.

It never rises above a whisper, it doesn't emote or project.

It stays home when it shoud've been out in the sunshine.

It's a tanning booth at the beach, NutraSweet (tm) over pure cane sugar, it's the patch when you wanted a cigarette.

It misses like an air ball lobbed from half-court.

You feel me.

Whatever happened to walking up to people and asking them questions?

Over-the-Rhine and the West End, two old and predominantly black neighboring neighbrhoods normally the wellspring of "urban" (read that *black*) voices, this time came up short.

Them niggas know something about niggadom.

The experts on niggadom is niggas.

I know one of the writers on the team of *N-quirer* reporters that produced this piece, and he's faking the funk if he don't know a nigga.

He can return his membership card for being derelict in his duties.

He could've pointed his colleagues toward some niggas.

I know it sucks being the Tour Guide. Playing Sojourner to their runaway on a cultural drive-by gets tired. It can also be a gimmick. But sometimes the risk is worth the truth you'll help them tell.

Rep' yo' 'hood, nigga.

Also, I *know* white people know some niggas.

It may not be Prince, Magic or Michael Jackson/Jordan, like the Italians said in Spike Lee's *Do the Right Thing*, but white people got some they can tag.

The word wouldn't be so electrically charged if they didn't.

That is, if only *we* owned it, its power would deplete from being left too long off the charger.

That's because, if we're not one, there's one in our family, on the street where we live, on our job or in our past and we fear we'll become one.

Again.

We've let it mean too much when white people spit it so it means too much when we spit it, regardless of the context. Randall Kennedy, a smart black man, published an entire book on the "troublesome word."

I agree with the poet/publisher jessica Care Moore.

"All words are lethal," she says.

For the squeamish Negro, the words "nigga" and its cousin, "nigger" — of the Connecticut niggers — are ripe with bad memories.

It's like the blues.

It's the plantations, the projects or the oppressive factories of the Great Migration from which black folks emerged from and that we've spent mass membership dollars on trying to blot out.

But for white folks? "Nigga" and its Klannish cousin, "nigger," are in a bag hewn from a white sale.

To whites: Nigger is shame, nigger is history, nigger is ownership, nigger is guilt and confusion. Nigger is the white man's co-worker by day and TV police drama thug by night. It's crossing to the other side of the street, switching the purse to the other shoulder and locking the car door with the elbow on the sly and turning on the alarm to the Lexus just as the brotha walks past.

It's a chorus chanted by Jimmy the Greek and Rush Limbaugh even though Oprah could buy and sell their net worth.

Nigger is downcast eyes, it's a burning cross, it's a news report on welfare and AIDS depicted in a black face.

Nigger is spoken in a whisper, a mumble; it's captured by a cruiser's internal tape recorder falling from a white cop's mouth when he thinks nobody's listening.

Conversely, nigga is Eminem tryin' to be Tupac and 50 Cent; it's the Backstreet Boys and 'Nsync aping the Jackson 5; it's Britney and Christina and J-Lo biting Janet's sexkitten schtick.

It's R. Kelly talkin' 'bout he got half on a baby. Nigga is Tupac's Thug Life tattoo. Nigga is white people saying, in all seriousness, "Don't even go there" and "You go, girl."

Nigga is blunts, dubs and freakin' a Black & Mild. It's head-to-toe FUBU, Tommy or Sean John when your mamma ain't got no air conditioning in the summer.

It's selling your food stamps card to buy a bag of hair.

Nigga is shootin' and runnin'.

Nigga is screwin' and runnin'.

Nigga is a dead-beat daddy and a crack-smokin' mamma.

It's the anonymity of white T-shirts, penguin saggin' jeans and boots.

It's the antithesis of Martin and El-Hajj Malik El-Shabazz. There's nigga in the sag and swagger of every black man you've ever stereotyped and in the switch and sway of every black woman you've ever sexualized.

It's Freaknik.

It's in the Alpha Kappa Alpha, the Delta Sigma Theta, the Omega Psi Phi and the Kappa Alpha Psi. Nigga is on our lips, in our minds and in some of our hearts.

It's irrevocably in our vernacular and in the canon of our literature.

A sure way to own your identity is to snatch off the taboo of the stereotypes that history has long told us will define us.

I collect mammy figurines. I'm shopping for a black lawn jockey. I'm often a nigga and, when I am, I'm just as comfortable with myself as when I'm not.

For me, nigga comes easily.

It frees me to say it, to own it.

"And the nigga metaphor is the genius of America," Donnell Alexander writes in his essay, "Are Black People Cooler Than White People?"

I can see why *The N-quirer* fumbled.

Honesty takes work. Hard work.

This shit is hard.

Nothing's harder than being a nigger/nigga.

All they had to do was ask one.

I'm available.

Street Life

Panhandlers are a nuisance.

Panhandlers are necessary.

It's that time again when people are debating the very presence of pan-handlers. In doing so, the lifeline of downtown's economic pulse always seems to come into question.

If I come downtown, will I be harassed? Should I make eye contact or keep walking? If I pull money out, will I be robbed? Why can't they just get a job?

To some politicians, pencilnecks and business owners alike, the answer to all panhandling-related questions is: They're killing business, so get rid of 'em.

Mayor Charlie Luken himself has drafted one of his infamously terse one-liners to the City Solicitor's Office: "I move that the Solicitor's Office draft an anti-panhandling ordinance that sets panhandling restrictions as strict as possible, consistent with constitutional guarantees."

I read that as: Wear down the dirty little buggers with as much harass-ment as possible without blatantly stepping on their constitutional rights.

The mayor sends another bouquet of love to the homeless at Christmas time, claiming the Greater Cincinnati Coalition for the Homeless (GCCH) is doing Cincinnati a "disservice" by "arming" homeless folks with newspapers. He's referring to *Streetvibes*, the monthly paper published by the GCCH cov-ering homelessness and poverty-related issues sold by trained, badge-wear-ing homeless people for a one dollar donation.

Vendors get to keep 80 cents of each dollar they bring in. The rest goes to the paper's administrative costs and other overhead.

The existence and selling of *Streetvibes* is the manifestation of the American work ethic that, ironically, anti-homeless and anti-panhandling naysayers accuse the aforementioned of being without. It speaks to pro-fessional disposition, entrepreneurship and a real bootstrap mentality that are the collective antithesis of what we think homelessness is.

For my (literal) money, I'd rather be hit up by someone with wares to sell. For the panhandled, exchanging a buck for a tangible item makes the quandary of "whatare theydoinwithmymoney?" easier to swallow.

For vendors selling *Streetvibes*, "panhandling" is a job. In this respect they're no different than hot dog vendors and the people selling all that loud, garish stuff during Jazz Festival weekend.

For Luken to say newspaper vendors are "armed" and doing us a "disservice" is a revelation of his shortsightedness and cultural alienation. Why not leave it up to Joe and Jane Schmoe as to whether they'd like to purchase a paper? Or is the idea that a "working" citizen just might have a conversation with a "panhandler" frightening to our public officials?

I buy *Streetvibes* when I can, just like a whole bunch of other people. And when I can't, I look a vendor in the face and say either, "No, thank you," or, "I've got one already." How difficult is that exactly?

Between the lines of all this brouhaha over the "panhandler question" is the subliminal picture painted by detractors that panhandlers love what they do and that there's glamour in begging all day long.

True, there are panhandlers who are sane, able-bodied, free from addiction and might very well be drawing some type of monthly assistance. For them, panhandling is a way to get over.

But even to that extreme, think about just how much they're getting over financially. Oh, the motherload of coins they dump onto their beds at night boggles the mind! They probably get naked and roll around on them until every penny sticks to their skin!

Let's get real. Panhandling in Cincinnati comes down to what every other issue in Cincinnati comes down to—class.

Panhandling is classless, it's dirty, it's degrading, it's humiliating and it's uncomfortable. And I haven't even gotten to what it must be like for panhandlers.

Ridding city streets of panhandlers has little to do with business fallout or safety and everything to do with aesthetics and how uncomfortable many people feel about dirty people asking for money.

I'll admit it's hard for me to ignore a panhandler as I clutch a frothy $3 coffee drink and a $7 bag of lunch or after I've just paid $5 to $7 to park my car. See, those are all amenities and not necessities.

I'm not trying to guilt anyone into anything. When it comes down to you and the panhandler, think about your own comfort level and give up the coinage or don't. If you don't, try not to walk away bad-mouthing the homeless for something the mayor is trying to socialize you into believing.

Hey, if we really gave this some thought, we'd all go down to Saks Fifth Avenue and panhandle them for some designer gear by Ralph Lauren, Prada, Gucci, Calvin Klein or Tommy Hilfiger. And maybe we'd get our hair done for free, too.

Oh, never mind. Saks already panhandled us for $6.6 million.

I understand if you don't have any spare change for the homeless.

Street Fight (Street Life II)

❖❖❖❖❖❖

Mayor. Charlie Luken, meet Riccardo Taylor. Taylor is a writer, *Streetvibes* vendor and activist. He wants you and every other frightened, uninformed and privileged Cincinnatian to know that, in the act of doing his job, he's not "hurting" downtown Cincinnati—and neither is *Streetvibes*. You'll recall that last month Luken called for the City Solicitor's Office to draft new anti-panhandling regulations and specifically pointed to the Greater Cincinnati Coalition for the Homeless (GCCH) as doing Cincinnati a "disservice" by "arming" homeless *Streetvibes* vendors with newspapers.

"I think Luken is misinformed about what it entails and what is at stake," Taylor says of threats to his livelihood. "It (*Streetvibes*) gives so much support to people who are homeless. He's not looking at the whole picture, just a few incidents or the bad behavior of a few vendors."

Taylor makes a good point. One bad vendor don't spoil the whole bunch, just like one bad mayor don't spoil the whole city.

Selling *Streetvibes* isn't a hobby or a way to make quick cash. It's not fun. Have you ever heard the collective butt-clinching of a pack of lunchtime pedestrians when a *Streetvibes* vendor approaches? It's a wonder vendors make any kind of living, but they do, and the ones who sell regularly are serious about it.

Vendors undergo orientation. They sign a contract stating they understand and will abide by GCCH's rules. There's a two-day waiting period, separating get-rich-quick vendors from serious entrepreneurs.

Then they're given a coveted badge, and their first 10 papers are free. Some do unload those first 10, never to be heard from again. But many others return and become long-standing vendors.

Luken claims to have had a "bad experience" with a *Streetvibes* vendor. He probably did. Disenfranchised folks don't like being steamrolled over, so the vendor probably had a few choice words for the mayor.

And based on that, Luken is trying to get City Hall to throw up roadblocks for vendors in the name of curtailing panhandling on downtown streets. Let's not confuse working people with beggars. Let's not confuse self-righteousness with classism.

It's true that some of the 32 or so badged *Streetvibes* vendors might be homeless. But when they're wearing a badge identifying themselves as vendors and engaging pedestrians huckster-style to move papers, they're not panhandlers. They're working.

I know it's an oxymoronic concept to wrap your psyche around — the idea of homeless people working for a living — but it does actually happen. And by bad-mouthing, demonizing and attempting to stifle *Streetvibes* vendors, Luken perpetuates the myth that our downtown streets are spooky obstacle courses for the uninitiated.

Plus, it just plain looks mean when you try to bully a bunch of otherwise downtrodden folks trying to make a living.

The vendors don't want sympathy. They want the right to make a living, just like all those Sunday *N-quirer* vendors who populate busy intersections across town waving papers. Will the city do unto Sunday paper vendors as it's trying to do unto *Streetvibes* vendors?

Not content to wait for the other boot to come down on them, more than a dozen *Streetvibes* vendors, supporters and volunteer organizers are meeting regularly to plan preemptive strikes. They fully understand their rights and the risks to their livelihood. They also know they'll have to present themselves as the antithesis to what the general public believes them to be. So expect to see these people on the news, in the papers and to hear them on the radio in coming weeks.

"Mayor Luken cannot magically wave his hands to make *Streetvibes* disappear," says Susan Knight, homeless advocate and a volunteer working to organize the vendors. "What the mayor can do is make it hard, make obstacles that would make it very difficult for vendors to sell *Streetvibes*. He can use his political savvy ... to work within the Constitution to hinder the program, the entire program.

"What we're trying to do is take the initiative before anything gets done. We're saying, 'Hey! Mayor Luken! You can't take this away.' "

Know that just because some in this class-stricken city think homeless people who have the gall to try to make a living are scabs on the city's otherwise unblemished candy-coated shell doesn't mean they can be swept under the pavement. Taylor, for one, isn't having it.

"It's obvious the paper itself cannot do anything to hurt downtown," he says. "This has allowed me to rebuild my dignity and regain my self-esteem." I challenge the mayor to stop making uninformed decisions. And he can thank me later for the introduction.

I Wish I Knew How It Would Feel to Be Free

⬦⬦⬦⬦⬦

Let's look forward.

In 2002, Mayor Charlie Luken must either lead or lead the way to someone who will. Alicia Reece, can you feel me?

People write, call and stop me to ask, "What is it with you and Luken?" It's nothin' with Luken and me. Let's flip the script. What is it with Luken and Cincinnati? What's with Cincinnati?

Criticizing Cincinnati is for me the equivalent of criticizing a family member. I do it because I love this city and I want better things for us.

If I didn't, I'd be gone in a heartbeat.

Sometimes I wish I could pack up and move on. I often think about getting a mind-numbing job so as to cut myself off from issues, people and problems. No matter how hard I try to alienate myself—to go home and close the door on the world—I always end up watching the news, listening to conversations and madly scribbling notes in my journal.

Then I reemerge with what I think are answers or, at the very least, a vantage point nobody's thought of. I'm always looking for the truth in things.

We don't get too much of that around here. It's like rain in the desert—it's a wish with little hope of fulfillment.

So as the mutha' of all holidays looms and year-end pensiveness descends, I am here to tell you that I'm tired but not beaten. In fact, I'm not even down on one knee.

But I am on two knees.

I'm praying that we can squash empty rhetoric and sloganeering and allow some room for divergent opinions, thoughts and ideas. Time has come and gone for the okey-doke we've been force-fed throughout 2001.

The disappointing court verdicts, the absence of justice, the alienation of citizens, the fear and loathing of so-called leaders, the name-calling, back-door deal-making, the pay-offs, the backstabbing and dismissals of all the wrong people have been biblical in nature.

And I know we're all tired. We're tired of trying to figure out what's right and correct. We're tired of explaining our actions and inaction to strangers and the initiated alike. We're beaten down from the relentless pursuit of slippery justice inside and outside the courtroom.

I don't normally get all off into making resolutions. Together, though, let's make some.

First, let's resolve to be honest. Don't internalize matters that have nothing to do with you. That way, when someone stands up to criticize, you won't be offended.

Next, let's be honest. Let's always be honest. When truth is the basis for all journeys, there won't be shock and horror when the truth is revealed at the end of that journey.

Don't be myopic. Life might be great for you. The sun might always shine on your street, your children might be perfect, your pockets might be swollen and you might never get sick.

Get real. Life ain't no crystal stair for most people.

If you live in a bubble of me-centered, suburban, privileged thoughts, the outside world (panhandlers, homelessness, racial strife and apathetic politicians) is a frightening proposition. But hitting the snooze button so you can keep catnapping is dangerous. It's life threatening.

Finally, let's be fearless. Let's try a new tact. The old ones aren't working. They just aren't. And in trying these new things, whatever they might be, let's not be afraid to call our so-called leaders on the carpet.

Get 'em for never having an original thought. Get 'em for asking for your vote and then squandering it. Get 'em for lying and for ignoring and disrespecting people. Just get 'em, and don't be afraid—they work for us, remember?

A new year is like a new chance. It's a do-over.

So let's not stuff anything else into our old baggage. It's already bursting at the seams. Grab some new baggage.

I've got mine, and it's by the door.

Dead Ringer

On the eve of Tony Ringer's trial for two counts of aggravated murder, visions of O.J. Simpson are dancing in my head.

It's laughable, spooky and democratic that Simpson is free to walk the streets and to... emcee concerts?

It's laughable because, well, it is.

You're thinking it's laughable because Simpson should be in prison for a certain murder.

I'm laughing because the man has never this closely aligned himself with Negroes to the extent that anyone would expect to see him—guilty, innocent or acquitted—emceeing a hip-hop show.

How black of him.

The Juice emceeing concerts?

Concert headliners Juvenile and Foxxy Brown don't give a good damn about gloves, Bruno Magli loafers, attorneys who rhyme and the whole nine. Some genius promoter or manager hooked Simpson up with the concert, distracting him from his tireless efforts to find his ex-wife's real killer.

What's all this got to do with Ringer, the celebrity barber accused of shooting his pregnant ex-girlfriend Cassandra Betts in the head while her then-7-year-old daughter slept in the backseat of the car?

It's about two smug black men.

It's about loyalties realized, dashed and then regurgitated.

It's about the disposal of women.

They're both tales of troubled relationships that sent battered women inexplicably back to the abuser.

We've seen the pictures of Nicole Brown Simpson, beaten and swollen. There were times that she returned to Simpson or at least left the door ajar.

We've read accounts of how Cassandra Betts, two months before her murder, applied for and received a restraining order against Ringer. The document details accounts of Ringer repeatedly kicking Cassandra, throwing her over a banister and down concrete steps.

She recounted how, as in previous breakups with Ringer, he'd call, come over and even show up at her job.

Cassandra later dropped the order.

Ringer later leveled domestic violence charges against her only to bail her out of jail.

What a tangled web.

Other similarities between Ringer and Simpson are more startling, more culturally specific and much more telling of how black folks deny the worst of who we are. When Simpson was acquitted of slaughtering his ex-wife and her companion, black folks weren't so much convinced of his innocence as we were glad a black man had finally gotten off for *something*.

Forget that many of us believed (and still do believe) in his guilt.

Here was one who got away.

Simpson's acquittal compensated for all the black men profiled, harassed and railroaded into prison.

Honest conversations about it ultimately collapsed beneath the weight of America's perpetually shabby race relations. To mention 'the verdict' today is to uncork a can of squirming intra-racial worms.

Remember when Ringer was first arrested and jailed for Cassandra's murder? A chorus of righteous Negroes rose up in support of Ringer, even posting his bail. Some big-money, mysterious Bengals player helped post his initial $500,000 bond.

Ringer's bond was doubled after a second manslaughter charge was added.

As more evidence was uncovered Ringer was painted with the brush of the sinister murder suspect.

Suddenly, Ringer's supporters became mute, pulling their money with him left to sit in jail.

When fingers were pointed squarely at Simpson, many were dumbstruck, too, that a hero could be capable of such rage. But that's where we're wrong.

Black folks like our heroes as much as anyone.

Real heroes rarely ask for the designation, however, and the ones who walk around wearing it usually have dressed themselves in it.

When we slap these tags on people without giving them the benefit of humanity and all its fallacies, we're setting everyone up for disappointment and even culture shock.

Truth is, if you love and support a black man on trial for his life, it's OK to do so.

But do it with the full knowledge of all his flaws and with the understanding that there's a possibility the man whom you love and support might be capable of killing a woman.

He might even be capable of killing her knowing she's pregnant.

That's chilling.

It's possible.

It might be the truth.

Ringer is allowed due process of the criminal justice system just as Simpson enjoyed it, albeit with less fanfare and without the sheen of celebrity.

Ringer isn't an athlete.

A barber, he just gave them haircuts and shaves.

There's a strangely harsh lesson to be learned from O.J. Simpson emceeing a hip-hop show: Life leaves us surreal, 3-D reminders of what can happen when justice is abandoned in the name of reparations.

A jury of Simpson's peers (that's a good one) said it wasn't (quite) him.

I hope Ringer gets a jury of people unlike himself.

I hope they're reasonable people fearless in the face of the truth and fearless when it comes time to tell it.

There are plenty guilty people walking free.

The last thing we need is Ringer one day emceeing a hip-hop show.

Although I hear the circus is in town.

Get Back/Stay Back

"What have you bought into/How much will it cost to buy you out?"

—POET SAUL WILLIAMS

Back in the day, I used to like Alicia Reece.

I voted for the vice mayor.

Twice.

Be clear that I empathize with that age-old pull of being black in a hard place.

Negroes expect one thing, while everyone else expects something else.

When you're black in a hard place, you can never be good enough, do enough good, be black enough or tame your blackness into its safer, older cousin, the Non-Offensive Negro.

It sucks, really. It's a trap, a gimmick and no Negro should bite the hype.

That doesn't mean there's room for an absence of integrity or that we shouldn't self-criticize.

More on that later.

Now for the roller coaster.

Orange fingertips, part one

I forgave Reece her unprofessional transgressions when she scarfed a bag of cheese puffs during our first meeting. While I was reporting the *CityBeat* cover story "Ware-ing Thin" about the sorry state of local black media, I interviewed Reece at WCIN (1480 AM), where she was executive producer of *1480 Talk with Lincoln Ware*.

I wasn't mad she excused herself and made me wait in her office while she ran next door to Walgreen's to get the bag of cheese puffs and a sugary red beverage.

I got over being offended by her orange fingertips.

I stopped obsessing over whether she'd have crunched cheese puffs and licked her fingertips had I been a white reporter in her office.

Maybe.

My Nigga Meter says nope.

Niggas do nigga shit in the company of other blacks out of assumed racial familiarty.

But who knows?

I respected Reece for attacking the vote in an old-school, grassroots style during her 1999 campaign for her first term on Cincinnati City Council. I even admired her for the way she worked her daddy Steve's business/political connects like those white prep boys who cash in their daddy's blue blood favor chips.

Why the hell not?

Since when has privilege been exclusively a birthright of the majority?

"You go, girl!" fell out of my mouth and, horrified, I'd look around to see who said it.

That soon turned into "Oh, gawd" whenever I read or heard about deals Reece brokered in her father's name, like the one with the Westin Hotel wherein anyone using Steve's Bond Hill meeting space Integrity Hall gets Westin discounts.

That mires her objections to the economic boycott in a self-serving agenda.

Suddenly, Integrity Hall sounds ironic.

Joe and LaToya

Negresses publicly scrutinizing one another puts us on shaky ground.

Folks would like nothing better than to see two black bitches go at it WWF-style in a weave-pulling match to the death. I ignored months of whispers from agenda-wielding blacks who tried convincing me I should shred the vice mayor.

I'd write it when Reece, by her deeds and arrogance, said so.

Until now I played my position.

Drama aside, now's the time.

Reece owes us.

She owes us more than her cross-promotional tactics of pushing her father's business interests. It's starting to smell like a conflict of interest. I'd rather they play out their Joe and LaToya Jackson stage-daddy scenario on their own time.

At least don't assume we're all stupid and that none among us can follow a paper trail.

What Reece really owes us is the firebrand persona that engaged us in the first place.

Before she joined council, Reece called for a U.S. Department of Justice investigation into the 1999 police shooting of Michael Carpenter, even writing a letter to former Attorney General Janet Reno.

This is the same Reece who, at the risk of alienating herself from council's other Negroes, brazenly and rightfully criticized the spending of the Greater Cincinnati African American Chamber of Commerce.

Then, as a muzzling-I-have-a-black-friend-tactic, Mayor Charlie Luken appointed her vice mayor.

I know, I know.

Black folks like their public Negroes crusading.

I'll cop to that.

But at some point in Reece's crusade, her Willona Woods *Good Times* feistiness morphed into the narcissism of *Dynasty*'s Dominique Deveraux.

It's the arrogance.

It's also the *oratio politicus* — the political speak — the talking in circles and all the time landing back on herself.

"Massa," "Mouth," "Slave"

After the April 12 signing of the Collaborative Agreement, when BET's Ed Gordon asked her about resolution, reparations and riots, Reece blathered on about how well she's done her job.

I thought the point of politics wasn't what you *did* but what you'll *do*.

Public service.

Not lip service.

It's not just me who's noticed Reece should be charged with LWI — Leading While Intoxicated (with Power). I heard she was booed and heckled when she took the microphone at the recent anniversary party of the demigods at WIZF (100.9 FM).

A cash bar will bring out the worst in some Negroes.

On April 7, a group of us leftover from the March for Justice commemorating the one-year anniversary of the police shooting of Timothy Thomas ended up at the shooting site on Republic Street.

Several 40ish black women held forth, clutching large signs.

I yelled for a *CityBeat* photographer to get a shot of one of the signs.

Later the photographer, a mature black man who often works with the Reeces, passed the photo to me.

"I've been thinking about a column about Alicia, and this is the headline," I told him, pointing to the sign in the picture.

"Don't put that in the paper," he said.

Out of deference to him and to keep this from teetering further into a niggerbitchfit, I'll say only that the sign contained the words "massa," "mouth" and "slave."

You connect the dots.

I'll put it more nicely: Reece is losing her grip on some much-needed street credentials.

She need only get back to where she once belonged.

Stay back

In my weariness I can see it.

Things are soon to get ugly.

Angela Leisure, Timothy Thomas' mother and her attorney, Kenneth Lawson, filed a federal lawsuit against Steve Reece, Vice Mayor Alicia Reece and James Washington, owner of Washington Limousine Service.

The suit claims the vice mayor and her father illegally conspired to intimidate political foes and enlisted Washington as an "agent" in their alleged dealings, including attempts to convince Leisure to drop Lawson as her attorney.

Dropping Lawson, recently named one of America's top-ranking black attorneys, would put Leisure on a faster settlement track in her lawsuit against the city in the April 7, 2001 police shooting death of her son.

Silence

This shit is curvilinear.

This doesn't happen often in life, but soon two points will intersect.

Believe it or don't, but when I write columns I don't do it to grind axes.

I'm minding my own business.

Wrong.

After "Get Back" dropped, Reece came to *CityBeat*'s new digs, missing me by only minutes.

In a public display of unprofessional bitchery on a public floor in front of more than a dozen of his employees Reece told John Fox, my editor and publisher, that she'd send a posse of black firefighters to convince me to stop criticizing her.

Black firefighters are somehow beholden to her. But to use them as her personal lynch mob is ludicrous.

Crazier still, Reece said she'd previously used the same tactic to silence another critic.

What?

This is crucial.

It speaks to character and small-town bullshit.

In what other racially divided city with a 40 per cent black population could one of the highest-ranking black public officials behave this way and not be run out of City Hall?

And Washington, D.C., don't count.

Think about this: The alleged suit-worthy behavior of the Reeces and Washington isn't news. What makes it titillating fodder for the city's radio talk shows is that the vice mayor led us to believe her reality was something else.

Reece's alleged behavior—including her paternalistic I'm-telling-your-daddy-on-you confrontation with my boss—is a bad black puppet show that's imitative of the white male power structure to which she begs inclusion.

Her bad.

Fox does not control or allow me.

Her alleged conduct squishes black ink into the buttermilk.

It's all alleged because Reece has yet to confront me directly.

I heard about her cursing, name-calling, threats and claims of my scorned lesbian attraction to her after-the-fact from Fox after I for hours and then days harangued him to tell me the full story.

All of it.

You're out

Besides idiocy, Reece is guilty of mimicry.

She long pooh-poohed the way white boys have been conducting business around town but then allegedly cashed in her daddy's favor chips and threw around her perceived political heft.

It doesn't make it right.

It merely makes it a bad imitation of life.

And she's mad at me for outing her on all of it.

You've heard of dumbing down?

I call Reece's backfiring double standard niggering down.

It's some kind of skewed SAT word association equation.

It's like Negroes crashing the Kentucky Derby—not to attend the races but to drink, smoke weed and have forgettable sex.

It's Freaknik as the ghetto home version of MTV's Spring Break.

It's why we never get invited to the big dance except to clean up afterward.

More importantly, it's a litmus test.

People all over town are singing in the comeuppance chorus, calling for the vice mayor's head. Others are choosing the Reeces' side and defending those good Negroes who never hurt anyone.

I wish this were as easy as a popularity contest, but it's not. It's a matter of right and wrong, and, while that sounds like absolutism, it's actually more complicated.

Truth is, the truth doesn't require us.

It doesn't need nor does it ask for any of our self-serving assistance, because truth always wins out in the end whether or not we decide to tell it.

In journalism, we say, "Let people talk long enough and eventually they'll tell the truth on themselves."

The Reeces don't need our help.

Never will.

If they're due to come undone, I think they've got it covered.

And if you think I'm taking the high road, you're right.

You can't see me

It doesn't make me soft, arrogant, naive, inflammatory or beyond reproach.

It makes me the one who wrote "Get Back" in the first place.

It makes me the one who, according to many of you hoarse whisperers, voiced some long-held but long-silent sentiments about a once-popular and now maligned public servant.

Since the column, the lawsuit and the *CityBeat* story detailing the vice mayor's behavior, my phone rings non-stop, e-mails trickle in and even letters appear in support of "Get Back."

I appreciate those acknowledgements and the words of support.

But let's be clear:

Don't look for me to validate your criticisms and don't expect to see me draped in the robes of spokeswoman for the race.

I've never laid claims to that.

I never will.

Anyone claiming as much hasn't talked directly to me about who I am.

Being spokeswoman would mean Negroes were organized, like a nonprofit.

We all know what a fallacy that is.

It'd also mean having to answer to someone, and that usually means being manipulated. Manipulation sucks.

Autonomy works for me.

And I write it like I see it.

O Brotha, Where Art Thou?

❖❖❖❖❖❖

"Truth is born/out of the mouth of a black man scorned/
I see you laughin' with swollen eyes/life be a mutha' when you playin' the losin' side

—"ALL THAT I AM," BILAL

Dear black males ages 13-55 years old:

You're scaring me.

I thought you were smarter than this. I thought you knew there are destructive forces standing and conspiring against you.

You don't need to ever battle one another. But still you do.

I see you. I'm no spy. I see you, though, sitting on ghetto stoops, saluting the sun with a French kiss to an up-turned brown paper bag. Others race around in bank-financed suits, dodging second mortgages and mistresses, blowing your children's college educations on blow.

And the rest?

You distance yourselves from the ones who need your example, afraid the dirt of their niggadom might stick to you. You're adorned in false happiness that hides volatility and anger.

What's up? Why can't you relax?

When you talk among yourselves, whom do you blame for failure and disappointment and whom do you praise when you gain ground?

I'm just wondering, because you're killing one another in record numbers. Not only that, the cops suspect you in most of these homicides.

See, you're hemmed up.

What level of big pimpin' would spin you into a rage sufficient to make murder an option or, dumber still, an excuse to rack up street credibility? Where do you get your examples, in videos, boardrooms, nightclubs, the news or sports?

That's where you're wrong.

Black athletes collect 'hos like I collect snow globes.

Mediocre black male warblers get caught desecrating all over somebody's under-age daughter like outtakes from their raunchy, record-company-financed pornos. (Can you say R. Kelly?)

Meanwhile, making money is celebrated and worshiped.

Sometimes it's hard telling the difference between a black-owned mansion and a black-owned church, yet the courts run on black gasoline.

Why are you so afraid?

Why must you be so hard?

Why do you make it so hard?

So far this year there's been 33 homicides in Cincinnati. Of those, there are 28 victims whose race and gender I know; 17 of them are dead black men and 17 black men are either suspects in or have been arrested for their brothers' deaths.

We're not yet even into the meat of summer and here we are, destroying ourselves at the speed of night.

No one wants responsibility for his or her actions. Responsibility in Cincinnati is a bastard; no Daddy. This includes you. And it's so tired now some of you blame the man, the system, the cops, the baby mamma, the war, the blah, blah, blah.

Don't you know whomever you deem your enemy delights in your genocidal behavior? They're laughing at how you look and behave.

They're moving away from you and brokering deals to secure a future minus you.

How does that make you feel ? Maybe you don't know how you feel because no one ever told you it's OK to rub up against your feelings without rubbing your penis up against everything.

You've bought into the game.

It's playing you and not vice versa.

I live out here, too.

I know there are things to acquire, women and men to lay and trails to blaze. In your empty quest for legacies, however, you're burning yourselves alive in the process.

Many of you have kept it clean and holy, but why is it only the black men on your pew benefit from your holy fellowship?

Your reach isn't long enough. (See Mathew 25:40: "Inasmuchas you did it unto one of the least of these, my brethren, you did it to me.")

Black women don't always make it easier, because we're dealing with a truckload of drama, too. We run to church without you, start dating Jesus and no one else measures up. We work you to an early grave to buy things we think we can't live without because we're still unsure of who we are.

(THERE WERE IN 2002 65 HOMICIDES IN CINCNNATI. THE NUMBER SET A CITYWIDE RECORD.)

We, like you, are afraid to be unadorned.

We're not always available.

When we are, we try to love away who you've become so we can re-make you.

That never works.

So we separate and play each other against the middle.

And the children we make, we foist them—incomplete and half-cloaked and cocked—onto the world and wonder why nobody else can fix them.

This cycle looks like a snake eating its tail.

If it sounds like I've slipped off into melodrama, I have.

The drama is biblical.

Don't worry about who else reads this.

I write to you in love.

So what if the other team knows we love one another?

I don't fear you.

I don't always understand you.

I accept you for who you are, wherever you are.

People died so you could be free to do better.

But today you're killing each other and it can't get much worse.

Let's make love.

Let's make it better.

Respectfully,

Kathy Y. Wilson, your sister

God Can See You Pee

◇◇◇◇◇◇

We need Jesus.

We know that, and so does the Rev. Billy Graham.

Unless you've been in a state of permanent Madeira, i.e. the white-washed suburbs, you know that Graham and his disciples will be shepherding more than 200,000 people into Paul Brown Stadium this weekend during a four-day mission organized by the Greater Cincinnati Northern Kentucky Billy Graham Mission.

I gotta hand it to these people.

"More than 964 churches and 67 denominations," according to the press material. They've marketed God, Graham and Jesus like a rock concert. If this were the regrettable 1980s, when benefit concerts overcompensated for President Reagan's "me, mine and ours" politics, Graham's road show would be like Live Aid or "We Are the World" redux.

I hear tell there's even a poster of Graham above a urinal in the men's bathroom at Kaldi's Coffee House.

"God can see you pee" is scribbled on his protruding forehead.

That's probably not what the mission had in mind when it charged underrowers with getting the word out.

Another, less guttural, slogan whispers, "God knows how it can change your life." Hmmmm.

Applying "god" in the generic, everyday sense, it's a tease that could sell a vacation, an alcoholic beverage or a time-share.

It's a stroke of shrewd advertising genius that's put God on mid-day radio, on the sides of busses and on car bumpers.

And why not?

Why shouldn't God and His son employ a public relations firm in the guise of intradenominational healing and bring it—like The Who or Rolling Stones—in trailer trucks to a sin-sick city?

You know you're on God's black list when Graham shows up.

He's like an employed Rev. Jesse Jackson without the rhyming couplets.

But there's something foreboding and sooooo Cincinnati about all this.

It's almost like that sticky, post-Sept. 11 patriotic tidal wave that washed over us.

Yeah, yeah, Cincinnati needs atonement, a round of rousing praise songs and group prayer. And, sure, we could even use a group hug.

But this is going to end up as throngs of suburbanites tailgating into downtown from points way east, west and north. These will be the people who've read about us and who've seen us on the news. They'll be the ones who've wrung their hands, rolled their eyes, clucked their tongues and maybe even prayed, all in exasperation, for us wretched city folk to find some healing.

They'll drive in off the expressway, take in the breathtaking skyline and marvel at the stadium rising from the riverbanks. They'll even feel safe surrounded by all that imposing development.

Their cherubic children and virginal teenagers will sing and dance together, and the hip (and Negroes) among them will git down with God to the Soul-filled sounds of Kirk Franklin, everyone's favorite New Jack Christian.

Later the stadium will empty and they'll go back to the 'burbs without so much as talking to one person living in Over-the-Rhine.

They won't have heard from Angela Leisure, Timothy Thomas' mother, and they'll leave without seeing one small business still boarded up, unable to rebound from last April's uprising.

It's a feel-good fest.

And there's nothing wrong with feeling good, so long as we're not slathering ourselves with positivity as a tortoise-shell shield from reality.

To those of us who've been knee deep in all types of racial, gender, economic and class warfare, Graham's mission is like a relief plane drizzling water on dehydrated people dying in the dirt of their own, unconcerned country.

It'll be enough to aggravate but not enough to ingratiate.

I say all this as a believer.

I know God for myself.

I know God loves a cheerful giver.

But He hates the drive-by.

Likewise, I'm Sure

People want me to hate Peter Bronson.

"How do you handle sitting next to him every week on that show?" they ask of our oppositional bantor on "Hot Seat," Channel 9's Sunday morning roundtable.

These folks are all ages, races and work all types of jobs.

As you read this you're just hoping I'm about to run the *Enquirer's* Metro columnist's ass through the shredder.

I do that—partly for entertainment value but more for the truth— enough on "Hot Seat."

Anything more and it's mean-spirited.

Plus, that's a gimmick—white vs. black vs. conservative vs. open-minded vs. establishment vs. alternative.

This city runs off melodrama.

We get off when people publicly hate one another.

The zing of sending and receiving character assassinating e-mails enthralls us.

Not me.

I'm a squelcher.

So when people bring up their amazement, I usually say: "If I get to say what I want, he gets to say what he wants."

It wasn't always like that.

Back in the day when "Hot Seat" co-creators and former co-hosts Aaron Herzig and Fred Nelson first invited me as a guest I came, butt cheeks clinched, and took a defensive seat beside Peter.

Black women must jump in or risk alienation.

I commented on everything during that inaugural taping.

What stands out in my memory is when I feigned punching Peter in the side of the head.

That was the extent of my Peter Bronson exorcism.

Herzig and Nelson eventually invited me to be a regular on "Hot Seat."

It's been an education.

First, there's diversity in the outward sameness of the Midwestern white male. They're not all alike and they're not as powerful as they'd have us all believe.

Next, they are skittish. Close proximity to the opposition fucks 'em up. Peter fits that white male mold perfectly. I do not hold it against him.

There's a touch of fearlessness in his cyclical attacks on boycotters, police critics, death penalty opponents, President Clinton, all liberals, all Democrats, homosexuals and all the other Others.

Some things he just doesn't get.

Most times we agree not to. We drop the pettiness and walk out smiling into the sun after "Hot Seat" tapings.

However, I know the recoil of being ass-out opinionated.

People attack not only his writing and subject matter, but also his character, intentions, associations and, most of all, his racial beliefs.

They do the same to me.

It's what you sign on for as a columnist.

Here's the short list of what's admirable about Peter.

He's a political scholar and a reasonable equalizer around the "Hot Seat" table and he doesn't back down.

It'd be easier to oversimplify him but people are always more complex than their opinions.

He loves God and his family.

From what I've cobbled together, I think he went from college hippie to conservative.

He's got nice hands and even my mother digs him.

But this ain't no Valentine.

Peter is myopic.

The threat to his status quo triggers all sorts of defense mechanism.

His blind pro-police stance is equal parts frightening,, funny and devil's advocacy.

More often than not he surrounds himself—on "Hot Seat," anyway,—with a parade of gun-toting white guys. I'm always the Flygirl in the Buttermilk whenever our third co-host, *Herald* publisher Eric Kearney, takes off.

It's the grown-up punctuation to a lifelong sentence of white-hot minority status.

So big deal.

I'm learning, always learning.

I don't pay attention to other local media, but sometimes I read Peter's column for quick tips on what not to do with the marriage of ideas and sentences. I am sure he has readers whose opinions are in lockstep with his own. Just like he has regular readers who hate reading him but who couldn't stop if therapy intervened.

I got those, too.

Sometimes they read us in tandem. Other times my readers wouldn't be caught in the dark with a Bronson column and vice versa.

And this is how it's suposed to be.

This is why comparisons between Peter and I are like comparing our papers.

It's a hot dog on a hamburger bun; there's overage.

But we do share our toys.

Neither of us—papers or columnists—never quite get it right, we could always do better and we're always looking for a comfortable spot to rest.

I was surprised by the appearance of *Cincinnati...For Pete's Sake*, Peter's new book (www.peterbronson.com) of collected columns culled from the *Enquirer*.

I assumed he'd serve up a heap more comfort food to his legions of loyalists.

His timing is perfect, though, because this collection was right on his heels.

Buy 'em both. Have a dinner party. Spend the evening arguing. Leave feeling the same.

It'd be like the "Hot Seat" home game.

"You are one fine writer," he wrote in the copy of his book he gave to me.

See, we agree on one point.

Nowhere Man

Upstanding Christian father and dedicated cop or a bald-faced liar hovering below the radar of departmental discipline? A pillar of the community deserving an outpouring of support or a spin controller epitomizing the cult of personality of cops who behave recklessly and skate wrongdoing?

Suspended veteran Lt. Col. Ron Twitty might be as schizophrenic as they come. Which is it? Will the real Slim Shady please stand up?

We all know people like Twitty. Then again, no one really knows people like Twitty.

A hero ain't nothin' but a sandwich, and black heroes operate on CP time. For the uninitiated, that's Colored People's time. They're late.

Yet Negroes in Cincinnati are so thirsty for black heroes that we've settled. And just as sediment floats to the bottom of a glass of murky Ohio River water, Twitty's been absolved from his half-telling-lawyer-speak-of-a-flimsy-excuse explaining what happened to his city-owned car.

"He can't explain what happened because he didn't witness the damage," said Sharon Zealey, Twitty's attorney. That's lawyer-ese for "He didn't witness it but that doesn't mean he doesn't know what happened."

Twitty's supporters are clinging to his nice-guy image, that of the former patrolman who kept a Bible in his squad car. That doesn't make him incapable of wrongdoing. Any cop worth his badge will tell you that along with all the honor and responsibility accompanying police work there's twice as much temptation and humanity.

And there are loopholes big enough to shove a misstep through.

Missing among the throngs of Twitty supporters is one who might counsel him not to lay back and enjoy this lap dance of misplaced black loyalty that's at direct odds with misplaced white authority.

Be mindful that, throughout the course of his career, Twitty was *thrust* forward. From jump he was never gung-ho to be a cop. Once he was, affirmative action—the right place/right time dumb luck of fate—conspired with the Cincinnati Police Department's need for a black face in the upper ranks. He became that Go-To Negro.

In 1993, the Fraternal Order of Police tried blocking Twitty's promotion over white cops with higher scores, citing affirmative action—an evil as necessary as cops themselves—as the wrong tool to put him in place near the top. Needing a less whitewashed division, city fathers created an extra captain's slot especially for Twitty.

Five years later, then-City Manager John Shirey added the assistant chief position to again add color to the force's upper ranks.

This begs the question: How would you feel if the yellow brick road to a comfortable retirement in a career you kinda fell into was paved with added positions and unspoken Golden Black Boy status? Would you feel put upon, like your smile would crack if you had to smile it just one more time?

By now, what happened isn't nearly as sexy as what *will* happen. That is, what type of race-tinged-not-quite-guilty-we-can't-catch-him-in-a-lie back-room deal will be brokered between Twitty and the city because Chief Tom Streicher commandeered an accusatory press conference?

Because the press conference was premature and overboard doesn't let Twitty out of the noose, though. But because only God and Twitty know what really happened, does that mean he shouldn't be punished? And because Cincinnati has an unprecedented and uncorrected record of under-disciplined and overcongratulated cops, is it time to set an example?

I don't think Twitty is coming completely clean about what allegedly and actually happened to his mysteriously banged-up Ford Taurus. Now that the investigation has landed on the desk of Hamilton County Prosecutor Mike Allen, I'm skeptical that a special grand jury will ferret out the elusive truth of the matter.

Indulge my Dionne Warwick psychic friendliness as I offer a few predictions.

This situation will fade to black under a hovering cloud of suspicion, whispers, innuendo and a gag order or two. Some type of settlement will be handed over to Twitty in lieu of an apology for the assumption of guilt put forth at the press conference. Then Twitty will either slink away with said settlement and his pension or, if white guilt rules out, get said settlement and return to work unblemished.

The point here isn't that the Twitty situation is another nail in Cincinnati's racial coffin or that it was responsible for the National Urban League cancelling its convention.

Here's the point: The Go-To Negro probably never was and maybe never wanted to be any of the things we foisted on him. He just happened to be a cop who now happens to be in trouble.

And he also happens to be a real nowhere man.

The Care and Feeding of Black Teenagers, Version 2.0

◇◇◇◇◇◇

I've written this one before.

It was another time, a different place and a different newspaper.

The more Negroes change, the more we stay the same.

See, the circumstances were identical.

Wild, careless, potentially violent, emotionally vacant, frighteningly under-parented and follow-the-leader stupid black teenagers left to their own devices.

Wearing expensive gym shoes and flopping Timberlands, black teens like these stomp down everything in their paths.

They don't think they're privileged because they're black or because they live in a certain zip code, but they're actually intoxicated on a cocktail of privilege, freedom and stupidity.

And it's not so much what they do, but how it appears.

They're either too young to fully realize the up-to-the-minute legacy of stupidity they're leaving behind or fully aware and they just don't care.

The latter might be worse.

There's a connotation of an ethical void, like they know better but "What the hell?"

Then these black teens who could be separating themselves from the pack are baffled when they're labeled as "roving packs" or when they're profiled because their behavior leaves little choice.

Torch my crib and I'll think you're an arsonist.

To that I say, "Behave how you want to be identified."

Try it.

It works.

We all know that what happened after the Saturday and Sunday close of the 14th Annual Midwest Black Family Reunion Celebration was shameful and embarrassing.

It's shameful because we don't need any of this banshee-girl/b-boy bull.

It's embarrassing because it proves that much of the displaced responsibility previously aimed at external forces instead lands squarely at our own feet.

This is one time when we can't point crooked black fingers at the police, the city, economic disparity or any other signpost of misplaced accountability.

Now what?

I'm not handing out Bad Behavior Passes or Get Out of Jail Free Cards because fits of destruction erupted in response to some perceived social injustice.

Nope.

Not gonna happen.

There should've been a disclaimer waved from a banner Saturday and Sunday: No unarmed black men were killed during the making of this fiasco.

And what of the rumors swirling about the free-for-all?

Girl gangs?

Neighborhood rivalries?

It doesn't matter, really.

Property was damaged, a Metro bus driver got punched in the face and vehicles were pelted with rocks and bottles. More than a dozen people were arrested. The cops showed restraint becoming of well-trained cops.

The national news reported on us, and the damage control is spinning. Some say it wasn't all that bad, that it was "blown out of proportion."

If one black child acts out, isn't that one bad black child too many?

Backpedaling in the deep end of denial is a sure sign of dysfunction and co-dependency worth a few trips to therapy.

I feel like a family member has brought shame and degradation on my name.

This isn't how we're supposed to look.

This isn't how we're supposed to behave.

This is whom we've given the world.

This debacle of antithetical Black Family Reunion behavior panhandles one question and only one question: Where the hell were the parents?

Hadn't they heard?

It's the Black Family Reunion.

It's not black church, where you send your kid so you can sleep in.

I know it's not only black postmodern families that are disjointed and non-traditional.

But our grandparents, aunts and foster and adoptive parents are raising Cain and Abel.

However difficult or different-looking, it still equals a family.

And every family's gotta have values.

So stop sending your unprepared children out into the world, hoping they'll get schooled, raised, loved, directed, arrested or otherwise taken off your lazy hands for a while.

That corny African proverb that "it takes a village" to raise a child is a bald-faced lie.

It takes parents to raise a child so that society isn't left to come up with excuses for your lackluster performance as parents.

I'm tired of writing this column.

I love your kids, but that don't make 'em mine.

Don't make me pull this column over.

Don't make me *write* this column over.

Brown Meat, Beer and a Bootleg Cabbie

The meat isn't brown.

I'd heard and believed the urban legend that said meat sold at the Over-the-Rhine Kroger was so near the end of its shelf life it was as brown as the customers who shopped there. But everything at the June 2 Grand Re-Opening—except the notoriously claustrophobic parking lot—was new and/or expanded.

And clean.

Cleanliness is next to gaudiness, right near shiny, which is in aisle 4A next to exuberance.

Out front, black men tugged a huge grill into the shade and off the parking lot blacktop. Personalities from WIZF (100.9 FM) operated a homemade roulette wheel for CD and T-shirt giveaways.

Inside, there's better lighting, wider aisles, bigger displays and more modern signage. Produce is arranged with surreal Martha Stewart accuracy. According to the board in the vestibule, Dave Miller is your store manager.

Cashiers spoke to customers in sing-songy tones, while other workers restocked shelves, helped old ladies retrieve Styrofoam coolers from high up and finagled brand-new carts.

There was no such hyperactive customer service the half dozen times I'd previously shopped there. But then this exhibition had as much to do with the proliferation of Kroger executives as with the refurbished digs.

I didn't know groceries exacted so much excitement and fanfare. The Vine Street Kroger, however, is more than a grocery store.

It's a landmark to the Kroger Co.'s prior lack of commitment to fulfilling Over-the-Rhine residents' nutritional needs beyond nicotine, sugary cereal, ribs, a rainbow of Kool-Aid flavors and 40 ounces. (More on that later.) It was an unspoken neighborhood joke. But wasn't shit funny. It was an eyesore among eyesores.

Nearly a blight.

So it's reasonable that a gaggle of Kroger executives wandered the aisles, surveyed the store behind baggers' stations and answered reporters' questions above the din of Jazz Muzak piping through the public address system.

Befitting most other O-T-R culture, the fanfare came down to loyalists and tourists. That is, residents have such fine-tuned radar they can smell an interloper at 10 paces.

All the media, suits and hoopla ain't worth a fistful of double coupons to the mostly old, mostly female black and white neighborhood folks who'll still need groceries once the new-car smell dissipates. A woman in a suit with a Kroger nametag on her lapel warned two female shoppers. "There's reporters in here," she said loudly. "Watch out."

The urban myth about the brown meat no longer holds true, but another surfaced. I'd heard about the expansive refrigerated beer cases, so after lunch at Tucker I returned to see for myself.

It's true. The cheap wine and wine coolers beg from stingy shelving, but across the aisle the refrigerated beer cases extend down the aisle. It's refrigeration's equivalent to the doublewide trailer.

Apples to oranges, the (wealthier/much whiter) Hyde Park Kroger has a state liquor agency and the Over-the-Rhine Kroger has every brand, size and flavor imaginable of malt liquor. It's offensive to discover marketing so race- and class-specific, but there it is—and on sale with your Kroger Plus card!

On my way out, a longtime employee confided her disbelief when she first heard the store would be overhauled. She's happy the execs kept their word.

The company is clearly recommitted to amped up and friendlier customer service and even a cleaner shopping environment. What about a response to the city's needs south of Central Parkway, however, where young, hip professionals are slowly answering developers' lures to live downtown?

Ask prospective downtowners what they want, and they'll answer that they need an accessible and well-stocked grocery store that doesn't close with the banks and with prices that don't skyrocket because most shoppers use Food Stamp cards.

On the edge of the parking lot, the spot is marked as an Ohio Historical Landmark. In polite language it traces Over-the-Rhine from its heyday of German and Dutch settlers to its present-day station where blacks live but few thrive.

Great, but what about making the store a viable landmark linking the two halves of downtown—those who have and those who have not?

The reopening is typical of Cincinnati. We look lovingly at the past, expecting laurels alone to propel us forward. Then we wrap it all in new packaging so folks believe they're getting something new.

In *Seinfeld* language, it's called the re-gift.

What's beauteous is that amidst the hoopla of corporate presentation and everyday reality, black folks—and our environments—remain unfazed. The acrid and heady smell of urine whoomped up my nostrils as soon as I stepped off Kroger's lot to the sidewalk. And just as when I first pulled up to the store, a black man caught my eye.

"You driving?" he asked, wondering if I was a bootleg cab driver.

"Naw," I said. "Sorry."

And Kroger should be, too.

'Shame the Devil'

Hal McKinney's dogs want to eat me.

Alerted by incessant barking, the 54-year-old Northsider appears in the doorway of his Chase Avenue home. Approaching the tall wooden fence, he assures his dogs are all bark.

Max and Baron, full-bred German Shepherds, push their full weight against the fence.

It sways.

I step back.

They back down.

I move forward.

We tango in anxiety.

It's Friday night, and a cold drizzle falls as McKinney opens the gate. Stepping inside his darkened yard feels like the last thing I'll ever do. I feel myself about to be devoured. But I owe him this visit.

On the porch, McKinney greets me warmly, regaling me with dogs stories.

"The rumor in the neighborhood is my dogs hate black people," he says. "They just don't like people hitting them in the head with two-by-fours."

Tails wagging, Max and Baron back away in retreat to the side yard.

During the next four hours, McKinney's dichotomies unfold.

This is about what I didn't know until I spent time with him.

It's about black boys and white men, crime, geography, class and culture.

It's about guns.

Harold "Hal" McKinney is the white man—hero to some, devil to others—who on May 8, shot Joe Person and scared the braggadocio out of DeMeico Hester, both 18 and black, in Junker's Tavern. McKinney emerged as a mythic, almost cinematic hero, Everyman's Man fed up with but unafraid of the clusters of young black dope dealers overruning his street.

Fear and anger are recurring McKinney themes.

"The only people making money in this city are moving companies and ADT," he says, in typical McKinney absolute succinctness.

"Is it citywide?" I ask.

"It's not citywide. It's countrywide."

He roots fruitlessly around his desk for an out-of-town editorial blaming crime victims for crime.

"I refuse to live my life in fear. I'd be hiding in the corner somewhere. When your number's up, it's up," he says, giving up on the article.

"It's not a color issue."

Is he talking about Northside specifically, Cincinnati generally or responses to the shooting? Drop the "not," and his pronouncement ironically befits all three.

"The worst thing about Northside is that we don't gain strength in our diversity. Diversity divides. It's our unity—the thing we all believe in—that pulls us together. It's not who you sleep with or what you sleep with," he says, a nod to Northside's unofficial status as a hub for gays and lesbians.

He's been courted by cops and, encouraged by a groundswell of support, announced his City Council candidacy.

McKinney, a Lutheran, looks like a fundamentalist preacher in his button-down white shirt, ink pens peaking from its pocket, subdued tie, dark suit pants and dress shoes.

He's come from meeting with Republican Party officials and doing the Endorsement Mating Dance.

Though he laments the slow to no police response for drug activity complaints, McKinney is unabashedly pro-police, a stance that might thrust him into a council seat.

"A cop told me, 'You'd make a good police officer, but you'd make a better friend to (us) on council.' "

The shooting and McKinney's subsequent pass by the grand jury on charges of felonious assault and carrying a gun into a liquor establishment sparked a maelstrom of talk radio pontificators, opinions and name calling culminating in appearances by McKinney and his attorney, Mark Naegel, on WLW (700 AM) and WDBZ (1230 AM), the latter a colored version of the former.

At the behest of *Enquirer* columnist Peter Bronson, they also appeared on the May 23 taping of WCPO Channel 9's local political roundtable *Hot Seat*, where we met.

During taping, I asked McKinney what he felt before he pulled the trigger on Person.

I questioned him for walking into Junker's with a .40-calibre semiautomatic pistol.

To understand guns and any rights to carry and shoot them is to more fully understand McKinney, who says he's clocked 300 shooting range hours.

He's lived in the mammoth house since October.

It sat vacant two years before that. Since, though, there have been three attempted burglaries. Some dealers McKinney confronted tried to feed his dogs in a ploy to win them over.

One threatened his daughter.

"I got the house for $43,000 because of the crack dealers. I think the property value goes down because of the crack," he says, pausing for a punchline, "$1,000 off for every dealer."

The large living room is neat.

The house has that damp and musty smell old houses emit when it rains.

Both sofas are covered with homemade Amish-looking quilts. His 6-year-old daughter's dolls, stuffed animals and toys are scattered about. A black-and-white picture of *The Wizard of Oz* leans on the mantle. I tell him it's my favorite movie and, as I rise to look closer, McKinney breaks into "The Lollipop Guild," singing it a la Alvin & the Chipmunks.

A flashlight, binoculars and walkie-talkie clutter a side table by the front door.

A 12-gauge tactical shotgun lies crossways on the table among the accoutrements of his citizen's patrol force work.

"This is my best weapon," says McKinney, holding up a camera he uses to snap pictures of people copping drugs.

We mostly stand in the different rooms he tours me through.

In the office, there's a picture of his bright-eyed daughter now living with her mother, and his late mother.

I spot a smallish holstered gun on a dining table. It's a .380 Bersa, and McKinney pulls it briefly from its case.

"Do you ever consider moving?"

"No more than I thought about walking out that door (at Junker's) and leaving four people behind," he says. "My life revolves around right and wrong. It sucks. My ideas are the same now as they were a few weeks ago, except somebody got shot. It's sad. My prayers go out to Joe Person's mother."

Before we leave for Junker's, McKinney pulls a bulletproof vest from a coat rack and slips it over my head, pulls the Velcro straps and I'm in, constricted and weighted.

"I was doing everything but sleeping in it," he says.

He suggests I wear it to the bar "under your shirt," but I decline. He slips on the same dark hooded windbreaker he wore to Junker's the night of the shooting. As we walk back through the living room I see a third gun, a .357 Magnum, nestled above a row of neatly arranged video-cassettes on the bookshelf.

He returns to the night of the shooting. "You know what the guys would've said if I'd let them get robbed and they found out later I had a gun? 'Girly man!' "

As we leave to visit his black neighbor, a similarly beleaguered citizen tired but undaunted by the gaggle of dealers on his stoop, McKinney says something quietly jarring.

"Now I'm not being armed tonight."

As we wait in the light rain for the neighbor to answer, I recognize several black boys by dress, swagger and duplicitous antics as probably street dealers. They take turns standing at the corner eyeballing us. Their stares are stale forms of street intimidation.

I stare back.

I think they recognize McKinney, and I'm unafraid.

Inside, the two men—a younger, plump and wild-haired black man from Evanston and a studious, practical, middle-aged white man born on 13th Street—commiserate about crime and fighting it.

The neighbor once soaked his doorsteps with bleach. When a velour-suited drug dealer rose to leave, he sported a skunk stripe across his ass.

"When he moved in I gave him a 'No Trespassing' sign and hollow points," McKinney says.

They're brothers in arms.

They both pray for inclement weather.

A rainstorm a day keeps the dealers at bay.

McKinney and I walk the dark, wet street to Junker's.

He's a conquering hero.

The bar is a dark rectangle cooled by whirring ceiling fans and popu-lated by People the City Forgot.

A woman with multiple face piercings sings karaoke to The Eagles' "Hotel California." Next, an old black man in a see-through shirt sings in a voice like a resistant car engine. The rest of the patrons comprise the cast—black, white, older, tired and retired, heavy drinking bar flies and a few youngish white men thrown in.

McKinney walks me through the timeline of the shooting, pointing out where he was when Person pulled his gun on bar patrons. Tony Coyne, the owner, is friendly.

Richard Wiggins, the man who dared Person to shoot him as Person held him at gunpoint, comes to our booth. Wiggins says McKinney saved his life when he shot Person.

McKinney downs his second and final Corona before escorting me to my car.

The rain has dissipated.

He strides quickly, nudging his body into mine as a signal for when and where to cross the street. Young black boys gather on the opposite sidewalk.

McKinney suggests we cross to them. As we walk through, McKinney greets them and I say, "What's up?" They respond in kind.

At my car McKinney says he'll take the written police exam the next morning "to show intent."

"You know a person by what they're willing to die for," he says. "I learned a lot about myself. I learned I can depend on me."

"Tell the truth," his mother used to tell him. "Shame the devil."

In McKinney's world of absolutes, black and white have little to do with race and more to do with the exactitudes of right and wrong.

His mother's directive fits the man caught looking through the cross hairs into his own destiny.

I Had a Dream (A BeBop for MLK)

❖❖❖❖❖❖

"Morals cannot be legislated, but behavior can be regulated."
—THE REV. MARTIN LUTHER KING JR.

Lemme holla at you today, my people, 'cause even though we're face down in these tripped-out times I still had this dream. It's a dream deeply dipped in the American nightmare.

I had a dream that one day black folks in this city will wake up and scream out the true frustration of their being: "We hold these weaves, these cell phones, these SUVs, these bored meetings, these addictions, these bad-ass children and every lie we've ever told ourselves to be self-hatred; that all folks are created equal and, though equality's been taken from us, we're here to reclaim it."

I had a dream that one day, on the corners of Madisonville, Walnut Hills, Bond Hill, Price Hill, Northside and Avondale, sons of former wage slaves and the sons of former owners of payday loan centers will cease using one another as a means to a dead end.

I had a dream that one day even the city of Cincinnati—grunting beneath the obesity of injustice, grunting beneath the obesity of classism—will be whipped into a sanctuary of impartiality and economic equity.

I had a dream that one day my two little nephews will live in a city where they will not be profiled by the color of their skin, nor by the expensiveness of their cars or educations, but by the range of their respectability.

I had a dream last night.

I had a dream that one day, down in Over-the-Rhine—with its broad daylight drug deals, with its residents flipping cracked mirror images of being trapped and disenfranchised—one day right there in Over-the-Rhine, little black boys and little black girls will be able to join hands with black mothers and black fathers and walk together as intact families.

I had a dream last night.

I had a dream that one day every guilty cop shall be prosecuted, every councilman and councilwoman shall be made accountable, the homeless will be given shelter and the crooked politicians will be made straight, and the needs of the unregistered voter shall be revealed, and the rest of us shall see it together.

This is my hope. With this faith I'll be able to mow down out of the mountain of status quo a stone of progressiveness. With this hope I'll be able to strangle dissonance into four-part harmony. With this vision I'll be able to labor, to pray, to struggle, to stand, knowing we'll get the picture one day.

And if Cincinnati is to be a reasonable place to thrive, this must become reality. So let empathy ring from the privileged private drives of Indian Hill. Let self-respect ring from the alleyways of the West End. Let justice ring from the benches of the Hamilton County Justice Center!

And when this comes down the pike, and when we allow empathy, self-respect and justice to ring, when we let them loose from every village and every township, from every community and every outlying suburb, we'll expedite that day when all of God's children—b-boys and white boys, gays, lesbians, Jews, Gentiles, Protestants, Catholics, anti-Semites and non-believers—will be able to hook arms and sing in the words of that old Negro spiritual, "Free at last! Free at last! Thank God Almighty, we are free at last!"

Then I woke up.

365, 24/7: Black History Month Everyday

◇◇◇◇◇◇

Announcer: February is American Heart Month.

It's also International Boost Self-Esteem Month, Library Lovers' Month and National Children's Dental Health Month.

Commentator Kathy Y. Wilson isn't particulalry interested in any of those celebrations.

But then, she's not interested in most Black History Month celebrations, either.

Didja hear the one about Black History Month being the shortest month of the year?

Exactly.

A day with the races has become such a debacle, such a slash-and-burn closeout sale that Black History Month isn't just the joke, it's its own punchline.

Every February we're spoon fed a diet of Negrodom so laden with guilt and permissiveness that surely the original idea is loathed by late January and lost by mid-February.

Add to the national menagerie some fill-in-the-blank Negroes from Your Town, U.S.A. who either owned, founded, started, invented or ran away from something, and you've got a Black History Month observation identical to ones in years past.

If Black History Month were a Broadway show, every famous Negro's name on the BHM All-Star Team would end with an exclamation point.

Malcolm! Harriet! Martin! Sojourner!

And PBS would undoubtedly option it for broadcast every single night.

So now how do we keep Black History Month from being, year in and year out, an old school black Baptist Church service where every Negro child with they baby hair combed down on their shiny foreheads gets up proclaiming how brave the slaves were for running, or how Madame C.J. Walker made a mint from selling the hot comb?

Aren't we better than this, when Black History Month starts to constrict and stifle like sitting through one of those chitlin' circuit black

Gospel plays?

Just how many times can we listen to "I Have A Dream" before we wake up?

Who knows because we haven't yet.

You wanna celebrate Black History Month?

Have a conversation with a black person away from the water cooler.

When you see a black face illustrating a story on crime, blue collar unemployment, welfare, illiteracy or AIDS drop all assumptions about class and economics.

Treat our elders like we treated yours when we stepped, fetched and drove Miss Daisy.

And give us the benefit of...no, the *right* to educate you the way you've educated us for ceturies.

That is, constantly and presumptively.

Then you'll know more about us than you could ever fathom in 28 days.

Make *that* your Black History Month celebration.

How Big Is Yours? The Patriotic Profiling of Flags

❖❖❖❖❖

Announcer: It's the middle of December, but Kathy Y. Wilson isn't just seeing plastic Santas and icicle lights everywhere she goes. She's got her eye on all that red, white and blue.

I have never been patriotic.

I've never thought about *not* being patriotic.

As an American I enjoy my rights just like the next American.

As a Negro I enjoy my rights just like the next Negro.

About blind patriotism I am judgmental, critical, cynical, distrustful and paranoid and especially now.

Just as surely as some Americans profile brown people with wrapped heads, long beards and alphabet-soup last names, we're now profiling one another.

Flag owners and the flagless alike are eyeballin' each other as if to say, "How big is *yours?* Where is it and why isn't your house red, white and blue?"

Yeah, Old Glory's taken on a new, mutated symbology.

Everybody's profilin.'

And it's paranoia at white noise levels born from our mistrust of each other based on external assumptions.

Flags in every shape, incarnation, derivation and size are everywhere.

Flags are to patriotic profiling what SUVs are to class status—the bigger, the better.

If you don't have a flag and you don't regularly and publicly display it then, well…somethin's wrong with you.

That means something's wrong with me.

Ohio's gone so far as to issue an obnoxiously patriotic license plate evidently designed by a blind person.

Sandwiched between its red-and-blue borders is *too much information*: Ohio's bicentennial is in 2003, Ohio's the birthplace of aviation and we *will* be patriotic as witnessed by the red, white and blue ribbons billowing beneath the state's name squeezed off to the left.

So now drivers of $400 hoopties (like myself) and drivers of cars worth more than my annual salary are *made* to appear prideful.

The Bureau of Motor Vehicles is forcibly turning us into Patriotic Stepford Drivers.

Still, I know there exists true-blue, blue-black Negroes.

I see them wearing, waving and holding Old Glory just like their white counterparts. And they're every kind of Negro—from war vets and the work-a-day blunt-smokin' grunts to the white-collar, business-class black Ken and Barbie, all the way up to the ultra-successful faux Huxtables.

They're *rockin'* the flag.

Yet just as many Negroes aren't piling onto the red, white and blue-stained bandwagon.

We're waiting instead for the bus that'll take us to an America where affirmative action isn't a dirty word, where crosses signify the crucifixion of Jesus and *not* racial hatred and where the Confederate flag's not allowed to fly *anywhere*.

As for me and mine?

We're still waiting for our 40 acres and a mule.

I've been repeatedly chastised for not bustin' a move to get a flag since Sept. 11.

I sense, no, I *know* there are other Negroes who see it like me because we talk about it in hushed tones.

So if you see, live near, know, have heard of or sense there's a Negro who—like me—isn't waving or wearing the flag with unabashed pride, then think about something.

Race remains America's great divide.

If America's now supposed to be one big family like the flag-wavers would have us believe, then race and its –isms are the crazy uncle in the attic no one wants to talk about at Thanksgiving.

And you want me wavin' my flag in the waiting room of reparations?

I'll take a number.

Get back to me.

Dead Nigga Blvd. (Cincinnati One Year Later)

❖❖❖❖❖❖

Announcer: On Sunday it will be one year since two white Cincinnati police officers chased an African-American teenager through a troubled neighborhood called Over-the-Rhine.

Police dispatch traffic: *Subject is last seen northbound on Vine towards The Warehouse.*

Male black, six foot, red bandana, Indy 500 jacket on.

Possibly in the store on Vine Street.

Timothy Thomas with 14 open warrants.

Subject is hopping the fence going towards Republic.

Announcer: It ended when an officer shot and killed Timothy Thomas.

In the days that followed, the neighborhood saw violent riots to protest the killing and the rioting spread to other parts of Cincinnati.

Timothy Thomas became a symbol of poor police/community relations, the flight of wealthy residents to the suburbs and the gentrification of parts of the inner city.

Over the past year nearly every person in Cincinnati has heard about Timothy Thomas and discussed what his killing represented, including commentator Kathy Y. Wilson.

She's concerned about what his death meant for the block of Republic Street where he was killed.

Nineteen-year-old Timothy Thomas fled through parts of Over-the-Rhine last April—hopping fences, dipping down narrow alleys and running through moving traffic.

He ran into a U-shaped alcove on a short block of Republic Street.

A neighborhood woman yelled to him a warning.

"That's a *dead* end!"

How prophetic and pathetic an omen that turned out to be.

No truer words have been spoken since the ensuing riots, curfews, lawsuits and boycotts.

It's a dead end.

Nothing more succinct has been uttered, written or hollered during a year when black, white, rich and poor Cincinnatians alike have uttered, written and hollered ourselves into fits.

It's a dead end.

Cincinnati is a city comprised of opposites, of absolutes.

Our spectrum has ends so high and so low sometimes the two don't know the other exists.

That is, until one year ago when a raggedy, drug- and sex-infested block on Republic Street made us shake hands.

Today, in the alcove where Thomas died, the shrine to him is tattooed with anger, sadness and aggravation.

It says things like *13th cops killed my friend.*

Next to that is God was here that night with him.

13th RIP Tim my nigga much love.

Down the street just a bit there's a sign affixed to a pole stating Republic was "formerly named Brenen Street. Renamed April 4, 1918, because of anti-German hysteria during World War I."

Ours is not the first time Republic hosted madness.

The street is like an atrophied limb.

And I'm not saying amputate it.

The part of Over-the-Rhine where poor people still live and die continues to be cut off from the rest of us. We were socially and culturally alienated before the Thomas shooting and today that's even worse.

For many whites that part of town is a cause.

For the blacks who don't live there it's the deadbeat relative.

But the people who live on and around Republic Street don't need our pity, either.

They deserve our *consideration*.

Because where they live was once so beautiful and so thriving that German immigrants named it after the place that most reminded them of home: Over-the-Rhine.

Cincinnati likes its poor people poor, insane, hustling, gaudy, stagnant and in one place.

We asked for it and got it on Republic Street.

Seeking refuge on Republic Street is like the lady said: It's a *dead end*.

Thomas couldn't find refuge there.

Places like Republic Street and the people living there don't need saving from themselves but they cannot be ignored, either.

If we do we'll run into the same dead end.

A Funky
Potpourri

Goin' Up Yonder, Dreams and "Kunta's Compensation"

Let Us Now Praise a (Not So) Famous Man

$\diamond\diamond\diamond\diamond\diamond\diamond$

You probably didn't know Dan Jenkins.

I didn't either, really.

But I have to talk about him.

I'm given 800 to 850 words in this space, and I've spent every day since last Thursday thinking of how to fill it. Then, on Friday, a friend at the Main Public Library showed me a clipping of an obituary, and I knew what I had to do.

The name in the headline was only vaguely familiar, but one look at the photo—the eyes disappearing into the subdued smile, the receding hairline and snow-white goatee—and I knew it was *that* Dan Jenkins.

It was a day less than a full week since I'd met Dan for the first time. Serendipitously, we'd seen one another twice in the same weekend after having never met at all.

On the evening of our first introduction, Dan's wife, Kathy Wade, a jazz singer and arts educator, was a sequined butterfly in Music Hall Ballroom. She worked the room like a squealing, bear-hugging politician.

Everyone was decked out.

It was a mellowed-out, black-tie affair. I felt like a grownup.

We were there to see Wade and jazz legend Shirley Horn perform as part of the main fund-raiser for Wade's baby, Learning Through Art, Inc. Wade calls the project "The 'Hood Is Bigger Than You Think," and that night was the finale, her crown jewel.

All kinds of dreams came true that night. After the show, Wade made it possible for me to meet and sit with Ms. Horn in her dressing room. I met Wade's mother and coincidentally sat at a table with her father, who introduced me to Wade's brother, Sylvester.

I went from having a solely professional relationship with Wade to catching a glimpse of her life away from the stage. Everyone comes from somewhere, the introductions seemed to echo.

And as her adrenaline drained after the head rush of planning, implementing and participating in such an event, Wade was running on sheer will afterwards. She grabbed garment bags, gathered congratulatory bouquets of flowers and hugged and thanked everyone in sight.

And there stood Jenkins, quietly standing by his wife's side smiling and basking. She introduced us, and he knowingly raised an eyebrow at the mention of my name. It was cool to finally meet the man who stood and worked beside Kathy Wade, a woman known for her tenacity and professionalism.

What must that guy be like, I thought as I finally left the ballroom, floating after a night of nightclub jazz.

The very next day at the Black Family Reunion, I barely recognized Wade and Jenkins in their shorts, jeans, T-shirts and sandals strolling hand-in-hand.

I nudged my friend and said, "Isn't that Kathy Wade and her husband?" We all greeted each other again, less than 24 hours after the gala. Walking on, I wondered if Jenkins ever felt like "Mr. Kathy Wade."

Then, as I read in his obituary how they met and how he aided in breathing reality into Wade's dreams of using music as an educational tool, I knew he was among that population of black men rarely spoken or written about: secure, intelligent, nurturing and, yes, average.

Here was a hard-working black man who valued family and education and the possibilities each afforded the other. He reminds me of my two brothers—no hustling, no BS and no running away from truths or responsibilities.

Yes, they do exist.

The real tragedy, of course, is that Dan Jenkins, 52, died suddenly of a heart attack before he got to lay eyes on his first grandchild, before the mayhem and exhilaration of organizing another fund-raiser, before another cup of coffee with his wife or before returning from vacation in Mexico, where he died.

This all makes me feel particularly fragile yet inspired. It just goes to show how quickly love and life ebb and flow. Everyone stops and pauses, their breath catching in their chests when they hear of such losses.

"Did you hear about Kathy Wade's husband?" people asked in hushed tones.

But what of the days following the burial? Death is synonymous for so many things, most of all change. So now that Jenkins is gone, will we change our lifestyles, our thinking, our perceptions, our work habits, our loving?

Dan Jenkins was one of those brothas we all need to remember. His death says don't slide down that slippery slope populated by generalizations about the sorry state of black manhood or the shadowy presence of "good" black men.

We had one. He left his legacy quietly and with a smile.

Touched by an Angel

❖❖❖❖❖❖

Prelude: Mable Harris, the subject of a springtime *CityBeat* cover story (issue of March 2-8), died suddenly on Sept. 22.

Mable blew my mind.

On Dec. 1, 1955, she was a 10th-grader sitting in the rear colored section of the public bus in Montgomery, Ala., when Rosa Parks was arrested for not relinquishing her seat to a white passenger.

Harris witnessed history and lived to talk about it, albeit much later and with much humility.

Even now as I think of Mable Harris and our brief, rambunctious time together there's a rock in my throat, that thing we get when we need to cry but do not feel like it.

Instead, I laugh.

I feel Mable.

I hear her saying: "Child, please! Honey, I got my flowers while I was livin.' Don't be cryin' over me 'cause I'm dead. It was time for me to go, so I went!"

She was just a *CityBeat* cover story at first, someone to rob of history for selfish reasons.

Then she became my hip aunt, my sassy grandmother and, finally, on par with my own mother. Why did she remind me so much of my mother? Because she could laugh at absurdities and keep an eye on reality, blemishes and all.

But she never held anything against anyone, even those who disappointed her the most.

That was Jesus in her.

I spent time with Mable—not nearly as much as I should have and, in retrospect, not as much as I could have. During our time together I tried in vain to maintain that professional veneer, but Mable wasn't having that.

In our initial phone conversation, she hemmed and hawed but finally caved in, allowing a meeting. She was sizing me up, trying to see if she could trust me.

Mable must have been sold on the idea of telling her story, because she invited me back to K&T's Mini-Mart on Reading Road in the black enclave of Avondale. The mart is a shotgun neighborhood bodega she financed and ran with Gwen, her sister-in-law.

During that initial evening visit we laughed raucously.

Book-ended between were stories of life in Alabama. My favorite vignette was the one about her explosive tenure as a salad girl at a chicken joint there.

When a patron called her a nigger for messing up his order, she dumped a salad in his lap, grabbed her coat and walked out.

When the cops showed up on her doorstep, her uncle smoothed things over with them but later told Mable she did the right thing. "You should have dumped it on his ass," her uncle said.

We laughed at the memory of that small early victory in the segregated South.

She paused her stories to chat and laugh with customers, some of whom she scolded for trying to buy Black 'n Mild cigars without proper I.D.

Had I known Mable my entire lifetime?

Ultimately that type of premature familiarity conspired against our relationship.

In the end I took her for granted. I assumed Mable wasn't going anywhere.

I figured I could always drop in and see her at the Hamilton County Administration Building, where she worked, or at K&T's any night of the week.

I thought I could always catch up but never did.

Life happened.

Then one day my mother, twinned by Mable's disposition and resilience, calls to say Mable is gone, that she just "dropped dead."

I lost my breath but ignored it, thinking that mindless activities would quench my guilt and comfort my grief.

Neither happened.

Mable is dead.

So every single person who ever knew her, however briefly or profoundly, must reconcile the fact that we didn't know her long or well enough. Death does this to us and that's life. But at least we were touched.

Postlude: A co-worker asked me about the topic of this week's column. "What's the fight?" he said. "There is no fight," I said. "No fight this week."

Just then I thought of Mable, of her salad days of bearing witness to and fightng against racism and sexism.

The fight had already been fought.

And won.

Half Past His Autumn

Fred Suggs Jr. was like Gordon Parks—innovative, tenacious, opportunistic, rakish, gracious and legendary.

Parks the filmmaker/photographer/writer/poet made *Shaft* and *The Learning Tree*, was a *Life* photographer and remains a Renaissance man. He smashed barriers not because he was a poster boy for revolutions or causes—he knocked them down because talents and passion left him little choice.

Suggs was the same. The two even resembled, Suggs with similar salt-and-pepper hair and easy elegance.

The photographer/publisher/activist/humanitarian died May 10 at the age of 82.

Death is allowed its suddenness.

But we weren't ready for Suggs' departure.

And his lengthy life does not salve the shock.

We weren't ready because Suggs hadn't prepared us. He was everywhere all the time, so we took for granted we'd see him everywhere all the time. And we did, until the final moment.

I'd just been on a media panel with him at the Grassroots Leadership Academy, a community-building agency that trains participants for media preparedness.

With typical aplomb and wisdom, Suggs railed about how ill-prepared our children are. He said we'd failed them—parents, civic leaders, teachers and society.

Denise Johnson, longtime freelance journalist and media critic, led the session.

It's to our benefit that Suggs was always invited to such discussions.

Suggs published Johnson in *NIP* magazine in 1983. It was her first pro writing gig.

"You just kind of know Fred from around town 'cause he's always just there," Johnson says. "He's either around in his jogging suit or with his camera. Fred's always been there when the newspapers were shaky."

Suggs did a lot, and we always assumed he'd continue.

He was born in Florence, Ala., and attended the University of Cincinnati for two years, studying business law, journalism and photography. Jim Crow sidetracked him, and he landed at Union Terminal working the train station as a busboy, soda jerk and trainer.

In 1952, he opened his first photography studio in the predominantly black West End neighborhood.

Like Parks, Suggs started making his own way. He would've died stepping and fetching had he not.

Suggs in 1955 started *NIP* (News In Pictures, then called News, Information and Pictures) as a medium for his own photographic work. He also showed the world that blacks dreamed, lived and excelled beyond domestic labor, rear entrances and separate fountains.

He headed *NIP* until 1990. Suggs sold it to Howard and Ruby Bond, who sold it in 1995 to the Sesh Communications partnership.

Jan-Michele Lemon Kearney, editor of the black weekly newspaper *The Cincinnati Herald*, also is a Sesh partner. Like many of us, she met Suggs at some forgettable function.

But Suggs was in the mix.

"I sat next to him at a function and he talked about being a photographer and not being able to get his work published, so he started *NIP* magazine," Kearney says. "I thought it was a great story. Here's this obstacle, so why not make your own opportunity? He was the ultimate mentor to everybody."

Meanwhile, Suggs emerged a human rights activist. During his early days here he helped integrate downtown Cincinnati lunch counters, theaters and stores.

Ernie Waits Sr. was already entrenched in civil rights struggles when Suggs arrived. He remembers Suggs, his camera and his interest in overhaulng public education. Suggs last year ran unsuccessfully for a seat on the Cincinnati Board of Education.

"His most fervent conviction was to start at pre-kindergarten through third grade and that, if children were taught well at that level, they'd get a good start," Waits says. "His gift was very great and his participation in the overall preservation of human rights has been steadfast. His interest was in humanity, in mankind itself."

Johnson says the fundamental preservation of a just society was Suggs' legacy. And he pursued by working to improve public education.

"I think 'involvement' would be the right word to describe Fred," she says. "Even at the end he was talking to me about restructuring some things for the school board, and this was after the man was defeated for school board. Every other word out of his mouth was about the kids."

Maybe it's what kept him interested, vital, energetic and around.

Then, he always had ideas.

He approached me recently about a story for *Tri-State Talk* magazine, another venture he started in 1996 that appeared a local version of *Jet*.

I told him I was interested but that I'd have to make time. Then I thought about a story about him for *CityBeat*.

Then it was too late.

But not really, because here we are remembering a legacy built on refusal.

And in the world I orbit, countless black professionals got started in Suggs' pages, by his referral or tutelage.

"I do feel honored to carry on his legacy," Kearney says. "He started something, and the key thing is anything is possible. It might sound corny but it's true. Nothing got in his way. He never thought he couldn't."

Goodbye, Jazzy, See You Next Lifetime

His people tell me his real name was George.

I knew him as Jazzy.

No one ever said how he got to be called Jazzy.

We all just called him that.

When my grandfather died, I shopped around for an old, wise curmudgeonly black man to stand in the gap.

Jazzy was there all along.

I met him when I was a sixth grader at Forest View Elementary School, where I was trying hard not to look like I was trying hard to fit in.

My family was splintering again.

Mina, my best friend since, held the ambitious middle-class black girl's prized trifecta.

She was pretty, popular and smart.

Plus, she had gear.

She clocked several pairs of Dr. Scholl flip flops with those unforgiving wooden soles; then there were all those tight Gloria Vanderbilt, Vidal Sassoon and Calvin Klein jeans that cut into the bends of the knees.

We listened to Prince, Rick James and Natalie Cole albums on her record player in her flowery bedroom, where I reclined beneath her canopied Barbie's first apartment bed and watched her try on new clothes.

Her family was intact.

I latched on to her and them — all of them.

One thick-aired summer Mina, her parents, her three brothers and I loaded into their Buick LeSabre ("Big Red") and rode to Mt. Sterling, Ky., to Mina's grandparents' house.

We were off to see Jazzy and Granny.

My house down the street exploded with testosterone.

My two brothers, two stepbrothers and one half brother were the all-black male cast of *Survivor*.

I needed a break.

Jazzy and Granny lived in a country house on a corner in a tiny community of nosy neighbors, Court Day, porch swings and cases of Ale 81 soda.

They raised Sidney, Mina's mother, and Joyce, Mina's aunt, in that little house. I didn't know this growing up, but Jazzy was Sidney's and Joyce's stepfather.

This surprised me. I knew stepparents usually spelled melodrama.

I didn't know having one could be a non-experience.

That's Jazzy and Granny, though—the Un-Cola of regular folks.

Their house is utilitarian, country-fried functional.

It is today cluttered but calm, small yet accommodating,; it's a house of sudden breezes and screen doors that squeak, yawn and wham shut.

Granny still lives there, and nothing much has changed except that Sidney redecorated her mother's front room with the heirlooms of family antiques.

I was nervous my first time there.

I was raised to revere, even fear, my elders; to stay just within earshot in case an errand was ordered and to lift heavy bags and chauffeur when I reached driving age.

I annexed Mina and her people. They were my refuge.

Meeting Granny and Jazzy was like being introduced to my grandparents all over again.

It was love at first sight.

They listened when I talked and remembered what I said, especially the details of my personal life. That weekend they fed me, loved up on me and laughed at my budding raucous humor.

It was the beginning of a three-way affair of mutual admiration.

Granny's middle name should be "Whatchulookinfer?" and Jazzy's could've been "Gitonawayfromme."

He was irascible, surly, outspoken, good-hearted, kind and hilarious.

Ignoring the seasons, he usually wore the uniform of a plaid shirt buttoned to the neck and a tweedy jacket. He had a high, "smart" forehead that chased away wild gray hair that stood up in tiny corkscrews like spun cotton.

His chin nearly always held gray pinprick stubble, and he had droopy eyes. When his mouth was pursed in a pinched grin, he was usually talking trash about somebody.

When I was a kid, he never treated me like the domestic interloper I was.

He warmed to me and expected to see me at Thanksgiving, Christmas, weddings, births and family reunions. When I missed one, he'd chastise me next time around, hug me and ask if I had a car because either I didn't or I was driving a hooptie.

We talked like fishing buddies. He was grandfatherly to me.

I loved fixing his plates so he could sit down. When they were headed back to Mt. Sterling, I never worried he was too old or his reflexes too slow to make the drive.

I knew he was old and tired. But I never considered him fragile or vulnerable in any way.

Mina is now three times a mother. She's still my best friend. After 27 years we're as close, serious and silly as sisters.

We trade phone messages before we catch one another on the fly.

When we spoke one recent morning, she was loading up her family on her way to Mt. Sterling to bury Jazzy. He had prostate cancer.

I didn't even know he was sick, a detail lost in the sofa cushions of being a grownup.

"You're my only friend who knew him," she said.

I could not make the trip to Kentucky because the hooptie at my disposal couldn't make the trip.

Jazzy forgives me.

But he's expecting me next time.

Pitiful

"I'm pitiful/Feeling sorry for me."

— ARETHA FRANKLIN

The best way to get a good wad of toilet paper going is to hold the roll aloft, right index finger through the spindel, and then yank the paper down with your left hand.

I learned a lot the last few days.

After losing consciousness twice the afternoon of New Year's Eve, I spent that most sacred of all party nights in a room on Six South in Christ Hospital.

Yep. I passed out. And not from the revelry of the pending new year. High blood sugar, low blood sugar, too much/not enough/no insulin. Stupidity.

Laziness. neglect.

Slothfulness.

A death wish. Call it what you will—my friends all have.

The last thing I remember is standing in the furniture section of the Goodwill store in downtown Oakley, an eastern, WASPy Cincinnati neighborhood.

I was holding a Nutrageous candy bar in one hand and a can of Hawaiian Punch in the other. I hadn't yet eaten or shot my first of two daily doses of insulin.

I treated with mountains of sugar what I thought was low blood sugar. Oops.

Must have been after 3 p.m.

It slammed across me suddenly, like a car wreck during a casual, un-seatbelted conversation.

I was thrown.

Inanimate objects moved, took flight actually.

Muddied colors bum rushed me.

Voices hummed. And the floor swallowed me whole.

Passing out is the best of all the body's strange sensations.

Everything is again possible at the outset of consciousness.

Coming to is like starting life over.

My mom says passing out is God's deliverance from unbearable pain. She's right.

Right there between the oatmeal-colored chair and a battered dresser, Nicole slapped and yelled me into consciousness. Her green eyes, bloodshot and teary, came first into focus. "OhmyGodKathypleasewakeupplease!"

Why's she yelling at me? What'd I do?

I swallowed the urge to laugh. I didn't know what was happening. But I assumed it was hilarious.

Faces loomed above my rolling head like a scene from *Rosemary's Baby*. I looked through a fish-eye lens.

There were these other people — kind, attentive, nosy, concerned strangers offering beverages, advice and phone calls. Two black ladies, in particular. One lady retrieved a green ceramic pot from the housewares section for me to vomit into.

It was already too late.

I'd projectile vomitted the Nutrageous/Hawaiian Punch stew all over the carpeting and the lower side of the dresser.

The can's contents made it to the other side of the store, in women's casual wear.

The second lady hung out in the aisle where the errant can of Hawaiian Punch ended up. Standing with her basket, she looked down on me and recommended food I should eat as soon as I felt up to it.

She wouldn't leave. She was like a fairy Aunt Esther.

I wanted to joke but there was nothing funny about my soon-to-be-36-year-old-ass laid out on the floor in the furniture section of the Oakley Goodwill on New Year's Eve. Neither was it funny that this debacle of poor personal care and diabetes — the bane of my fragile existence — crashed headlong into one another.

Damn.

It was time to stop screwing around with my health. I feared for my life for the first time since I'd been diagnosed with diabetes. (When was that exactly, anyway?)

So I sat there, slump shouldered and soles together, drinking water, looking around and muttering apologies.

I asked finally for paramedics, vomited, refused transport, staggered to Nicole's car and asked to come here to Christ Hospital, where I'm writing this.

Another black out and more than five hours later, I'm in a hospital bed with a portable heart monitor taped to several points on my chest, 15 needle pricks across my body and a snoring roommate.

(Ever heard water being sucked down a drain?)

I scoot out to the nurse's station pulling my portable monitor. I'm nearly too weak to stand, but too agitated to sleep beside the snorer.

"I hate to be a bother," I say to the interrupted night nurse. I'm good at inconveniencing people while appearing otherwise.

"Could I have a different room? I'm exhausted and my roommate's snoring terribly."

Two hours later and I'm in a different room, alone, watching a gangster movie marathon on the USA Network.

(It's an escapist's wet dream: All three *Godfather* flicks, *Carlito's Way, A Bronx Tale* and *The Suicide Kings*.)

I wondered what everyone else was doing and how I'd explain this to those who hadn't already heard.

True, dealing with a disease is personal business.

I'm obviously not equipped to do this on my own.

Hell, it took me two years to reconcile the fact that diabetes is a *disease*.

I shakily started my relationship with diabetes.

The day my grandmother died I was learning to shoot myself in the stomach in a rear exam room in Fort Hamilton-Hughes Hospital in Hamilton while a patient nurse talked me through it.

I didn't get a chance to process it all through.

Shit!

Food was still my nemesis and now I knew why it'd been mocking me; now I knew why my body was failing. I had the power early on to reverse my body's revolt. But I didn't know what I was mourning during my grandmother's funeral

I was too tired and overwhelmed to sort it out.

With only a few shining exceptions, my diabetic track record ever since is littered with missed doses, finger sticks, vomiting, diarrhea, dehydration, night sweats, weight loss, lying, cheating, passing out, excessive peeing, mood swings, depression, denial, hopefulness, wretched days and mediocre days.

But this is it.

I want all the feeling returned to my toes.

I want my crisp, defined vision back.

For the people who love me, I want for them the restoration of my good nature and even temperament. I want a liver, eyeballs and legs that'll last me to my grave.

I want good days and the good health that define them.

I'ma die trying.

The Closer I Get to You

◇◇◇◇◇◇

I never knew Chuck Wilson as a free man.

I never saw him walk down the street, run from the rain, bundle against the cold, play on the floor with his children or stroke his wife's arm.

When I was 4, he violently forfeited his rights to those freedoms.

In 1968, he returned to the store he and his brother, Eddie, were robbing. It was brotherly love gone haywire.

They'd gotten away, but Eddie, greedy for what he assumed the man withheld, went back for more. The man seethed at the brash stupidity of two young black men violating his life's work. He took aim at Eddie and shot him in the head.

Chuck went back for his brother, for retribution and for payback.

Chuck emptied his weapon into the white shopkeeper, ending three lives.

Back then in Hamilton, the fiasco was the stuff of black folklore, straight out of a Zora Neale Hurston or a Gayl Jones novel.

Chuck fled to Canada and then California where, assuming his young son's identity, he prostituted women for cash. Califonia cops even nabbed him on some charge, but kicked him 'cause they didn't know his true identity.

He eventually surrendered.

He went back for Eddie.

Amazingly, during his sentences at Lucasville and the London Correctional Institute, all of his brothers and even his son have done time along side him. Add it all up, and the tragedy enveloping this family seems surreal, almost nightmarish.

But I watched it intently as a young girl. For a kid on the other side looking in, there was a sexy intrigue to their nightmare. Growing up and into a writer I wondered if I'd ever be mature enough to write down their bones.

I conceived a feature-length *CityBeat* cover story, stirring girlhood memories and rescucitating long-neglected relationships with Chuck's family.

Observing Chuck back in the day was like watching John Shaft without the popcorn.

Chuck was the crumbling cornerstone of a disintegrating family who shared my last name but who couldn't have been further from what I'd been taught was the definition of family.

That didn't make my Wilsons any better than their Wilsons.

It just made us different. It made us the other Wilsons.

And that for me—sheltered, spoiled, fragile and precocious—was a good thing.

Because Chuck's sisters, Lena and Malinda, and their six brothers have always been part of my life. They knew about me before I knew about myself.

They are signposts in my childhood. Rudolph would sing The Stylistics' "Betcha by Golly, Wow" in his tender tenor falsetto whenever my mother would give him a ride somewhere in our Ford Fairlaine stationwagon. I'd crack up laughing while Gilbert, Eddie and Romeo imitated their mean, blacker-than-a-thousand-midnights father, J.E. Then there was Lena's irreverent and insane flights of imagination and her sandpaper, Jimmy Durante-like laughter would trip me out.

Collectively, they taught me how to accept different people. They reassured my wild imagination, one that others probably will never understand.

So really the subsequent story has been all our lifetimes in the making. There were times I wanted to write it, but doubted its relevance. Further, until now I never wrote for a publication that allowed such journalism.

A family's survival is always relevant. But you just don't mine someone else's experiences without paying something in return.

This story was an emotional boomerang for me and the Wilson women I spoke with.

When I saw Chuck's mug shot morph onto my computer screen, I felt dread.

I neared the end of gathering information for the story and I was verifying the Wilson brothers' prison records.

I hate the wallop of responsibility that love packs.

I squinted at his now-bloated face and receding hairline.

I hunted the blurred mug shot for the man of my early 1970s girlhood, the shutchomouf motherfucker who was a newly converted Black Muslim named El Rashid with a perfectly picked-out Afro.

But it was all gone. His eyes didn't glisten like they used to.

He looked resigned.

What's he supposed to look like?

Chuck was the last of the Wilson men still locked up. He got out this year after outlasting the demise of Ohio's death row statutes and cheating the commuted life sentence.

He evolved from Black Muslim to born-again Christian. He remarried his once-estranged wife. When he was locked up he saved souls who were as broken as he once was.

I imagine he's suffocated by free society and all the blips, beaps and conveniences of technology advanced during his lock down.

We didn't speak while I wrote the feature story and I haven't seen him since he's been out. But I reconnected with a family who helped me remember just how close we once were.

And who reminded me of how far apart we remain

Spiritual Walkers

✧✧✧✧✧✧

"Haven't you ever encountered the spritual walkers?"

—STEVIE WONDER, "SPIRITUAL WALKERS"

Looking quickly through the bedroom blinds, I thought it was someone else.

The bell had such a friendly ring to it.

But by the time I got into the hallway, it was too late.

They'd already seen me, so I had to answer the door.

Something like dread engulfed me.

"Jehovah's Witnesses," I whispered to myself. "Aaah, maaan."

I don't know what made me think this particular Saturday should be different from any other. After taking a more careful peak through the blinds, I'd previously either ignored the J Dubs or narrowly missed them by being out of the house on weekend errands.

Picking eye boogers from my eyes, I wiped a hand over my oily face and smoothed my T-shirt, pulling it down past the fly of my boxer shorts.

My breath was a weapon of mass destruction.

"Good morning," the dark-skinned woman said.

"Hello."

Interrupted dreams fell from my mouth.

She said something about God's kingdom and spreading the good news. She wanted to leave a *Watchtower* magazine. She stumbled through her memorized script. She perked up when I said I'm familiar with *Watchtower*.

Or maybe she was relieved I wasn't slamming the door in her face.

"Oh! You know it?"

"Yes, ma'am."

The older black woman interjected: "She's new. What we'd like to do is leave you a pamphlet and ask if we might leave them every two weeks. And maybe later you'd like to have a personal Bible study."

I took a *Watchtower* and never took the Bible study bait, instead leaving it open but remembering to dodge the J Dubs sure to come on future Saturdays.

I can be a passive/agressive Houdini when I wanna.

The exchange was pleasant, painless and quick. I never moved my body from the front door and left them on the porch lest they think I'd be open to that much God-talk before noon on a holiday weekend.

We've been socialized to demonize Jehovah's Witnesses.

And why?

You can't honestly say they're anything like the red-faced zealots — using God, the Bible and scripture as foundation and/or reasoning — who bomb and protest abortion clinics and other destinations of women's reproductive rights.

They don't murder with dissenting viewpoints and practices.

The J Dubs are nearly passive.

They're miles from the insanely conservative right who preach God's way but who really mean their way and to hell — literally — with anyone who doesn't quack quite like them.

But that's really so many apples and oranges.

What I'm saying is we compartmentalize religion just like we do every other nook of our lives. So the J Dubs have somehow warranted farm team/sweathog status.

We mainly hate 'em 'cause they come to us and knock on our doors.

How dare they interrupt our self-medication/escapism/idiot box daydreaming/child neglect/domestic violence/bliss?

It's the home version of *Guess Who's Coming to Sinner*?

Damn them!

But give them their props, too.

In the work that is clearly God's and in a city dotted on every other corner with churches, the J Dubs walking the streets of my neighborhood are consistent, visible and tenacious foot soldiers.

I've never encountered people from those neighborhood churches where I live now. And when I lived in Walnut Hills — Land of the Lord — the only time I saw parishioners from surrounding churches was when they were littering my doors with car wash leaflets or blocking my driveway on Sunday mornings.

We fear what we don't understand.

I literally grew up in black Baptist churches.

I'm no biblical scholar, but I've got a working knowledge of scripture and a shoddy prayer life.

I see through it and to whatever the agenda of whatever religious leaning.

I'm not easily swayed or sidetracked.

Divergent religious practices and beliefs don't bother me.

Hell, maybe I'm spiritually vulnerable—and we all know that many religions count and feed on vulnerability to thicken their plots and pots.

The J Dubs probably will be back.

Now that I've engaged them, they'll work the room.

Oh well.

It's probably karma boomeranging around to bite me in the ass for all the jokes in my repertoire with the Jehovah's Witnesses starring as punchlines.

Sometimes I tell friends I ignored them at the door because I thought they were J Dubs, or next time they come I'll act like they're J Dubs and turn off the lights and hide until they leave.

I know, I know.

This isn't a free advertisement, and it lacks damnation.

Relax yourself.

I'm not converting, just elevating.

Because, really, what *would* Jesus do?

He'd knock on doors and get them slammed squarely in His face.

And Jesus would keep walking.

Empires (Greasy Haiku)

❖❖❖❖❖❖

Bring me men/bring me men/men with empires in their purpose.

— "EMPIRES," LAMYA

1.

Twenty-five-day war
Palm Sunday Jesus walked palms
Baghdad goes to town

2.

Nauseated now
unemployed undertaker
shores oil shores oil shores

3.

It's wall-to-wall oil
while in Asia SARS scares US
brown people get used

4.

Seven are alive
sun beats down sandstorms of change
Saddam's DNA

5.

Beat around the Bush
he who convinces US to
send him send her, them

6.

Coalitions forced
looters snatching newfound rights
abandoned palace

7.

Troops first took a shit
to prove that global shitting
isn't all missiles

8.

While running down streets
gargantuan torso goes
a boy smacks its head

9.

In Hussein's Tikrit
U.S. soldiers sun themselves
in khaki relief

10.

Guided by voices
is Syria next in line?
Five more years, he said.

11.

Wearing White House briefs
makes Rumsfeld, Powell and Rice
Oreo axes

12.

Televised liars
tell truths we don't want to face:
"We'll run that city."

13.

Arms countered by will
bomb suicidally bomb
coalitions dumbfound

14.

In America
box-office receipts are up
sunshine returns home

15.

Rita Dove wrote that
she's "crueler than government"
poems often are

Versus

Follow for now.

You have Kenny G, we have Charlie Parker.
You have Bette Midler, we have Chaka Khan.
You have George Washington, we have the Rev. Jesse Jackson.
You have Dennis Rodman, we have Prince.
You have Prince, we have Dennis Rodman.
You have Chet Baker, we have Miles Davis.
You have Grateful Dead, we have Parliament Funkadelic.
You have Al Sharpton, we have Al Sharpton.
You have Andrew Dice Clay, we have Chris Rock.
You have Seinfeld, we have Rock.
You have Jesus, we have Haile Salassie.
You have Buchanan, we have Farrakhan.
You have constellations, we have consternation.
We have demanstrations, you have affiliations.
We have John Edgar Wideman, you have Ernest Hemingway.
We have Tupac, you have Shakespeare.
You have Alice Walker, we have Zora Neale Hurston.
You have Truman Capote, we have James Baldwin.
You have TV doctors, we have Dr. Ben Carson.
You have Phil Spector, we have P. Diddy.
You have Henry Ford, we have Garrett A. Morgan.
You have Edith Piaf, we have Aretha Franklin.
We have James Brown, you have Elvis Presley.
We have Elvis Presley, you have Elvis.
We have Malcolm X, you have Martin Luther King Jr.
We have MLK Jr., you have MLK Jr.
You have Joseph Papp, we have George C. Wolfe.
You have Anne Sexton, we have me.
You have Alanis Morissette, we have Kina.
You have Max factor, we have Madame CJ Walker.

You have the Beats, we have The Last Poets.
We have Miles, you have Miles.
We have Spike Lee, you have Martin Scorcese.
We have bell hooks, you have Gloria Steinem.
We have Gordon Parks, you have Ansel Adams.
We have Ken Griffey Jr., you have Ken Griffey Jr.
You have O.J. Simpson, we have O.J. Simpson.
You have MTV, we have BET.
You have BET, we have BET.
You have PBS, we have The Heritage Network.
You have *American Idol*, we have *Showtime at the Apollo*.
You have *The Washington Post*, we have *The Amsterdam News*.
You have Mumia Abu-Jamal, we have Mumia Abu-Jamal.
You have networking, we have happy hour.
You have Lenny Bruce, we have Richard Pryor.
You have chain letters, we have gossiping.
You have, "I see dead people," we have, "Him downstairs."
You have *Rolling Stone*, we have *Vibe*.
You have Keith Richards, we have death.
You have *Joe Millionaire*, we have scratch-offs.
You have slavery, we have temp agencies.
You have *Life, Newsweek* and *Forbes*, we have *Ebony, Code* and *Black Enterprise*.
You have zero tolerance, we have three hots and a cot.
You have Jack Kerouac, we have LeRoi Jones/Amiri BAraka.
You have David Sedaris, we have Paul Beatty.
You have Christina Aguillera, we have Janet Jackson.
You have Howard Stern, we have Don King.
You have Oprah Winfrey, we have Oprah Winfrey.
You have JFK, we have JC.
You have Selma, we have Soweto.
You have Soweto, we have Selma.
You have Tiger Woods, we have Tiger Woods.
You have Larry Bird, we have Michael Jordan.
You have Michael Jordan, we have God.
You have God, we have Michael Jordan.
You have Ted Koppel, we have Tavis Smiley.
We have Oscar Micheaux, you gave D.W. Griffith.
We have Rock, you have Rickles.
We have prolotariat chariots, you have carpools.
You have support groups, we have family reunions.

You have support groups, we have beauty parlors and barber shops.
You have therapy, we have church.
You have therapy, we have talk radio.
You have church, we have talk radio.
You have talk radio, we have talk radio.
You have Christmas, we have Kwanzaa.
You have *The Wizard of Oz*, we have *The Wiz*.
You make 40 oz., we drink 40 oz.
You had slavery, we've had reparations.

My Brother, Myself

i have faith
in who you are becoming
in who you are
you are the wolf
having run through a stream
to stand on a mountain peak
dripping wet

— SAUL WILLIAMS

Let me tell you about my brother, Kenny.

He comprises snatches of men I know, anonymously familiar men I see during my daily treks and even the fellas I think I know but don't really.

Kenny's like a pair of patchwork pants, like a mosaic of refracted pieces best considered from a comfortable distance.

It's apropos and ironic that he's a father.

For years I'd sold him short.

I never thought Kenny could be a father. I assumed he lacked the selflessness or was wholly incapable of suspending his ego long enough to raise a child.

See, it was, most of all our lives, about Kenny.

And he came by it honest.

Our father, Clarence, is the (god)father of the self-orbit who authored seven children because he had sex, not because he'd necessarily planned to have that many—if any at all.

Likewise, I just knew Kenny would play out a similalry self-centered life wherein kids would be an afterthought, the answer to intercourse.

All our lives he rarely showed anything to the contrary.

He was always zipping his cocoon shut behind him.

Despite Kenny's strong physical resemblance to the Hills, my mother's people, he is nearer in temperament, conservatism and paternalism to Clarence Wilson, our shady and well-preserved Mighty Oak.

They're both these old-school men who know how to fix things and put furniture together. They cut grass and empty garbage, lift heavy things, dock tight finances.

They are rescuers of the stranded.

I witnessed and missed nuances of Kenny's transformation.

The former juice-guzzling, hoop star, cartoon-watching ladies man is a gentle man who holds open doors, checks on our mother and disciplines his children.

I watched this cat topple fixtures in the downtown Hamilton Elder-Beerman and sock-skate the basement floor in Israel Baptist Church.

But I couldn't picture it.

All the times he called me names, yanked my chain and coveted my attention, it was unfathomable.

After all the expensive gym shoes he ran through, the stamp collections he bored of, the *Sports Illustrated* subscriptions he amassed, the smacked-out 10 speeds he begged for and polyester leisure suits he rocked, there were no signs pointing to the possibilities, to the future.

I couldn't see it beneath the hut of his blow-out combed, beach-ball Afro.

This dude is a study in contradictions cloaked in an amazing (techni)colored dream coating also known as the machinations of contemporary black male survival.

He's all: Coding, switching, sagging, baby mamma drama having, BET beater, *Wall Street Journal*/King James Version Bible and wing-tipped Tim's.

He's a shrewd businessman and a vaudevillian emcee. His Volvo plates declare: IDOPRAY and inside he bumps gospel rap and black talk radio. His six-figure income doesn not salve the sores created from attaining the abundant entitlements his two sons already assume they deserve.

Like every Negro I know Kenny's got a hope chest filled with lynching stories, of being profiled, followed, suspected and blamed.

He is Donald Trump and P. Diddy. He can be a disciple and a linchpin.

He's an under rower and a captain.

He's arrogant, bombastic, perfunctory and sarcastic.

But, then, so are all my mother's children.

His redemption is in the fact that his attributes dwarf his blemishes.

Kenny—my nemesis, my hero, my brother—is affable, intelligent, gracious, talented, energetic, sensible, insightful and tender.

He's a Christian before and while he is black.

He's a man before he is a Christian.

He is a Wilson—son of Clarence and Gladine, husband to Kelli, father of K.J. and Kyler and brother of Randy, Kathy and Devin—above all else.

If you're against him, you'll wish you were with him, and if you are with him, be thankful he's on your team.

That's what I know of him after the pit- and pratfalls of a 38-year relationship.

Here's what's new.

Divine order manifested the first time I saw Kenny wrap his basketball-palming, extraterrestrial fingers around a newborn Kenneth Vance Wilson, Jr., his first son. Suddenly, the past was a backdrop and that moment sum-totaled both our lives.

That was it.

Kenny's fatherhood remains the identity of both our selves —together and apart

We are twins with half selves yet to go.

He gets to live out God's purpose and I get to transfer all my unfulfilled maternal longings onto my nephews.

His children are the measurements of us.

They make us want to be good people. Through them we know we're only as good as our children.

Finally, I am proudest of Kenny's interpretation of black manhood.

His black male self is the antithesis of the sorry Sambo we've been socialized to believe black men to be. He's not ostentatious in the responsibilities of fatherhood and manhood. He takes care of his wife and children because he's supposed to.

He is the priest of his household. He's an overcomer. He's a prince.

Kenny is the man I never expected.

And Father's Day is a day I never expected him to celebrate.

But he sure deserves to.

Princess in the Promised Land

✧✧✧✧✧✧

Welcoming another's baby makes grieving a dead infant unbearable. There goes Kennedy Anne Wilson. Here comes Francine Anne Blase.

Three days after Kennedy, my niece, died at home from complications from a birth defect, Francine's daddy, Darren, left me this message: "Dean had the baby last night at 8:55 p.m. Francine Anne. We're at home, where we'll be for the next 18 years." Funny.

Since then I've misplaced the giddiness I'd felt when I first learned my friends were having a baby, one who would be Kennedy's friend, her playmate, her pigtailed buddy.

I'd kept meaning to call. To stop by. To promise to love and baby-sit. But I didn't.

I'd have to answer for Kennedy. "How's your niece? How do your nephews like her?" Any question.

Sound your death knell in one fell wail when a baby dies. It eases the pinch of repeating your speech.

I made a round of calls to close friends between the early morning, the day of Kennedy's memorial service. Though I took three days off from work, I honored all my public engagements.

I honored Kennedy by going through. She'd fought for 25 days.

I never took to my bed out of grief. I didn't rope off my emotional self. I moved. Grief can't strike a moving target.

Then I just gave out. My heart was broken.

I'd seen Kennedy only through a half-open car window; never even held her.

Then her memorial service set me free.

Wife Kelly at his side, my brother Kenny dispelled rumors and speculation about Kennedy's illness and death. He described her birth defect and the turmoil it wreaked on him. During the throes of self-pity, he smashed his hand through a wall.

"God," he said, "is a stud finder."

Kenny always jokes inappropriately, but this time his humor wasn't a shield. It was an outspread blanket.

He stitched together a timeline of catastrophes felling his family this year culminating in Kennedy's diagnosis, Kelly's premature delivery, the prognosis and the hope Kennedy would live defiantly. She died on Oct. 23, what should have been her actual birth date.

My nephews, K.J. and Kyler, said goodbye to Kennedy at home. They called her Princess.

She taught everyone to stand up. K.J. promised his dad that he and Kyler would be everything Kennedy would've been.

Sadness wants a home. Sometimes I let it rest, but it cannot stay.

My favorite way to trick myself is to cry in the shower. Tears mix with water, and I can't tell the difference.

In the days since Kennedy's service, I've meditated on family. It takes work to untwist decades of domestic damage—hurt feelings, unrequited affection, emotional aloofness, selfishness and abandonment.

Our family is complicated. Multiple marriages have produced stepchildren and half-siblings whose paths rarely cross except for reunion hugs at weddings, funerals and occasional holidays.

I have three half-brothers, a half-sister, two stepbrothers, a stepsister and countless stepnieces, stepnephews and on. Then there's Devin, really my half-sister from my mother's marriage to her second husband. But Devin doesn't get the "half" designation except for genealogical explanations.

All the mixed blood bleeds tangled emotions and bloodstained relationships. When my folks split for good and my father remarried, his new union divided my two brothers and me so decisively that where we spent our holidays sometimes was a testament to parental loyalty.

And we were known by the company we kept. Once a daddy's girl, I leaned toward my mother. Randy, my oldest brother, went where the food was. Kenny, the middle child, learned to look at life from both sides now. He remains closest to our father.

In all this holding a tight grip on my immediate family—two brothers, a sister, a sister-in-law and two nephews—comforts me. The swirl of our blended family was tumultuous for me, and I haven't sustained those relationships as well.

Going back to the blood. I've got work to do. Reconciliation is the greatest task before me, and I have never felt so small and so mighty.

Writing this took three days of hand-wringing and head-holding solitude, and it still isn't close to how I really feel about an infant I didn't know and a family I sometimes don't want to know. But Kennedy's making me be a woman.

Losing her means letting go. It means losing control of emotions I'd depended on to keep me bound. I took being bound up by disappointment and hostility—I took it all for granted.

I didn't know I was allowed or supposed to be free to forgive my father his improprieties, my brothers their male-centered arrogance and all the in-between emotional interloping.

I've forgiven myself for doing what I had to do to get through it. Today I am free.

Kenny, Kelly, K.J. and Kyler gave me the high sign to get through my grief any way I please. I choose to tell the truth and to reconcile those truths, to pick them apart not to obsess myself into anger but to put it finally behind me.

Kennedy's name means "helmeted warrior." Her life and death mean freedom to me.

I'll see her when I get there, and this time I'll hug her.

Hymn to Him

Heroes are at home.

Randy is my aesthetic yardstick, my operative, deputized spy and intellectual paramour.

Peerless in his frustration, anger, rage and truth-telling, he's the O.G. Negro Tour Guide. Hear me?

Do you believe in magic?

When we were kids I did, because he did.

I even climbed onto his bed in the stuffy rear bedroom on South Fourth Street. Reciting a spell from *Bedknobs and Broomsticks*, Randy said we'd fly and I booked passage. Kenny, suffering, middle-child syndrome and a skeptic, talked trash about the likelihood a bed with three kids attached would leave the floor.

To this day I believe his skepticism kept us grounded.

Do you believe in Randy?

As grown-ups I do, because sometimes he doesn't.

In the backyard of our pasts, I was sometimes the only audience member for the one-man puppet shows he staged. Our mother's best sheets billowed from clotheslines. And I'd see everything — Randy changing puppets, jostling his arms and straining his throat to different voices faked to fool me/us.

He hated Gino, our German Shepherd, who customarily broke his chain to follow Randy's marching feet and drum beats in the junior high school's band.

In his down time, Randy came into his strangely beautiful self by rummaging clothes from family members. He'd rip, resew, alter and reattach until he had costumes that earned him askance glances, showers of "how could you" ridicule and lockerroom beat downs.

He roller-skated his demons down until sweat left. He danced solo/so low at teen parties in the Booker T. Washington Community Center. The Isleys, The Ohio Players, Aretha Franklin, Sly & the Family Stone and James Brown good-footed dark child anthems in the gym.

The basketball court doubled as a dance floor, and he'd never be invited to join black teenaged reindeer games on that floor once the lights came up and people connected the moves to the man-child.

Much to our father's dismay and growing aloofness, Randy wore down Diana Ross and Judy Garland records back when album covers told stories. Later, he graduated Diva School to Patti, Chaka and Phyllis. And the Three Negress Graces soundtracked this black alien's future love paradise, which today remains unfulfilled.

Put all this in a blender and pour yourself a Randy Shake that tastes of the brilliant, bitter alienation of James Baldwin with a hint of Black Panther Pride.

What happened next makes and breaks black men.

And Randy's been made.

Our citywide talks of anti-gay hate crimes, boycotts and ever-morphing definitions of black is/black ain't and "the black community" remind me that Randy went there and did that. He's still ostracized from the cliques of gay black men who fear and envy him. Aghast that he dare speak his mind, they clutch the pearls and recoil at his identity and how far it is from their own.

They appear equally frightened by his dissention and jealous of the artistic talents that sustain him despite their lack of support. He's bored and tickled by the minstrel showing of black talk radio, an arena he conquered and enlightened at its dawning.

He's too sexy for this city.

Randy's physique is malleable, and its armor is a response to violence perpetrated against him during childhood and as an adult.

He's been bashed, banged and threatened. He is loathsome of gay black men who can't and won't keep pace, and he's wary of gay white men whose tastes run to black men.

Yeah, he's got issues.

Many of which curl up in his own dichotomous lap.

His male-to-male relationships in our family ain't been no crystal stair. Kenny, 40, and Randy, 43, are just now doing a drive-by on brotherly love.

There's silence between Randy and our father.

Not to dismiss anyone else's culpability, but it's also because Randy is as complicated as he is sometimes absolute, layered as he is in his Randyness.

He's Randy-ful.

He keeps his sights fixed on Randy, even as he moves his gaze from the rear view where he's just passed Randy.

He's entering Randy, got his hand on his Randy.

I invoke this prayer for him. It centers on reconciliatory expansion.

His birthday isn't 'til July 31, so it's not a hokey black Hallmark. He may never be a daddy, so Father's Day is out.

All rise.

It's time to sing his hymn.

Turn to page Randy in your Randy Manual.

And it goes like this: A hero ain't nothin' but a sandwich, but a brother such as mine is a refrain whispered by God.

Amen.

Going Dutch

*"As a teen-ager I dreamed to see the world.
But how could I do this; me, a poor black girl?"*

— "TRY" BY JILL SCOTT

I'd always wanted to go to Amsterdam, mostly because it seemed tolerant and exotic. I didn't know how or when I'd get there, but I knew it would come to pass.

I repeatedly fought the urge not to go. I had to silence the voices of my childhood that told me I didn't belong anywhere but where I was. Little black girls from Ohio were not supposed to go to Europe, much less Amsterdam.

I put Amsterdam on the back burner as my 36th birthday approached, but still I dreamed of going there.

Work to do

I was born and grew up for a time in Hamilton, Ohio, where I became a young writer, a little girl too sensitive for my own good, too attached to my father, then my mother.

On the corner of Pershing Avenue and Fourth Street is a mailbox where I used to drop letters addressed to God.

I had a lot of questions. Mostly I wanted to know why I couldn't shake the notion of always, always, always watching people and internalizing the nuances of my surroundings.

Why was I the one always soaking up everybody's BS when everybody else seemed to be able to shake off life's drama?

I had no choice but to write for my life. I knew this early on.

Fast-forward through my parents' divorce, an uprooted childhood spent bouncing around, an abrupt change of custody from mother to father, a life as a lazy student and ultimately as a wandering college drop-out — then there I am, scared to death as I sat behind an orange metal World War II-issue desk in the newsroom of the *Journal-News*.

My hometown newspaper never left an indelible mark on me as a kid who read everything I could get my hands on. The paper was something for white people. The only blacks in it were always dead, dying or on their way to jail.

I spent the first few months convincing myself that I had a job to do there.

I did.

Something in the earth shifted

Anne Frank hid from the Nazis in the attic of a building behind her father's job on what is now a main avenue in Amsterdam.

She was a writer and a sensitive girl. She was always, as my mother would say, "in grown folks' business." Anne is known the world over for her diary and as the young girl who personalized the atrocities and abruptness of the Holocaust.

Hannah Gosslar, one of the last people to ever see Anne alive, is an old Jewish woman who lives now with her family in Israel. She, her daughter and granddaughter travel around speaking candidly about tolerance. I dragged my sorry butt out of bed early one morning before dawn and made the 45-minute drive to hear her speak.

All I knew was this Jewish woman was going to talk to students about being Jewish. It didn't interest me so much personally as it did professionally. Journalists, you see — especially those who toil away at small dailies — are measured not by the breadth of their talent, but by the size of their output. I needed bylines.

Hannah Gosslar could've been my own grandmother. She was beautiful in a handsome way.

The hour was too early and I was not prepared for her story, for the history in the lines of her face and her thick accent. I sat there paralyzed by the reality that this woman had gone through hell and back. There she sat, calmly talking about seeing neighbors and friends disappear, about losing her family, about finding a place in the world to settle.

She told of being Anne Frank's friend. She told us how, risking her own life, she would have clandestine meetings with Anne at a barbed wire fence constantly awash in the sinister light of a sweeping Nazi searchlight.

She tossed rations over the barbed wire in a ratty blanket to Anne, who was starving herself to death trying to keep her sister alive.

Hannah Gosslar was a teenager in a Nazi prison camp who saved the life of another teenaged girl in a Nazi prison camp. Hannah was the one who told Anne her mother was dead — and so, too, was her father.

Anne's will, frayed and ragged, gave way and she died.

History proved the prison camp rumor mill had been wrong. Anne's father, Otto Frank, was still very much alive. But Anne didn't know this, and she died thinking she was alone in the world.

Hannah and Anne were friends from their last days of freedom when they could still walk the streets in Amsterdam, go to school and attend each other's birthday parties.

That morning in the Hamilton High library, my life opened up. I flowered a little bit, and my flowering made the drudgery of churning out stories about school levies more bearable.

It was a moment I felt something shifting in the earth and in myself.

I filed it away and wrote a moving, front-page story of this woman's experiences not only as Anne Frank's friend, but also as a survivor.

Grilled cheese and grifters

Years later I opened the mailbox and found a letter from the *Journal-News*. I was asked to settle my retirement account, because the newspaper had been sold. I signed the form, mailed it and soon got a check for several thousand dollars.

Amsterdam became a possibility, an obsession even.

Who would I go with?

Last July, I lit Nicole's cigarette in the Greenwich Tavern and we've either talked on the phone or seen each other everyday since. She is impetuous, adventurous, smart and energetic.

She cruised the Internet, reserved the tickets and I purchased them. We paid extra to have our passports extradited.

Timothy Thomas hadn't been dead long. We were all still edgy with anger and frustration. The citywide curfew was in effect. It seemed a good time to leave.

We spent almost 10 days walking the streets of the Red Light District, trying not to look like hicks with our lives strapped on our backs in borrowed backpacks.

We navigated public transportation, dodged crazed bicyclists and were awestruck by the painful strokes of Van Gogh's brush.

We ate our share of grilled cheese sandwiches, watched late-night porn and changed hostels for what seemed a million times.

We met newly graduated American med students, an Irish bar maid, a black British bus driver and a local psychiatrist and her doctor girlfriend. We toured the canals, got invitations to live with strangers, and received detailed advice from a grifter on how to use an international calling card at a public telephone.

The first time I walked through the heavy doors of Centraal Station and set foot in the main square, I stopped cold. Looking over my shoulder, I saw that ominous steel sign: Centraal Station. I felt history at my back.

Inside, the platforms were dirty and sat high above the tangle of tracks, and it felt like the Old World.

True to the memories

Back home I had serious jet lag of the bedridden variety for nearly one month. I thought Europe in general and Amsterdam specifically would've changed me.

But it didn't wash over me. I wasn't badder. I didn't feel freer. I didn't look like the world traveler I thought I'd become.

Then one Sunday night *The Anne Frank Story* came on television.

I was mesmerized. I studied each scene looking for familiar landscapes and landmarks. I didn't even know if the movie was filmed in Amsterdam, but I knew I'd been there.

Then the scenes of the relationship between Hannah and Anne, true to my memories of Hannah's recounting, came across my television screen.

I wept, because I'd met and known Hannah Gosslar; I'd hugged her — the woman who tried to save her friend.

I wept because I was overcome, old as the story was, by the weight of the loss of all those lives.

I wept because I'd strolled across the floors that Otto Frank had walked with anticipation before he read the lists posted outside Centraal Station that included names of family members returning from the camps.

Had I stood, posing for a silly tourist's portrait, in the very spot of one of those long-ago signs? Had I stood, waiting for a train to the airport, on one of the very same platforms as Otto Frank?

In the movie, when Otto Frank steps outside the station and takes in the view of the city that betrayed him, the camera pulls back to reveal the sign above his shoulders: "Centraal Station."

I was blown away by the cosmic serendipity of the whole thing. I was different, after all.

People kept asking, "How was your trip?"

I didn't have much to report, because I didn't really take that trip.

It took me.

Thanks for the Mammaries

Seventeen years ago, I caught my aunt Dorothy's prosthetic breast.
It was high and outside, but I saw it coming.
The thought was more frightening of it exploding against the wall of her den.
"Kathy, you ever seen a prosthesis before?" she asked as the jelly bubble-cum-breast-thing wobbled through the air like a pregnant Frisbee.
I used the left side of my body to catch it, smashing it against myself with my left hand. It hit me with a soft thump, sorta like a snowball without the disintegration.
It slipped out of my hand and down into the Lazy Boy recliner.
It was still warm.
She'd just slid it from the pocket in her special James Bond breast cancer bra.
It was smooth and squishy.
The fake breast was flesh-colored like a white Barbie, or more the color of Oscar Meyer's Beef Bologna. It wasn't made specifically for Aunt Dorothy, this semi-brown black woman.
I balled my right hand into a fist, punched it into the underside and let it rest there.
The nipple was very faint. It danced from beneath my finger like mercury.
The prosthesis hardly duplicated the size and texture of her removed breast, but she was trying for a semblance of normalcy.
Boy, was she trying.
By this time, Aunt Dorothy still had a three-years head start on death.
She wasn't going quietly or tragically.
But it was tragic to watch her hissy fit vanishing act.
Chemotherapy zapped her hair, leaving her with wiry patches.
Cancer had spread to her lymph nodes. She was hot, tired and uncomfortable most of the time. My uncle John, a retired small-city cop, ran himself aground caring for her.
Normally I wouldn't have been spending any sort of down time with

them.

They were, after all, my square aunt and uncle. My three cousins had all moved out and on.

I was there because I'm Dependable Kathy.

Uncle John hired me that early October morning to drive a spare car back from Columbus, Ohio.

Aunt Dorothy hit the Lottery.

There was a brand-new champagne-colored Merc Cougar courtesy of The Ohio Lottery Commission with her name on it, a prize she'd won when her ticket stub was pulled from a hopper of thousands at a Cincinnati Reds game.

I was to drive back in John's burgundy-and-white car—a Lincoln Continental, Delta 88, a boat—and they'd cruise home in the new Cougar. I was just back from a two-year stint in Denver, fresh off dropping out of college for the second of three times.

I was broke, bored and adrift.

There was $45 in it for me.

"God, I bet this thing is hot," I finally said, still holding the silicone blob.

What was I supposed to say while balancing atop my hand Dorothy's life and death?

"You know it is," she said. "I burn up in it. And it's really hot when I just wear it inside the bra next to my skin without sliding it in that pocket. When I do that, I have to watch what I wear, because if something is low-cut it shows 'cause it can slide up and down, 'specially when I'm sweatin.' "

I have total recall of the conversation because I wrote (for no one's eyes but mine)"A Day with Uncle John and Aunt Dorothy," as soon as I got back to my mother's house.

I compulsively write things down.

Words I've read but don't know, entire overheard conversations, rap lyrics, haiku, invented langauage, whatever.

I do it because I fear losig an instant's truth.

Mostly I'm afraid if I don't write things down, there'll be no record we were ever here.

The whole thing was surreal, a jolt.

I was so self-involved then, self-pitying for dropping out of school, ashamed for not having, at 21 years old, concrete plans for what was turning out to be my sorry-ass life.

And on and on.

Aunt Dorothy's cancer was mythic in our family. My people—mainly my gaggle of hen-like aunts—bad-mouthed the cancer like it was a person.

Truth is, few of us had actually gotten up on it.

I'd gotten all up on it, smelled it, took note of it and refused its invitation to embarassment or awkwardness.

I felt blessed Aunt Dorothy trusted me with the information written on her body.

In a dream-like procession: the air-borne prosthesis, the horrific scar where her breast had been, Dorothy massaging her chest, Uncle John talking—apropos of nothing—ad nauseum about his tour in the military, falling asleep on the backseat en route to Columbus and waking up to Lou Reed singing/speaking—"And the colored girls sing doo da doo da doo doo da doo doo da doo da doo doo da doo doooh" —on some far-away radio station we'd picked up on the way.

But her cancer became a nightmare rife with foreshadowing.

By the time she died three years later, she headed a literal funeral procession of family members to the grave.

Ed Hill, my maternal and only known grandfather, died of brain cancer one year later; Uncle Clarence Hill died of cancer of the gallbladder the following year; Aunt Dorothy Saunders died of lung cancer; Mary Hill, my maternal and lone grandmother, died from complications from Alzheimer's; and Clarence's widow, Valerie, died from kidney failure.

Aunt Dorothy, an aunt by marriage, was ribald, unapologetic and rock hard.

Profanity was her vocabulary and gossip her pasttime.

She knew that most of Uncle John's people, my mother's people, never liked her and she never tried courting their favor.

She didn't suck up.

She was scrappy when she was alive. She died mad, fighting mad.

October is National Breast Cancer Awareness Month.

With the proliferation of cancer in my immediate family, it's my pleasure to get my mammaries mashed and, because of Aunt Dorothy, my memories rehashed.

A Dream Referred

We're the reflection of our ancestors.
We'd like to thank you for the building blocks you left us.
As your spirit possessed us, yo, you blessed us.
Thank you very much.
Thank you very much.
Thank you very much.

— "AFRICA DREAM" BY TALIB KWELI AND HI-TEK

For a 17-year-old black girl whose failure seemed imminent, guaranteed and certain, finding Nikki Giovanni meant possibilities existed for me after all.

When I first saw a book of poetry by a black woman for sale in a bookstore, it was like looking in a mirror and seeing not a face but a reflection of a future that didn't include heartbreak, disappointment, suicide or anguish.

No more vicitm.

Rather, I saw a future of intellectual introspection, spiritual reckoning and writing.

Always writing.

The writing proved to be the most difficult.

The black teenaged girl I was in 1982 knew I would, most times, be writing for my very life.

Soon as I committed to it, writing immediately turned me into a selfish bastard.

I knelt to the solitude it demanded.

And I knew early on that writing, and any recognition to come from it, would slam a wedge of jealousy between envious onlookers and myself.

But I knew there'd also be as many lovers.

In the winter of my junior year, I bought a $2.95 copy of Giovanni's *The Women and the Men* at the bookstore.

I didn't know what I was getting into.

I understood enough of those poems to know they were over my head, just out of reach.

So I bought it, anyway.

Back then, I was getting five bucks a week for allowance. I combined it with babysitting income to buy gas, lunch, recreation, books and magazines.

Three bucks for a book set me back.

Twenty years later, I still have it. Sometime between high school and dropping in and out of college, I studied it when I first thought I was a poet.

A few weeks ago, I dialed up Giovanni at Virginia Tech University.

I interviewed her for a *CityBeat* preview piece in conjunction with her appearance at the University of Cincinnati. I did I don't know how many drive-bys on the phone before I finally dialed. While the phone rang, I hoped she wasn't there, that the line would be busy, that she'd tell me to blow off.

I did and did not want the interview.

It sucks fakin' the funk when your shero becomes your subject.

I panicked suddenly at the it's-too-late-now thought of having scripted lame questions.

The phone was ringing.

I know, I'll just be charming.

I'd done no real research.

I was an idiot.

"Giovanni," she answered, not with anticipation but with interruption.

Chatter over her minor computer problems alleviated the nag of the pregnant pause while my hand caught pace with my brain.

I managed to eke out a short story.

I had to name that tune in about 700 words, and I could've easily gone on for 1,000 more.

It's not easy or comfortable boiling down an American idol to bite-sized portions of history, poetics, respect, nuance and stature.

As a journalist, I've met, interviewed or been introduced to real legends. I'm talking now about people on album covers in my living room who've lived the notes sailing from my speakers.

Journalists live disconnected lives.

We're supposed to act unfazed by, be knowledgeable about and then spin un-startstruck copy about people we idolize and imitate. For me, a stack of musicians are usually my feature material.

I've interviewed and/or met jazz titans Ron Carter and Dave Brubeck, Freedom Singers founder and Sweet Honey in the Rock anchor Bernice

Johnson Reagon , classical composer John Adams, Wynton Marsalis, jazz/rock drummer Cindy Blackman, hip-hop impresario Hi-Tek. I've even interviewed Fiona Apple and The Fairfield Four and gotten laudatory e-mails from Chocolate Genius. I've hung out with jazz organist Dr. Lonnie Smith, jazz vocalist Renee Marie and jazz legend Shirley Horn, who invited me to her Washington, D.C. home for a fish dinner.

And a few writers — namely poets jessica care Moore and Saul Williams — have made the list of interviewees.

I name-drop to make a point.

These people rock my world.

But they didn't make me nervous.

They didn't rattle me.

Giovanni was different.

Could be because she's the only writer with saved-up history at her back.

She's not a peer.

She's an elder.

She hails from a burg in Cincinnati and I've whiled away the most time and develeopmentally rich years here developing my craft and myself.

Giovanni lives. She traversed and transcended.

Therefore, despite all it's put me through I know this city cannot possibly kill, stifle, extinguish or rid itself of me.

Giovanni thrives as her tattooed and outspoken self.

That means I can, too.

My potential percolated 20 years ago as I tried deciphering *The Women and the Men*.

My brush with Nikki Giovanni returned me to a hopeful simmer.

A Picture Is Worth 74 Years

◆◇◆◇◆◇

Where were you when Halle Berry got her best actress Oscar? Like other life-defining phenomena—the assassinations of presidents and pop stars, acts of terror and the births of our children—this history deserves to rank in our memories for posterity.

I took it personally. I was sitting Indian style in the middle of my mussed bed holding my breath and envisioning Berry's victory but anticipating her loss. When her name was called and the camera caught her transfixed and paralyzed, I exhaled and cried.

The next day I bought a copy of *USA Today* with Berry's picture above the fold. Once at work, I played India.Arie and with 'Video'—the black woman's I'm-not-too-pretty-but-I'm-not-ugly-either anthem of self-love—as my soundtrack, I taped above my desk that photograph of a tearful Berry clutching her trophy to her right side.

Her mouth is open and her teeth are bared in anguish, disbelief and relief. Her wail is frozen. Her left arm is extended. Her hand is aloft, outstretched as in an unreciprocated handshake. She reaches out to me.

When Russell Crowe announced Berry's name as best actress of the 74th Annual Academy Awards, Berry spoke to me. She spoke for me.

Egomania and skittish hormones aside, Berry's win has nothing and everything to do with me and more to do with Hollywood's brand of big-budget racism, history, sacrifice, all that other skewed socialization that fertilizes racism and mostly what *Salon* arts and entertainment writer Stephanie Zacharek calls 'cultural conditioning.' History depletes us, forcing us to deceive us.

Judging from the Academy's legacy of sprinkling flies in the buttermilk, we might buy into the lie that blacks haven't been worthy of Oscar-caliber roles. Furthermore, even when we landed them, we weren't rewarded with gold statues.

Long-forgotten Lonette McKee should've been at least nominated for *Sparkle*, *'Round Midnight* or *Jungle Fever*. Oprah Winfrey deserved a win for *The Color Purple*, as did Diana Ross for *Lady Sings the Blues*.

Ruby Dee deserves at least a look every time she's on screen. Cicely

Tyson has nearly done herself a disservice with her patented emoting, traits for which Meryl Streep, Sissy Spacek and Jessica Lange have all been lauded. *Sounder* still breaks my heart.

And what about Angela Bassett as an otherworldly Tina Turner in *What's Love Got To Do With It*?

The Academy is fickle and manipulative. It plays into Hollywood's stultified thinking, and it doesn't give us credit for suspending reality for two hours. It doesn't know we can accept a black woman playing an 'un-black' character.

Instead, Hollywood likes its Negresses as bitches, 'hos, maids, crack heads, mammies, comic foils, inane sidekicks, martyrs and monosyllabic judges. So blacks—as moviegoers and moviemakers—are relegated to roles of co-dependency.

We wait. And our rewards for waiting have been scarce.

In 1939, when Oscar was just 11 years old, Hattie McDaniel won best supporting actress for her role as Mammie of the World in *Gone With the Wind*. Twenty-seven years later, Sidney Poitier, who this year received an honorary Oscar, won best actor in 1963 for *Lilies of the Field*. Whoopi Goldberg, everybody's favorite asexual, guilting Negress, won best supporting actress in 1991 for *Ghos* .

Denzel Washington won best supporting actor for *Glory* in 1989 and made history this year when, with his best actor win for *Training Day*, he and Berry became the first blacks to snag best acting nods in the same year. He's also the first black man since Poitier to win best actor, for a film that's not his best or worst work. He should've won for *Malcolm X*, but that would've meant rewarding black dissonance, and that's a no-no.

Part of the reason there's a paucity of reasonable roles for black actors is there's an anemic cast of Negroes in positions of power in Hollywood. And when the pool is that shallow, it's easier to spot, mimic and deconstruct mediocrity.

Think of the lop-sided ratio of questionable and vapid black flicks to every strong, well-acted and directed one. That we can name names is my point. That there are about equal numbers of good and bad white movies is also my point.

So when Halle Berry cries, clutching all that history and squeezing the breath from naysayers at her side, I cry. And I cry because I'm filled with the recognition of validation.

I know what it's like to be walking head first and nearly parallel to the ground into icy, bone-slicing winds. Turning finally to fully face the glory of the sun is enough to make anyone cry. And a picture says it all.

Sorry, Miss Jackson

"Sex is not the one string on the guitar. There are nine other Commandments."

—THE REV. JESSE JACKSON CONDUCTING DAMAGE CONTROL
FOR PRESIDENT CLINTON DURING THE MONICA LEWINSKY SCANDAL.

Rev. Jesse Jackson was so taken with 39-year-old Karin Stanford while she was writing a book-length doctoral dissertation on his foreign policy that he gave her a job running the Rainbow Coalition in Washington, D.C.

They had sex and a daughter.

Then there was an avalanche of financial deals—a reported stipend of $10,000 a month in addition to a $40,000 payment allotted before Stanford took a maternity leave and relocated to Los Angeles.

Sure, we're all used to Jackson in all his savior modes.

Spewing rhymes deffer than Rakim and always showing up uninvited, he's saved white politicians from themselves, whites from blacks, blacks from whites, fallen American soldiers from any number of America's foreign enemies and, perhaps most notably, blacks from ourselves.

Jackson once co-starred as Martin Luther King Jr.'s earthy, Afroed Soul Brother No. 1.

Back then, Jackson was Maceo Parker to King's James Brown.

Now, he's not so much pitiful as he is fallible.

He's just that baby daddy.

Well, as Jesuses go, they've all gotta be revered, hailed, followed, misunderstood and ultimately crucified.

Let us now escort Jackson up Golgotha. His custom cross awaits.

The official White House photo depicting Jackson, Stanford and Clinton is about the only thing more despicable than Jackson—the married, iconic family man—knocking up a staff member. The picture was snapped while Jackson acted as "spiritual adviser" to the Clintons during the Monica Lewinsky debacle.

This means Stanford was at least four months pregnant with Jackson's child while he was praying with and for the Clintons.

Hmmmm.

I wonder what Jackson "advised" the president.

Not getting caught?

Baby names? Stain removers?

Lord knows they had a lot to talk over, 'cause pimpin' ain't easy.

As Jackson reveals himself to be a fallible man, however, we're sucker-punched into believing in and trusting yet another flesh-and-blood person who we thought deserved our trust and reverence.

And the fact that Jackson—the bastard son of a teenaged mother and a married next-door-neighbor man—fathered a bastard daughter says as much about the erosion of our collective fiber as it does about his male weaknesses.

Forget for a moment the mammoth societal implications of Jackson's part in the Civil Rights Movement, his association with King, the founding of Operation PUSH, the Rainbow Coalition and his participation in the countless marches, rescue missions and opportunistic appearances at every lynching and at each fallen Negro's bedside.

Dismiss all that.

Now look at Jesse Jackson as a man with a woody for a woman who, 20 years his junior, probably slobbed him with compliments, praise and adoration.

Whad'ya get?

A baby, scandal, disappointment, bewilderment and resignation.

That's what the public might be going through.

Or maybe not.

Except for its sexiness as a point of newsworthiness, maybe nobody really cares about Jesse Jackson anymore. If he were a musician, he'd probably be eligible for a "Whatever happened to ..." segment on VH-1.

As it is, he's ripe for a "Behind the Music" spot.

I mean, is it just me or had Jackson's penchant for assuming he spoke for all blacks worn thin?

Is it me or had he made himself into a caricature, a remnant of black America's glory days when we cared about ourselves for the sake of self-preservation?

Is it me or had he become little more than Al Sharpton's handsome older brother?

Of course, we'll never know anything more than what we cobble together via the media, because Jackson now is stepping back from public life and refusing to publicly discuss or explain his illegitimate daughter.

Maybe he'll use the time to concoct some nifty new rhymes: "Don't legislate! Masturbate!" Or, "When you've hit bedrock, have a child out of wedlock!"

Who'll be his "spiritual adviser?" Will any of the thousands he's counseled and rescued return the favor?

Nah.

He's probably better off alone to reconcile his shortcomings like the rest of us.

Sacred Cow

I'm a lapsed Christian.

Then so is my pastor.

And it disturbs me to say so.

The Rev. Freddie T. Piphus has been disengaged from leadership at Lincoln Heights Missionary Baptist Church (LHMBC). The village of Lincoln Heights is an old and all-black hamlet on the northern skirts of Cincinnati.

Hometown to the Isley Brothers is often its greatest claim to fame.

The reasons for Piphus' dismissal aren't evident, because no one besides God and Piphus really knows what went down. Oh, there have been years of speculation, accusation and frustration.

Many of the die-hard, faithful tithers have left the congregation.

There were meetings. Rumors of meetings. Loyalties have been decided and divided. Rightfully so.

Piphus brought the sprawling church—with its outreach, three Sunday services, progressive ministries and effervescent messages—up from its humble Byrd Street beginnings on the tucked-away side street.

The old building looks identical to every other red brick, post-slavery black Baptist church built by free, north-seeking coloreds. The new place is grandiose, airy, bright and modern without the intimidation.

Young, dynamic and anointed, perhaps Piphus' greatest gift was integrating the needs of the Old Saints (the members whose faith, prayers and loyalty sustained the old church) with the needs of the younger, affluent and spiritually rootless members who, together, built his dream of a cross-generational progressive black Baptist congregation.

With his sermons on finishing—a prayer, a task, a job, a relationship, you name it—he was antithetical to the Old Jack/Up From Slavery preachers spitting into handkerchiefs, rubbing their brows and ignoring Scripture.

His messages were practical, his progressivism notorious.

Newspapers profiled and quoted him. Other preachers and congregations requested audiences with him.

During a series on depression, he introduced to the congregation Christian-based therapists. It saved my life.

I connected with one, navigated my depression and emerged more sane and stable.

If Piphus hadn't veered from tendencies of typical black Baptist ministries, I wouldn't be writing this today. He was the Kirk Franklin of the postmodern black Baptist pulpit.

And like the Gospel impresario who weds grinding urban hip-hop to the traditional mores of old-school Gospel, Piphus was a hip Pied Piper. He preached in jeans and sweaters. Congregants came to church relaxed and casual. Everything he touched and every word he spoke was golden.

He was fond of saying the church was "doing a new thing."

And it worked.

For a while.

Then somewhere there was a shift, then a rut. There was trickery of biblical proportions.

These are the rumors: an extramarital affair or affairs, a drastic drop in membership and noticeably low tithing. Plus a closer move to Charismatic Christianity, which embodies a reliance on personal religious experiences, divinely inspired powers and speaking in tongues.

And it looks like trouble in paradise.

I'd stopped attending LHMBC about three years ago, mostly because of transportation issues—the church is a 20-minute drive away.

But also I'd grown disenchanted with black churches after years of faithfully attending the 8 a.m. Sunday service.

Once I missed it was easy to keep missing.

I started back, coincidentally at this tenuous time, because I'd bought a hooptie.

So here we are. And now a pall hangs over the church.

Congregants—some, not all—splintered off into factions of the pro-Piphus kind, the never-mind kind and the let's-get-on-with-the-business-of-kingdom-building kind.

Pro-Piphus campers issued a recent letter stating his innocence and that the board of deacons and trustees overreacted. That's fraught with denial. If it weren't, he wouldn't have shown up to meetings with an attorney.

Piphus had been banned from church grounds and the locks changed, but his supporters called for a meeting at the church the following midweek. Prior to it, a statement was read at all three services. It said Piphus had signed and agreed to a "separation package."

Severance?

Who knows?

What I do know is Christians, would-be Christians and play-acting Christians and their churches aren't immune to weaknesses — flesh, financial and otherwise. In fact, they're *especially* in the cross hairs.

I columnized this breakdown in the body of Christ to document and testify that we've all sinned and fallen short.

Sinning preachers aren't new.

Do they owe us more than who we're capable of being? Yep.

Remember when they first took the pulpit? They claimed a calling.

They're supposed to be special, so disappointment is mandatory; yet, disappointment cannot sustain.

This normally isn't the space for such conversations. The Piphus debacle has been washed in the blood of secrets and lies. LHMBC sailed for years on a glorious sea of abundant blessings. Its members seemed empowered, infallible, even haughty.

There's now a new crop of members who think their way of worship and biblical scholarship supercedes all others. To them hell is the resting place for anyone dissimilar.

Proverbs 16:18 says, *"Pride goes before destruction, a haughty spirit before a fall."*

When Piphus shepherded the church, he'd never tolerate divisive, classist and arrogant thinking. But he's not there anymore.

His dismissal, his absence and the sadness that an entire congregation is wandering in the wilderness is itself a tale from the Scripture.

And just like in those biblical stories, we need Jesus.

All of us.

Rated: R. (Kelly)

❖❖❖❖❖❖

This is war.

God and Satan in an ancient grudge scrap in a *Celebrity Death Match* for R. Kelly's soul. God keeps losing.

Deejays make jokes ("some brothas just freaky like dat") and open the phone lines ("whaddya thank, callers?"). Kelly keeps feelin' on our booties, vomiting sound-alike songs sung in nasal drone tones like a man possessed.

He is. With sex.

He's set adrift on misery's bliss, cast out by arrogance, narcissism, stupidity and immoral lust.

No pedophile is an island unto himself. Since slavery, black girls have been sexualized and objectified and disposed of properly like pink razors.

But it's always been this way. We've for years inhaled mediocrity hidden in ass-shakin' goodness.

Kelly is lower than the ick of resulting public intoxication. He's a tortured man so mired in pedophilia that the people who made bank from his "skills" held their noses only long enough to finish the track.

They're complicit. They've known what was only hinted at in 1994 when Kelly secretly married martyred Black Barbie Aaliyah, then 15.

Then there was no looking away.

He was arrested in Florida after a Chicago grand jury indicted him on 21 counts of child pornography. The arrest stemmed from the infamous videotape that allegedly showed Kelly having sex with a 13- or 14-year-old girl.

Shortly after, Chicago cops investigated four copies of yet another Florida videotape rented and returned by men claiming to be Kelly's employees. Investigators soon threw out further charges surrounding these tapes, though it was reported they showed the same girl as in the original tape.

Six months later, Kelly was arrested again in Florida and charged this time with 12 counts of possessing child pornography. This arrest, too, reconnects to the previous Florida bust. Florida cops, when carrying out the original Chicago warrant, found a digital camera containing a dozen images of an underage girl.

Kelly is allegedly having sex with the girl in three of the photos.

Cops say they took so long to file the latest charges because they were verifying the girl's age.

It's under.

At least four lawsuits have been brought against the singer, three of which accuse him of having sex with underage girls, according to stories in the Canadian press.

Kelly's settled two.

Meanwhile, his colleagues drove their customized Cadillacs and Benzos away from Kelly. Dr. Dre, Ashanti, Nas, Jay-Z and even Sisqo have either publicly dissed or privately dismissed Kelly. In an industry rife with playalistic images of bitches, hoes, money, misogyny, Cristal and private jets, even Kelly's illness is too ill to chill with.

While the aloofness seems a career move, however, it's really a drive-by on humanity. Why didn't these people, otherwise hyped by his formulaic Midas touch with an annoying song, confront him on what's amounted to an out-of-control disease?

If he was a drunk, there would've been an intervention like Whitney Houston's never seen.

There was a time when Kelly appeared to wrestle down his demons, publicly hanging out with the likes of Kirk Franklin, that New Jack Gospel Pied Piper. Then there'd be a full-out Gospel cut smacked up, flipped and rubbed down in the middle of Kelly's bordello soundtrack CDs.

Then he'd go back to fucking.

Kelly supplanted therapy with warbling.

"I Believe I Can Fly," a song he calls " a song for kids," followed the annulment from Aaliyah. "Heaven, I Need a Hug" was his post-traumatic soundtrack to the widely circulated tapes. Since then he's been going down on his preoccupation with sex, and we keep lettin' him feel on our booties.

That's startling.

It says the troubled celebrity's entertainment value is worth stomaching his flaws. It says we delight in devaluing little black girls. It says we'd rather hear a bumpin' beat than reconcile what he's bumpin' on.

Robert Sylvester Kelly is sick. Forget Iraq. This here's war.

I believe it because I've seen it close up; grew up in proximity. There are brothas among us who struggle with Kelly's addictions.

You'd never know it by the packaging.

But it's a dirty open secret in what's left of our village.

Money and access to stringless sex is what separates Kelly from the work-a-day brotha, the one who goes home to a woman who can't possibly measure up to and/or satisfy images he's been dry humping all day. So somehow it's hidden or dormant.

But Kelly's arrogance, narcissism and denial will vulture off whatever corpse his pedophilia leaves.

That brotha don't need no hug.

He needs some black-on-black love.

From people his own age.

Fallin'/Fallen

The lure of anonymous pussy trumps mortgages, diapers, family vacations, carpools and all those other trappings of domestic bliss.

While work-a-day men bet the farm on pussy, athletes and entertainers seem especially susceptible to throwing it away over six minutes of pleasure. That lure tempts even the most well-meaning, well-respected multimillion dollar man.

Take Kobe Bryant. The allegations of sexual assault against Bryant, by a 19-year-old woman employed at a Colorado resort, aren't at all that shocking.

Take it in the context of my sanctified imagination.

A young, black, beautiful, exceptionally talented, insanely wealthy professional athlete has an eye for young white girls while his young half-white wife—whom he engaged while she was in high school—is at home with his infant child.

He's miles from home in an otherwise non-descript resort town.

He's horny.

Why not?

Bryant and his entourage were encamped there, and reports verify there was brief contact between Bryant and his alleged victim after her shift ended the night before he was to receive minor surgery. She left the front desk and went to his room. There's a 20-minute window unaccounted for.

"Nothing that happened was against the will of the woman who now falsely accuses me," Bryant said in a prepared statement, copping only to adultery.

Meanwhile, the media are frothing, concocting a brouhaha more concerned with Bryant's fall from squeaky clean and his potential loss of millions in endorsements than they are with examining why America keeps unjustifiably endowing our sports and music heroes with undeserved high moral codes.

They're athletes and musicians. Not God and gods.

And there it is. We're just as busted as Bryant.

Every single time this happens—good guy athlete/singer charged with sexual improprieties—we navel-pick the perceived character of said athlete/singer and come up with nothing.

That's because we're in denial about the realities of the pressures and the fast-forwarded adolescence of being the youngest player ever drafted into the NBA. We don't want to know what life's like behind the propped-up persona of being the youngest person to start an NBA All-Star Game.

We're too busy living vicariously.

We're too busy feeling good.

Even by America's Super-Size Standards, Bryant has it all—more money than he can count, a Quaker Instant Family, three NBA championship rings, houses, cars and, most importantly, access.

Lately even Bryant was beginning to believe his own hype, waxing poetic about role models in interviews broadcast just days before the allegations became public. Maybe, knowing what he knew, he was trying to convince himself that what he was saying was true.

I'm on a limb.

I don't think Bryant sexually assaulted the woman. I do believe, however, there was sexual contact. I think Bryant is quietly raging against the machinations propelling him as this too-good-to-be-true almost raceless sports hero (once) safe to leave alone with your kids.

He's acting out.

He's been scrutinized, idolized and held aloft since before high school, and now in his infidelity he's acting like most of his NBA colleagues he somehow managed 'till now not to emulate.

And the former *American Idol* hopeful and alleged victim had to do something with all that guilt and abandonment remaining from what was probably brief and unremarkable sex.

Speaking of guilt and abandonment, in all this there's something to be said about America's love/hate relationship with the strapping male Negro. America treats its black men like they're stuck with them in a revolving door. Chasing after or running from? Revering or reviling? Accusing or accosting?

In the name of the game of falling from grace, Kobe Bryant got a triple double he'll never forget.

He cheated on his young wife with a young white girl, he stands to lose most of what America respects and admires him for and he learned what it's like to be another young black man in the criminal justice system.

Priceless.

Treacherous Bunnies' Lament

It's Bugs Bunny's 65th anniversary.

I wanted to write solely about Liberia, our lyin'-ass president and why he don't particularly give a fuck about a country of dusty-ass Africans 'cause can't no precious crude belch from their black, bloated bellies.

I so wanted to weigh in on political racism.

But fact is, after an afternoon of feeding library copy machines to duplicate 10 days of articles on Liberia and after shouldering cultural ignorance in my Gap bag—even still—I know the same about Liberia, which isn't much.

It's in Africa, and its capital is Monrovia. Charles G. Taylor was the worrisome president, and we're not supposed to like him.

He wouldn't leave.

The study of Liberia nearly overshadowed its point.

I'm stunned over a Saturday, June 28, 2003, *New York Times* front-page picture of a flip-flop wearing African boy whose face is flattened by fear and terror. Falling out of a crouch onto his left knee, he clumsily aims an automatic weapon straight for the camera.

Strapped to his back is a pink teddy bear-shaped backpack.

Anguished that I lacked the words to articulate my bewilderment and frustration, I watched *CBS Sunday Morning* on the hunt for good sentences to steal.

There were a few, but nothing worth shoplifting. Then, a segment on Bugs Bunny.

When I was a lazy, Saturday morning cartoons kid, I always felt that Bugs' hip and flip attitude was lifted from the caricature of the black man.

Had to be. I don't care how much Warner Bros. might refute this. Bugs is a brotha.

Actually, he's in reverse drag. He's a little like my dead great aunt Peg, a truth-spittin' curmudgeon who always secretly held the last laugh though we rarely, if ever, saw her laughing.

And now as much as I need to, I cannot laugh.

Ain't shit funny.

During my tango with bunnies I came across a card with a John Updike quote.

"America is a vast conspiracy to keep you happy."

I took it as a sign.

I had to come clean.

And it's this: Africans do not respect or place in high regard black Americans and our tireless search for identity. They're in fact aghast at the notion that our quests have unfortunately and incorrectly come to rest at "African American."

We're as African as Kwanza observed but not understood.

Likewise, we've become packaged and mass marketed in a plan to keep us sedated and groggy off the Black Status Quo Buffet.

And that, brethren and sistren, ain't being African.

It's a drive-by, a drive-thru.

When do we unhyphenate ourselves and become one/won?

I'm disturbed but not surprised by President Bush's deadly slow response to Liberia.

It says motherfuck the assumed nobility attached to Africanness—thy middle name is AIDS.

You's still a bunch of niggras with no oil.

I've studied the front-page photos of Bush looking askance at African children assembled for his size up, of crumpled and grieving African women and, finally, of crazed-looking African males brandishing automatic weapons.

And my soul cries out. What is going on?

It dawned on me that embattled black Africans are depending on all black Americans for help as much as—if not more than—they're depending on America's white male power structure.

They're looking to us, especially since we've co-opted and gotten rich from the African Diaspora (TM). They need those black Americans who blithely adorn themselves in African heritage as a fashion statement but who sidestep accountability when the Mother(fuckin') Land is under siege.

If we claim—not pledge—allegiance to the America that works for us, why don't we demand the rest of it work for us as well?

It's no longer enough to selfishly use up all the empty gaudiness of the America we can digest, then bitch about the wrinkles and remain unwilling to jeopardize colored status quo to make the Bush League beholden to the descendants of the country that supplied his foreparents with the Original Temp Service.

I'd be willing to table all other forms of reparations if our federal government halted the mayhem in Africa with the vim and vigor with which it hunts Saddam Hussein and trots out his dead family like Southern lynching photos sold as postcards.

And I'd even forgive black Americans of all our repeatedly stupid, genocidal behavior if we used all our might—economic, spiritual and physical—to at least question Bush's slow-mo.

We can be citizens of the world.

Right now we're merely renting ZIP codes.

And it's so African American.

Dancing with the Devil

❖❖❖❖❖❖

In 1970, Sen. Strom Thurmond hired Thomas Moss.

A black South Carolinian and director of the Voter Education Project, which advocated black voter registration, Moss was the first black person hired by any member of Congress hailing from South Carolina.

Thurmond, however, isn't going down as racially progressive, supportive of civil rights or a friend to the colored.

That's too easy.

More like an elder Klansman than an elder statesman, Thurmond — who just withered away at age 100 — worked hard to pause America at attack dogs, fire hoses and separate entrances, even attributing integration to Communism.

Actually, I don't recall Thurmond as anything less than what he was: the southern racist who, when he'd say "Negro" and it came out "niggra," made me feel like I needed a shower. You know, a stereotypical bigot so blatantly racist it almost made sense.

And he was. But it didn't.

Thurmond's hiring of Moss, who for 25 years parlayed the senator's clout to improve conditions in South Carolina's black communities, was a political preemptive strike.

See, Thurmond had just felt the pinch of supporting Gov. Albert Watson, a boisterous bigot who "stood up for hardcore rednecks." Watson lost, and Thurmond saw the colored section turning against him for his penchant for trying to defeat civil rights legislation — once with a 24-hour, 18-minute filibuster against the 1957 civil rights bill.

So to keep the darkies happy at home, he had to show good faith.

As long as he kept Moss performing grunt work, there was sure to be dancin' 'round the campfire.

Thurmond returned again and again to the Senate.

This is the thumbnail version of Strom Thurmond, the man whose work realigned white southern conservatism with racist Democrats. Of how this World War II veteran — a Democrat, a "Dixiecrat" and then a Republican, foe of civil rights and hater of integration — got away with it as America's longest-serving senator.

Reading, thinking and ultimately writing about Thurmond is like a root canal—it's a painful but unavoidable extraction of infectious roots.

To affix time and place to their time and place in history, folks of that generation recall their whereabouts when Kennedy or King were shot. I did the same with Thurmond, making a mental note.

As a TV newscaster ran through his obituary, I turned to catch a glimpse of Thurmond's Bitter Beer Face.

"Is Thurmond dead? He must be dead," I said.

"Yes, thank God," my friend said, herself relieved.

Relishing Thurmond's death is a guilty pleasure

I can only compare it to the mental unraveling of a long-ago editor who'd shaped up to be an intentional adversary. He lived to test my character. He rejoiced at my failures, sabotaged my successes and stared in disbelief when I prevailed. I believed he was evil.

The day he slinked from the newsroom, weighted by the collapse of the infrastructure he'd devised for grinding me down, was the day I made another mental note.

It was historical. It was hysterical.

Relief and triumph returned when I read Thurmond's *New York Times* obit.

I know, I know.

It appears I've taken too personally the inevitable death of a bigot.

But consider the closeted (and not-so-) support of Thurmond's ideologies held aloft by his history-making political career. And then there's Sen. Trent Lott's tribute to Thurmond on his 100th birthday, which bears repeating: "America wouldn't have had all these problems over all these years" had Thurmond been elected president in 1948.

Scary.

Scarier still is how close Thurmond came. Facing President Harry Truman in 1948, Thurmond, then still a Democrat, got 1.1 million votes and 38 electoral votes from a gaggle of southern states after southerners balked at Hubert Humphrey's plea for civil rights during the Democratic National Convention.

In 1981 and again in 1995, Thurmond was elected president of the Senate by his Republican colleagues, placing him third in line to the presidency behind VP and Speaker of the House.

Scary.

Just because it never happened doesn't mean it couldn't have.

History's a toothy road that'll rise from behind to bite us in the ass if we move too slowly outrunning it.

I was raised not to judge a man's salvation.

For now, I summon my sanctified imagination: Thurmond has cleared security. He's charging up his Miracle Ear for the long haul. He's throwing back a cold one with Satan at a whites-only bar.

For eternity.

Kunta's Compensation

❖❖❖❖❖❖

Cut to Kunta Kinte, Alex Haley's distant relative and icon for a generation. Kunta is making his way down Wall Street. The street and sidewalk are jammed with dark-suited, money-gittin' men and women, all yapping into cellular appendages.

Kunta's loincloth is replaced by a pinstriped, charcoal, custom-tailored Ralph Lauren suit.

A raw silk necktie hangs where once a slave catcher's rope snatched at his neck.

His spear is a two-way cell phone, and his watch and wedding band are platinum.

Off the backs of his foreparents, this Kunta Kinte is an Ivy League-educated, elegant and insanely successful young millionaire who doesn't go back to the 'hood much anymore.

Cut to reality: Reparations are us. Making reparation means making amends for a wrong or injury.

Since postmodern Kunta Kintes abound, isn't that reparation enough? Never.

You know how we Negroes can be.

We're always in search of that leveled-off playing field.

Deadria Farmer-Paellmann, a 36-year-old former law student, found evidence during the course of research that Aetna's corporate predecessor "insured human slave owners against the loss of their human chattel." FleetBoston Financial and CSX Railroad were named with Aetna in a lawsuit filed in March on behalf of 35 million African Americans, with promises to produce 100 more "guilty" corporations.

The suit claims conspiracy, human-rights violations and unjust wealth from slavery but doesn't seek specific damages.

According to CNN, it estimates that slaves performed upwards of $40 million in unpaid labor between 1790 and 1860.

By today's standard, that labor comes in at $1.4 trillion.

Besides re-igniting the ever-smoldering conversation about race in America, the lawsuit comes with a promise, albeit unspoken—that despite whether slave reparations become a cashable reality check, we all must reconsider American history, America's legacy of the payback and the manifestation of the postmodern reparation.

Reparations will make victimologists of some Negroes, apologists of others and race traitors of still more. At least the debate might, once and for all, settle the upset stomach of Negroes constantly demanding ideal weather conditions before they play.

Meanwhile, all around us, other teams play on during thunderstorms.

Larger unanswered questions, however, might be whether white neglect is responsible for racial disparity and whether the involvement of whites can alter the conditions of blacks.

I don't trust the American process of righting wrongs.

We all know this country has participated in the 'R' word.

Without the benefit of heavy-handed debate, committees, reports or rallies, the U.S. paid off ancestors of Native Americans and Japanese Americans.

This makes me think slavery is different and that implied guilt is attached to slavery payback.

As it should be.

While Japanese Americans were interned in camps, Negroes died segregated deaths in World War II. Those names don't even turn up during Black History Month.

Further, black illiteracy, low test scores, fatherless black households, black teen mothers and northern black ghettos are all direct descendants of the transatlantic slave trade.

Male slaves were ripped from their families to reproduce and work.

Left alone, black women learned sex as survival — givin' it up to Massa' equaled a longer life, but making too many babies put Kizzy out of commission in his fields.

During the Great Migration, millions of Negroes arrived in urban centers fresh off farms, camps and plantations, yet they never stabilized. Uneducated and unskilled, they choked factories with cheap labor.

Like spirits in the material world, slave DNA is smeared today all over cities like Chicago, Indianapolis, Detroit, New York City and Washington, D.C.

Reading for slaves was a life-and-death choice, so Negroes haven't been reading (or educated, en masse) as long as our white counterparts. There's a direct correlation between our legacy as slaves and our devaluation of education; we were taught not to learn, and it stuck.

Black and white Americans crouch today at the crossroads of a cliché.

Opponents of slave reparations know Negroes have it good.

Supporters know it, too. To many, the fish-are-jumpin'-and-the-cotton-is-high status has everything to do with the mythic slave heroes who made the rows easier to hoe.

Reparations manifest in black men marrying and dating white women; black CEOs with seven-figure incomes; historically black colleges; Tiger, Venus and Serena; Condoleeza and Colin; Oprah, Michael and Magic; black panhandlers; black homeownership; black voters; Martin Luther King Jr. Day; Farrakhan, Sharpton and Jackson; and black talk radio.

I know what you're thinking.

If you want FleetBoston Financial, CSX, Aetna and the others to cut a check, that list doesn't amount to a hill of black-eyed peas.

And if you think paying reparations is the worst idea since the end of slavery, you're thinking Negroes need to get over it, once and for all.

After all, you didn't own slaves, and I'm not a slave, right?

Don't be narrow. Truth is, Negroes *do* need to get over it—the shameful, self-loathing, genocidal, sacrificial and unproductive legacy wrought by slavery.

America still eats off the meal that slaves prepared.

It's food grown by slaves from dirt worked by slave hands.

America is morbidly obese off that food.

Don't skip out. Pay the tab.

Kunta and his 10 million or so shipmates thank you in advance.

About the Author

Kathy Y. Wilson is an award-winning writer and weekly columnist for *Cincinnati CityBeat,* the alternative newspaper in Cincinnati. Her commentaries can be heard on National Public Radio's "All Things Considered." She is also a regular guest on WCPO-TV's "Hot Seat," a weekly political program. She has written for *Newsday* and has won awards from the Ohio Associated Press, the Association of Alternative Newsweeklies, the Society of Professional Journalists and the Knight Center for Specialized Journalism at the University of Maryland. She also works with the Christ Church Cathedral Racial Reconciliation Initiative and has attended the Neiman Conference at Harvard University. She lives in Cincinnati, Ohio.

Books of Interest

My Mother's Eyes
Holocaust Memories of a Young Girl

By Anna Ornstein

Art by Stewart Goldman

Twenty-five years ago, at the family Seder gathering, Anna Ornstein's family asked for a story from her past. Since that day, she has shared a short essay every year describing her experiences as a teen caught in the horror of the Holocaust. These stories of how a mother and daughter survive the death camps gain power through their simple, understated grace.

Includes 16 illustrations

1-57860-145-2 HC $20.00

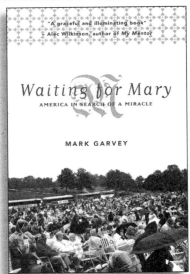

Waiting for Mary
America in Search of a Miracle

By Mark Garvey

Mary the Mother of Jesus seems to be appearing everywhere—from California to New York. To investigate this phenomenon, Mark Garvey visited nine sites, talking to visionaries and skeptics, the faithful and the doubtful. *Waiting for Mary* is the fascinating account of his journey. With w and wisdom, he delivers an informed look at a world that is strange and captivating, moving and, in its way, miraculous.

1-57860-138-X PB $12.99

To order call: 1(800) 343-4499

www.emmisbooks.com